A Geography of the Hutterites in North America

Simon M. Evans

UNIVERSITY OF NEBRASKA PRESS
Lincoln

Library of Congress Cataloging-in-Publication Data
Names: Evans, S. M., author.
Title: A geography of the Hutterites in North America /
Simon M. Evans.
Description: Lincoln: University of Nebraska Press, [2021] |
Includes bibliographical references and index.
Identifiers: LCCN 2020057441
ISBN 9781496225085 (hardback)
ISBN 9781496228321 (epub)
ISBN 9781496228338 (pdf)
Subjects: LCSH: Hutterian Brethren—Canada. | Hutterian
Brethren—United States. | United States—Population. |
Canada—Population.
Classification: LCC F1035.H97 E93 2021 | DDC 289.7/7—dc23
LC record available at https://lccn.loc.gov/2020057441

Set in Questa by Laura Buis.

Contents

Figures

Tables

Acknowledgments

My first all-embracing thank-you must go to the Hutterite ministers and managers who have been so generous with their time and
hospitality over the years. This book could not have been written
without them. One well-remembered incident must suffice to illustrate their kindness. My wife and I arrived at one South Dakota colony just as the minister and his family were unpacking after a long
car journey back from the Peace River Country in Alberta, where
they had been visiting their daughter. We said we would come back
later, but within minutes we found ourselves sitting down to an
impromptu lunch with the family. A helpful interview and an exploration of the various colony activities followed. The only practical
help I remember giving to the Brethren was when I helped paint
a barn (inexpertly) while I talked to the minister. I hope that this
book will be some recompense for all the hours they have spared
me. It is written with respect and admiration.

My friend and colleague Peter Peller has been a stalwart and
invaluable support over the past five years. Together we have coauthored four papers on Hutterite diffusion, demography, and cultural
landscapes, versions of which are incorporated into this book. These
papers are identified in the endnotes. Peter's skills in handling spatial data complemented my own work in the field and with the writing. Often he was able to make what seemed impossible to me into
a routine exercise. I have enjoyed our working lunches immensely,
and having Peter at the end of the telephone as a sounding board
has helped again and again. Thank you so much Peter.

I would like to acknowledge my wife, Stephanie, for her contribution to this book. As well as nurturing me over the years, she has
been my field assistant, driver, interviewer, scribe, and sounding

board. Thanks too to my diligent readers who did so much to polish the manuscript, Barbara and Alex Holliday in Manitoba, Julian Marshall in the United Kingdom, and my daughter, Dr. Emma Anderson, at the University of Ottawa.

Robin Poitras, cartographer at the geography department of the University of Calgary, has been turning my sketches into clear and meaningful maps for fifteen years, to him many thanks. During the past months the preparation of the final draft has become a truly family affair as my son, Dr. Benjamin Evans, manipulated maps, tables, and photographs to be ready for the press and edited the entire manuscript in preparation for publication. Thank you all.

Introduction

The Hutterites are a German-speaking religious brotherhood, and it is their Anabaptist faith that both holds them together and sets them apart. They attempt to mirror the life of the early Christian church and to hold "all things common."[1] Members of the colonies have few personal possessions and receive no wages; the community provides for each member from birth to death. Theirs is an all-encompassing faith in which they hallow God's name by living in community. Work in the fields or in the kitchen is esteemed as worship just as much as time spent in their daily church services. Each family occupies a separate apartment in multifamily dwellings, but food is prepared in a single large kitchen and the community members eat their meals together. This communal life separates the Hutterites from other Anabaptist groups such as the Mennonites and the Amish, with whom they share much common history.[2]

Unlike many other ethnic groups that have settled in the Canadian Prairies and northern Great Plains, the Hutterites have resisted assimilation and have maintained their language and culture since their arrival in North America in 1874. The colony is the essential unit of Hutterite culture. It is a farm village occupied by around fifteen to twenty families in which all members have prescribed roles to play and contributions to make, whether it is a ten-year-old girl babysitting younger siblings or a bearded *Wirt* (business manager) wrestling with next year's cropping plan. It is within the borders of this community that Hutterites struggle to live in harmony with one another. They meet for meals three times a day and for church in the evening. No doors are locked, and old and young move from home to home to visit, borrow items, or exchange the news of the day. Children regard all adults as family and address them as "uncle" or "auntie," and the adults keep an eye on all the youngsters as if they were their own.

To preserve this intimate sense of community, when a colony becomes too large it is divided into two and a new "daughter" colony is established. This complex process of colony division, often referred to as "hiving" or "fission," has become formalized over the decades. Years before a colony reaches a threshold size of 120 to 150 people, planning already begins to acquire a new place. As a strategy, colony division has served the Hutterites well; indeed, one might argue that it is an important reason for the group's longevity.

The Hutterites are divided into four clan groups, or *Leut* (people). One of the communal groups, which undertook the hazardous journey from Ukraine to the Dakota frontier, was led by Michael Waldner, a blacksmith. They became known as the "smith's people," or Schmiedeleut. Another group followed Darius Walter and were soon referred to as the Dariusleut, while a third party was loyal to Jacob Wipf, a teacher, and were christened the Lehrerleut.[3] At first relations were close with noncommunal Hutterites, the Prairieleut, who had moved from Russia with them, and intermarriage was common.[4] By 1914, however, boundaries between the three communal groups and their neighbors had become less porous. When the Hutterites were forced to leave South Dakota in 1918, an important spatial division took place. The Schmiedeleut moved just across the Canadian border into Manitoba, while the Dariusleut and the Lehrerleut moved to Alberta.[5]

During the 1990s a split took place in the large Schmiedeleut clan. Differences between the more conservative groups, who venerated tradition, and those who were prepared to countenance some changes proved to be irreconcilable. The Hutterites now recognize two groups: Schmiedeleut One (the more liberal group) and Schmiedeleut Two (the more traditional group).[6]

Alberta is home to the Dariusleut and the Lehrerleut. The differences between the groups may seem slight to outsiders, involving nuances of dress, custom, and idiom. Nevertheless, the two clans have grown apart during the past century and are endogamous. The Lehrerleut tend to be more conservative with regard to their church services, music, dress, and socialization processes. Dariusleut colonies enjoy more individual autonomy with regard to when, where, and how they establish new colonies. They are regarded as dangerously liberal by the Lehrerleut. However, the generalizations of "liberal" and "conservative" apply only to social and cultural norms. Pragmatically, the Hutterites regard making a living as a vital contribution to the maintenance of their way of life. In this sphere they are prepared to embrace the best machinery and the most innovative science. Thus it would not be unusual to observe a well-run Lehrerleut colony that adheres strictly to every facet of Hutterite culture while at the same time adopting progressive, even aggressive, agricultural technology. Likewise, there are supposedly more relaxed liberal Dariusleut colonies that pursue activities like keeping sheep and geese or maintain a shoemaking and harness shop, which are traditional but not rational in an economic sense.

Differences between the clan groups are matched by diversity within each Leut. A brief anecdote will illustrate this. One group of Dariusleut colonies protested being required to have their photographs on their driving licenses, for they regarded photographic images as an infringement on the second commandment concerning idols. They took their case all the way to the Supreme Court of Canada. Meanwhile, the three Wipf brothers, from another Dariusleut colony, were happy to pose for an advertisement for Alberta Milk in a major periodical.[7]

Hutterites draw strength and direction from their four hundred years of history.[8] This history becomes an integral part of every Hutterite's worldview through the repetition every Sunday of sermons dating back to the seventeenth century.[9] Their religious belief—the cement that has held them together for so long—is based on three closely linked principles: "yieldedness," sharing, and separation.

Perhaps as a reaction to the religious-based conflicts and persecutions that were so much part of his experience, the founder of the Hutterites, Jacob Hutter preached "yieldedness." In his view all creatures were created in the image and likeness of God, and all Christians were called to yield their own lives rather than to engage in violence.[10] The Brethren's adherence to pacifism has often involved them in conflict with the host societies in which they found themselves. This resulted in a series of moves: from the Tyrol to Moravia, from Moravia to Ukraine, from Ukraine to South Dakota, and finally in 1918 from South Dakota to Manitoba and Alberta.[11] Once again during the Second World War hostility flared up against the Brethren in Alberta. During the war years all sales of land to "enemy aliens" was forbidden, and in 1947 the Communal Property Act was passed by the Alberta Legislature. This act prescribed where the Hutterites were allowed to purchase land and had a profound effect on the Hutterite settlement pattern.

The Hutterites are often described as an "ethnic isolate" because one of the foundations of their way of life is to be separate from "the world." They perceive themselves as an ark adrift on the stormy sea of secular society. The little flock must keep themselves apart as far as possible from contagion from all that is worldly. They aim to be in the world but not of it.[12] To this end they pursue agriculture in rural locations and may purposely seek out isolated locations for their colonies. Moreover, each colony is self-sufficient to a considerable degree. Staples like meat, poultry, eggs, milk, and vegetables are all produced on the colony. However, there is always tension between their deeply held spiritual aspiration to maintain separation from the world and their absolute need to interact with the market economy to make a living and for their healthcare needs. One strategy they adopt is to entrust necessary business contacts to the hands of a few senior members of the community and to establish long-lasting relationships with a limited number of outsiders, such as accountants, lawyers, real estate agents, and dealers in agricultural machinery. Of course, maintaining separation from worldly influences is increasingly difficult in an age of cell phones and the internet.[13]

The Hutterites are also a "genetic isolate" because their attempts to maintain separation from the host society have been so successful. They do not evangelize, and very few individuals or families have joined them over the years. Thus their gene pool is somewhat limited and relationships can be traced back for many generations. Their carefully maintained records of births, marriages, and deaths provide invaluable data on their family trees. For this reason, the Hutterites have been sought out as case studies by demographers, geneticists, and medical researchers.[14] Anthropologists and sociologists have also been drawn to study the Brethren.[15] They are of particular interest precisely because they have achieved their goal of living apart from the host society, and yet the necessity of making a living draws them into sophisticated relationships with agribusiness. This is another of the contradictions and complexities of Hutterite culture.

One final attribute of the "Hutterite way" deserves mention. The Brethren aspire to a simple ascetic lifestyle. They are Plain People like the Amish and the Old Order Mennonites.[16] They make their own clothing and furniture and try to limit purchases of consumer goods. While the communal kitchen and laundry display the most up-to-date appliances, most living rooms and bedrooms in contrast are quite austere, the only wall decoration being a calendar from an elevator company. The number of community-owned vehicles and their use is strictly controlled. There are no televisions, and computers, if present, are confined to the school and the colony manager's office.

By pursuing agricultural activities with the aid of modern technology and science while at the same time adopting a self-sufficient lifestyle and having strict limitations on consumer spending, the Hutterites have been able to accumulate capital on a scale, and at a pace, that would be the envy of any family farmer. In the past, these savings have been urgently needed to purchase land for the next daughter colony. Today, with the period between colony divisions extended to thirty years or more, it is harder for leaders to curb demands for more consumer goods. Change is manifest everywhere. In the kitchen there may be commercial ice cream bars and prepared kebabs from enormous supermarket chains, and plastic toys and scooters have replaced most of the homemade wagons and wooden toys. Indeed, some new colonies look like upscale row housing in a suburb, complete with finished basement and several bathrooms. Folk in Lethbridge, Winnipeg, or Sioux Falls come across Hutterites shopping in Value Village or selling goods at farmers' markets, and they are impressed with their "old world" clothing and their apparent adherence to traditional ways. Yet closer observation over several decades has shown that the culture is dynamic and the pace of change is increasing. As the number of colonies has doubled and doubled again, so the range of contrasts among colonies and clan groups has increased. As Rod Janzen observes, "Writing about Hutterite life is complicated."[17]

The Hutterites have been well served by scholars who have studied their way of life and narrated their history. Two recent books provide an up-to-date review. Rod Janzen and Max Stanton have crafted a nuanced account of the "Hutterite way" that emphasizes the increasing diversity within the sect but also reflects an empathy for the spiritual foundations of colony life.[18] Yossi Katz and John Lehr provide some insights into the progress of the Manitoba Schmiedeleut and have made the ordinances of that clan group available to a wider audience.[19] These authors built on the solid foundations laid by John Hostetler in the 1960s and 1970s and are buttressed by a range of more specialized studies, such as those of John Ryan and John Bennett on economics, Joseph Eaton on demography, and Karl Peter on social dynamics.[20] There are also studies in German that provide another perspective, notably the works of Thomas Winkelbauer and Astrid von Schlachta.[21]

These studies, however, have paid scant attention to the geography of Hutterite settlement in North America. *A Geography of the Hutterites in North America* explores three geographic themes. First, it describes the diffusion of colonies from the "bridgehead" established in Dakota Territory in 1874 to the present distribution of some five hundred colonies spread over four prairie provinces and six U.S. states. The analysis goes far beyond simple maps of locations. The book also examines relationships between parent and daughter colonies, explains the cultural and demographic forces that have driven the diffusion process, and weighs the internal and external factors that have shaped the developing patterns of settlement.

The second theme of this book is the contribution of the Hutterites to the cultural landscape of the prairies and Great Plains.

Hutterite colonies are easily identifiable both from high-flying jet aircraft and from dusty rural backroads. The assemblies of barns, workshops, grain bins, and feed mills are on an entirely different scale from that of even the largest family farms. The multifamily housing units grouped around the communal kitchen, and often masked by windbreaks and shrubs, contrast with the single-family bungalows of other rural folk. Whether you are on the banks of the James River in South Dakota or the Peace River in Alberta, the farm villages of the Hutterites strike the observer as both distinctive and homogeneous. However, this study establishes that significant changes are taking place in both the layout and the housing types adopted on the colonies.

A major topic discussed in the contemporary history of plains settlement has been depopulation. This outmigration has affected the smallest "central places" in particular. The villages and small towns, which used to provide schools, post offices, grocery stores, and elevator services, have all but disappeared. The expansion of Hutterite colonies, each representing a community of about one hundred people, is doing something to mitigate this trend.

The third theme is how Hutterites make a living and interact with the land they occupy. For most of their sojourn in North America, they have concentrated on agriculture, and they have been very successful. The size of their operations has yielded economies of scale and has spread risk, while the available labor force has allowed them to balance field crops with animal husbandry. This diversity in their operations has provided jobs for their growing population and some margin of protection against environmental and economic vagaries. They have been more than willing to adopt any technology that will contribute to their profitability. Indeed, they often adapt and improve an idea or a bit of equipment for their specific use. This success, when combined with an ascetic lifestyle, has allowed them to accumulate capital to buy land and to establish daughter colonies for the next generation. It has also meant that the Hutterites "punch above their weight" in the agricultural economy, producing far more products, such as milk, eggs, and turkeys, than their relatively small numbers would lead one to expect.

Since the beginning of the new millennium, profit margins of many Hutterite farms have been squeezed as prices for their products have remained stable or declined while costs have increased inexorably. More and more colonies, especially among the Schmiedeleut in Manitoba and South Dakota, have adopted light manufacturing activities to balance their agriculture and boost their bottom line. In some cases this transformation has gone all the way, and colonies have become wholly dependent on manufacturing enterprises. This trend is spreading among the Dariusleut in Alberta and Montana, and even some conservative Lehrerleut colonies are establishing pilot projects.

This book explains how their culture and way of life has channeled their population growth into a vigorous pattern of expansion diffusion. It looks at how the multiplication of Hutterite colonies has added a new and distinctive element to the cultural landscapes of the northern plains and how their contribution to both the agricultural and manufacturing economies of their home states and provinces is considerable and growing.

The first six chapters of the book describe the diffusion of Hutterite colonies. The story starts in chapter 1 with the establishment of three founding colonies in the Dakota Territory in 1874. Chapters 2–4 cover the exodus from the United States during the First World War, the quiet expansion of colonies during the Depression years, and the far-reaching and lingering effects of the Communal Property Act. Then chapters 5 and 6 look at the more recent period, examining the growing confidence of the Brethren in their dealings with governments and their neighbors and charting the development of their settlement pattern now that they have freedom of locational choice.

The second part of the book (chapters 7 to 11) consists of five essays. The first two evaluate the demographic pressure driving the diffusion process and weigh some of the recurring factors that have shaped locational decisions. The third focuses on the cultural landscapes that have resulted from the multiplication of colonies, and the last two discuss how the Hutterites have sustained their unique way of life for almost a century and a half in North America.

A Geography of
the Hutterites in
North America

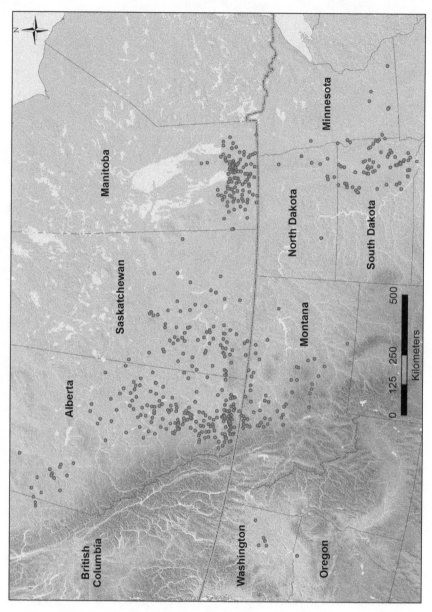

Fig. 1. North American Hutterite colonies, 2015. Drawn from locations in
Birch Hills Colony, *Hutterite Telephone & Address Directory*, and GAMEO.

1

Forging a Home on the Frontier

Dakota Territory, 1874–1918

While the Hutterites have preserved written records in diverse forms throughout their history, there is a dearth of documentation about their arrival on the Dakota frontier and subsequent efforts to make homes for themselves.[1] This is a pity, since it would surely make an epic story. Perhaps for this reason, historians have tended to gloss over the first decades of settlement, stressing the relative isolation and low profile of the Brethren, then moving on to describe the prosperity they had achieved by the first decade of the twentieth century. This makes light of the achievements of the first generation of North American Hutterites. They soon shook off the trauma and tragedy of their journey and relocation; they worked through their relations with their fellow travelers and kinsmen who elected not to live communally, losing some families to the Prairieleut and gaining some others; they built substantial new homes, wrestled with a new ecosystem, and coped with droughts and grasshopper infestations; they learned to live together in their *Bruderhofs* and drew up by consensus the rules that helped make this life harmonious. This was especially crucial to the Lehrerleut, who had not practiced communal life back in Johannesruh. When the strong and charismatic leaders who had brought them to this new land died, new leaders were elected without controversy. Finally, and most important to this book, they established the process of colony division and formulated parameters concerning colony threshold size and the division of people and assets.

The original party of 200 to 250 Hutterites arrived in Yankton, South Dakota Territory, on August 8, 1874.[2] They had been traveling for two months. First they had moved by train across Europe from Ukraine to Hamburg. Then they endured the rough Atlantic

1

crossing on the SS *Harmonia,* which landed them in New York on July 5. After interminable waits and chaos during the immigration process, they moved by train across another continent to reach Lincoln, Nebraska. Here they were housed in immigrant accommodations, and tragedy struck when an epidemic of dysentery swept through the facility. Thirty-six Hutterite babies and vulnerable young children succumbed, leaving few families without heartbreaking loss. Moreover, the land they were shown proved unsatisfactory. Interviewed years later, Michael Waldner from Bon Homme Colony recalled that they had sent two delegates to revisit the land in Dakota. These scouts came back with favorable reports. John Funk of Elkhart, who accompanied the delegates, confirmed this: "I think the climate was agreeable to them—much like what they had in Russia. The rivers and undulating surface of the land and the soil had to do with it."[3] So the party left Lincoln and entrained once more for Yankton. The *Dakota Herald* announced, "Sixty families of Russian Germans will arrive in Yankton. They were induced to go to Nebraska by land-sharks who much misrepresented things."[4]

Within a month the Schmiedeleut group, led by Michael Waldner, found an attractive site perched above the Missouri River. But here, too, the newcomers were exploited by an unscrupulous landowner. Walter A. Burleigh, a former Indian agent, sold them 2,500 acres of unbroken ranchland for $10 an acre.[5] They paid $17,000 down and arranged to pay the balance in yearly increments. This price was exorbitant. Paul Tschetter, on his journey of exploration a year or two earlier, had been offered land at only $3 an acre, and land values in South Dakota did not rise to $10 an acre until the twentieth century. Of course, if the party had been prepared to abide by the provisions of the Homestead Act, they might have acquired 12,800 acres of free land as individuals and obtained an additional 6,400 acres for only $8,000. But this was not an option for those who wanted to live in community.[6] Not surprisingly, this land purchase left the group in financial difficulties, and Waldner contacted the Harmonists in Pennsylvania. This communal group, which shared Anabaptist roots with the Hutterites, proved extremely generous and supportive.[7] They provided $3,000 to cover immediate expenses and later another $3,000 to enable the nascent Bon Homme Colony to build a mill that operated until the 1950s, when it was drowned by the water ponding behind the Gavin Point Dam.

A county landownership map dated 1893 shows the colony headquarters, some ten buildings situated on a bluff above the Missouri floodplain (fig. 2). The colony's lands stretched westward to Charley Creek. It had few neighbors, and the citation "Hutterische Bruder Gemeinde"—literally translated as "Hutterian Brethren local community"—suggests that the Hutterites were accustomed to using the breaks along the river to the east for pasturing their flocks and herds. Homestead farmers in the vicinity had been struggling for some years with droughts and grasshopper infestations, but the harvest of 1875, the first year the Hutterites planted a crop, was truly blessed. It was one of the best years the territory had experienced. Two years later a curious and intrepid newspaper editor from Yankton provided one of the few eyewitness accounts of the colony. He reported excellent crops, with rye yielding 42 bushels an acre. He predicted that the Hutterites were "bound to get rich, struggle against it as they may, that fate will sooner or later overcome them."[8]

The Dariusleut group, under the leadership of Darius Walter, spent a bitter winter in sod huts on government land at Silver Lake. In the spring this group found a site for a colony on the James River at Wolf Creek, about 40 miles north of Bon Homme.[9] An 1898 topographic map shows the colony located where the creek debouches onto the floodplain (fig. 3). The site was relatively safe from flooding but had access to water from the creek and was sheltered by the coulee. During the first years, the colonists used the natural grassland of the prairie for pasture and the rich soil of the floodplain for arable crops and a garden. This site location set a precedent for a string of colonies later established along the James River.

The third group of Hutterites arrived from Russia in 1877. They were led by Jacob Wipf and his brother, who were both recognized teachers, so they became known as the Lehrerleut, or "teacher's people." This party of thirteen families established Elmspring Colony (later known as Old Elmspring) on 5,440 acres a few miles up the

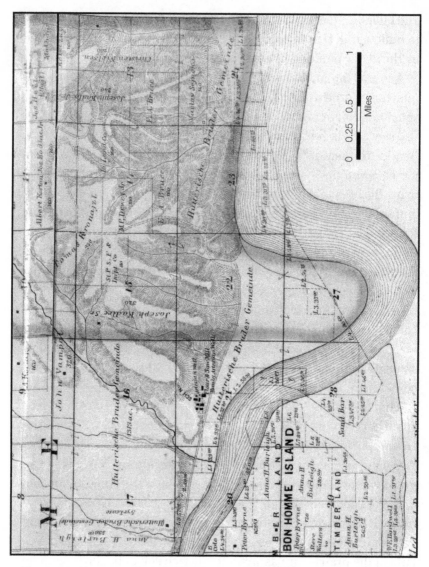

Fig. 2. Bon Homme Colony on the Missouri River, 1893. Scale: 1.6 inches to 1 mile. *Map of Bon Homme County, South Dakota: Compiled and Drawn from a Special Survey and from Official Records.* Vermillion SD: Rowley and Peterson, 1893.

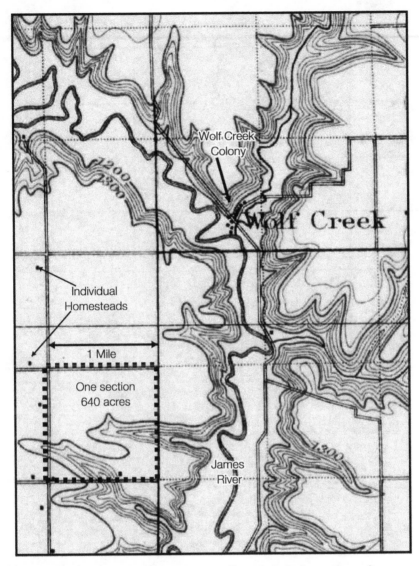

Fig. 3. Wolf Creek Colony, James River Valley, 1898. Scale: 1:125,000 (topographic). U.S. Geological Survey (USGS), *South Dakota Olivet Quadrangle*. Washington DC: USGS, 1898.

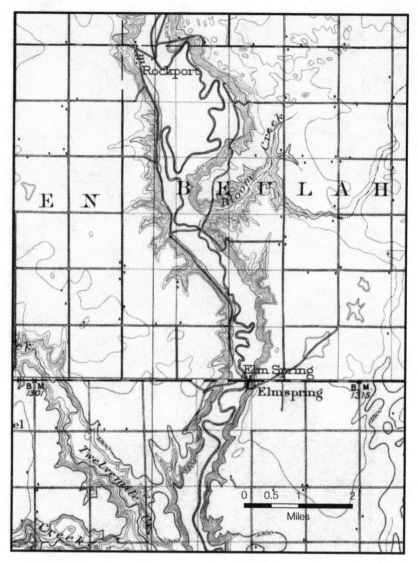

Fig. 4. Elmspring and Rockport Colonies, 1898 and 1899. Scale: 1:125,000 (topographic). USGS, *South Dakota Alexandria and Olivet Quadrangles.* Washington DC: USGS, 1898–99.

James River from Wolf Creek (fig. 4).[10] A year later they purchased a mill some 6 miles north of their site. In due course it would become the nucleus of their first daughter colony, Rockport.

In their new home on the Dakota frontier, the Hutterites took the scriptural admonition to "be fruitful and multiply" to their collective heart. In Russia their population had hardly doubled over a century, but according to data from the U.S. Census, in North America their numbers increased rapidly from 443 in four colonies in 1880 to some 1,700 in fifteen colonies in 1915. Family size grew to an average of ten children, and their population doubled every fifteen or sixteen years. Within a decade of arrival, they were set on an extraordinary demographic course that was to last until the 1970s.[11]

This demographic vitality meant that each founding colony grew quickly, and this might have threatened both the intimacy of the communities and the efficiency of their agricultural activities if it had been allowed to continue unchecked. Fortunately, colony leaders found a way to channel their growing population so that it contributed to their survival and expansion. They established the principle that when a colony reached a threshold size of 130 to 150, it would divide in two and establish a daughter colony. There was no precedent in their previous history to guide them, and they thoroughly debated ideas about the management of this traumatic process until eventually protocols to ensure a fair division of both people and assets were established. It was a remarkable achievement to develop a system that has worked well for more than a century.[12]

In 1878, after only four years, Bon Homme Colony established a daughter colony at Tripp, 25 miles to the north. However, this embryo colony fell into financial difficulties in spite of some assistance from the Amana Society in Iowa.[13] Its members decided to respond to the entreaties of the Harmonists in Pennsylvania and try their luck in the East, supported by the generosity and deep pockets of their fellow believers. Nineteen families sold their land at Tripp and arrived at Tidioute, Pennsylvania, on May 1, 1884. There they struggled for two years in the unfamiliar hilly and forested environment and found it hard going. Longing for the open vistas and big skies of the prairies, they returned to South Dakota, where they established Milltown Colony and finally put down lasting roots. Bon Homme branched again to Maxwell in 1900 and to Huron in 1906. In its turn, Milltown hived to Rosedale in 1901 and then to Buffalo in 1908. This colony failed, however, and the people ended up moving to James Valley in 1913.

The founding Dariusleut colony, Wolf Creek, also established a number of daughter colonies over a relatively short period. First was Jamesville in 1884, then Tschetter in 1890. When the Spanish-American War broke out in 1898, the Dariusleut, fearing conscription, established Dominion City Colony just across the international border in Manitoba, Canada. It was peopled by families from Kutter Colony and Jamesville. After spending the first winter camped in a big horse barn, the community built stock barns and frame houses. However, the small group struggled with heavy land prone to flooding, and in 1905 it sold its Canadian holdings. The families moved back closer to their coreligionists, buying a place near their kinsmen at Spink Colony, which had been founded a year earlier, in 1904. They called it Lake Byron, although it was also referred to as Beadle County Colony.[14] Meanwhile, Kutter Colony had been established in 1901, followed by Richards, also in 1905. Next, in 1912–13 two separate groups were sent to find homes in Montana. Twenty families moved in a special train during the spring of 1912 to Spring Creek, near Lewistown, while a smaller group occupied a property at Warren Range, Montana.

In comparison, the Lehrerleut were less eager to split and founded only four new colonies before 1918. Old Elmspring established Rockport in 1891, New Elmspring in 1900, and Milford in 1910. Rockport did not establish a daughter colony but sent families to both New Elmspring and Milford.

During these early decades the three clan groups began to display the characteristics regarding colony division that would become more marked later in their history. The Schmiedeleut, apart from the necessity of finding a new place for expansion after only four years, set up new colonies at a well-spaced and regular tempo. The Dariusleut, on the other hand, established daughter colonies in an irregular and unpredictable fashion. Tschetter and Kutter were

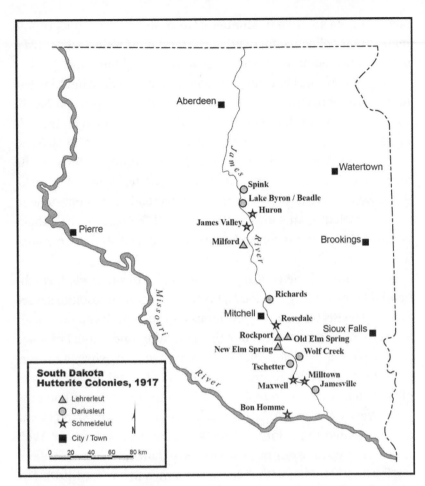

Fig. 5. Map of South Dakota Hutterite colonies, 1917, showing the colonies'
distribution just before the move to Canada. Drawn from various sources.

started within a year of each other, as were Richards and Spink. The
two moves to Montana also occurred within a year of each other. It
is clear that these were not formal fifty-fifty splits, but rather groups
of families—perhaps volunteers—who acquired relatively small
properties and settled down to add to them over the years. The
Lehrerleut, for their part, were prepared to let their communities
grow rather larger and were more careful and measured in allocat-
ing families to new daughter colonies. On the eve of the exodus that
was about to take place in 1918, there were seventeen colonies in

South Dakota and two in Montana. On contemporary topographic maps, their collective farm villages stand out in marked contrast to the dispersed homestead farms of their neighbors (fig. 5).

Surprisingly, the Hutterites brought no appellations from Ukraine. Rather, the founding colonies took their titles from local North American sources. Bon Homme was the county in which the colony was located, and Elmspring and Wolf Creek were local physical features. Rockport derived from earlier Rockyford, which got its name from a quartzite outcrop. Even Tschetter, a truly Hutterite term, was so called for a swampy area that had been homesteaded by a Prairieleut man. However, over time, fifteen large-scale topographic map sheets in South Dakota were named after the colonies in those areas.[15]

By the turn of the century the memories of bitter cold, earth-floored homes, droughts, floods, fires, and "locust" infestations were fading. The Brethren were now housed in substantial stone houses with effective wall furnaces burning hay, dung, and wood. Livestock were sheltered in thick-walled stone barns, some of which have survived to today. When representatives of the Canadian Department of the Interior visited in 1898 to evaluate the Hutterites as potential immigrants, they were impressed by the productive mixed farms and estimated the colonies' total assets at over $750,000.[16] Wolf Creek Colony, for example, owned more than 8,000 acres stretching for 6 miles along both sides of the James River (see fig. 6). The prosperous colony had 400 head of cattle, 21 teams of horses, 2,300 sheep, 200 hogs, 7,000 geese, and 200 ducks. Twenty-seven families lived there, making a total population of 160.

As soon as they could afford it, the Hutterites secured the most up-to-date farm equipment. Gasoline engines were used to power cream separators and butter churns, generators powered lights on some colonies, and water was piped from artesian wells. By 1912 large steam tractors were being used to plow and break new land, working alongside the ubiquitous teams of horses. The Hutterites owned five water-powered flour mills along the James Valley, which provided an invaluable service to their neighbors. Each colony engaged in

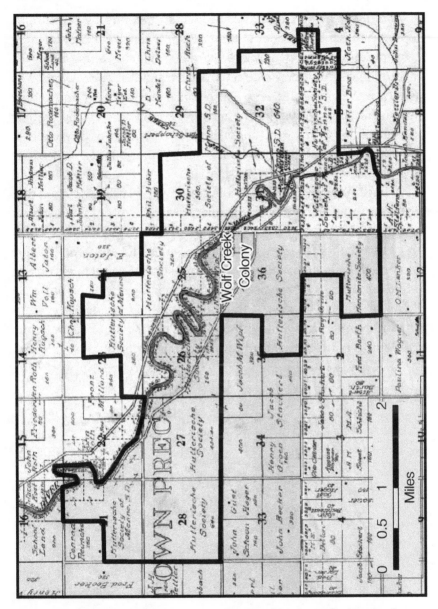

Fig. 6. Map of Wolf Creek Colony, 1910, showing the extent of colony lands. Scale: 1.75 inches to 1 mile. Created by Peter Peller from four adjacent maps in *Standard Atlas of Hutchinson County, South Dakota, Including a Plat Book of Villages, Cities and Townships of the County*. Chicago: George A. Ogle, 1910.

spinning, weaving, carpentry, shoemaking, tanning, blacksmithing, broom making, and bookbinding. Their extensive mixed farming operations, augmented by large gardens and burgeoning orchards, combined with their craft activities meant that each colony was more or less self-sufficient. The colonies, tucked away and almost invisible along the banks of the river, were "distinguished by their stone buildings, by their herds of geese and flocks of pigeons, and by their ice houses and tall flour mills."[17] Their relations with their neighbors were amicable, as they shared a common language and heritage. Even businessmen and town leaders acknowledged that the Brethren were excellent farmers and honest and forthright in all their dealings.

Thus the refugees from Russia had indeed made good in their adopted home in the New World. After some years of lively debate and sometimes dissension among the clan groups and with the noncommunal Hutterites, they now lived in harmony both within their communities and with their neighbors. Unfortunately, the fallout from the Great War brewing in Europe meant that this harmony was not to last.

2

The Exodus

Crossing into Canada, 1918–1920

The Hutterite leaders, for all their social and spatial separation, followed world events carefully, and they were well aware of the enormous conflict in Europe. The war, which had started in 1914, had drawn in country after country and had spread to affect shipping lines and colonial territories around the world. Closer to home, Woodrow Wilson had been reelected in 1916 on a platform of non-involvement in Old World quarrels, and at that point it seemed likely that the United States would continue to remain aloof from "Europe's war."[1]

Nevertheless, the Hutterites regard themselves as sojourners in this "vale of tears." Constant repetition of their history of persecution, martyrdom, and forced migration merge the past with the present. The Brethren always felt that they must not put down roots that were too deep or get too comfortable, and that they must always be prepared to flee when their principles—especially their pacifism—were challenged by the state. When the United States went to war with Mexico in 1898, the Hutterites lost no time in investigating the possibilities of moving to Canada. They were assured that the promises made earlier by the Canadians concerning exemption from military service were still in effect. Indeed, Canadian authorities attempted to persuade more colonies to move. However, the war was short-lived and the threat subsided, and plans for a wholesale move north were shelved. Nevertheless, the incident made it clear that Hutterite leaders were prepared to take radical action if their core beliefs were threatened.[2]

How quickly things changed. The sinking of the British ship *Lusitania*, with many Americans aboard, and the revelation that the German High Command had been conspiring with Mexico pushed the United States into the war. President Wilson was under no illusions as to what this meant for his country and made this prescient observation in an interview: "Once lead this people into war, and they'll forget there ever was such a thing as tolerance. To fight you must be brutal and ruthless, and the spirit of ruthless brutality will enter into the very fiber of our national life, infecting Congress, the courts, the policeman on the beat, the man in the street."[3] Almost overnight the five million Germans who had found new homes in the United States became objects of suspicion. Many had maintained close links with the motherland, and their clubs and publications extolled the superiority of all things Teutonic. Now German newspapers and periodicals were banned, and German intellectuals came under increased scrutiny:[4] "Amid an outpouring of government propaganda about war being waged at home as well as abroad, a hyperpatriotic fever swept across the land, turning neighbor against neighbor in a relentless search for traitors. When these neighbors formed mobs, they set about their business with hanging rope, whip, tar and feathers, yellow paint, and midnight fires."[5]

Nowhere was this violent hostility demonstrated more forcefully than in South Dakota. The first indication of trouble came when Hutterite elders were assaulted and humiliated when they visited town to do business. The colonists' unwillingness to buy war bonds made community leaders and newspaper editors apoplectic with patriotic rage. Hutterites were referred to as "yellow bastards," and state bureaucrats described them as "a rabidly pacifist body . . . considered dangerous and under investigation."[6] After weeks of sporadic harassment, a mob attacked Jamesville Colony and drove off 100 head of steer and 1,000 sheep, the idea being that the stock would be sold and the proceeds used to buy Liberty Bonds. The Hutterites—true to their pacifist principles—did nothing to intervene. The *Sioux Falls Press* supported the theft, adding, "If the Hutterites do not like the idea let them pack up what they can carry away and return to that part of Europe whence they came."[7] A photograph of the proud "patriots" was printed in the Yankton paper.[8]

Hutterite leaders conferred together and agreed to allow young men who received draft papers to travel to induction camps. They thought, perhaps naively, that when the draftees explained their pacifist beliefs, they would be put to useful alternative service. This proved to be a strategic error with fatal consequences. Even on the train to Fort Lewis the Hutterites were picked on, their beards roughly shorn, and their colony-made clothing ridiculed. On arrival at the camp, all military personnel, from officers to enlisted men, took the Hutterites' steadfast refusal to put on uniforms or conform to military discipline as a personal insult and set out to break their will. The men were subjected to beatings, water tortures, and sensory deprivation. Some fifty Hutterite men were drafted, and all suffered mistreatment to differing degrees.[9]

Although they were often referred to as "boys" in the literature, it is sobering to remember that most of these Hutterite men were baptized and married, the fathers of growing families. Examples include the three Hofer brothers and Jacob Wipf, who were court-martialed and condemned to thirty years in prison. David Hofer was twenty-eight and with his wife, Anna, had five children ages six, five, three, two, and a newborn. His brother Michael had been married for only a year but had a little girl, born just two months before he was inducted. The third Hofer brother, Joseph, was twenty-three and the father of two children, and his wife was pregnant with their third child. The grim story of their fate is well known. After suffering torture in Alcatraz for several months, they were transferred to Fort Leavenworth, Kansas, where Joseph and Michael died from the abuse they suffered.[10] This sad story of steadfast faith in the face of state-sanctioned injustice is retold again and again on the colonies today, as these recent martyrdoms take their place alongside the atrocities faced by the Hutterites in previous centuries.

Meanwhile, the colonies at home were facing a new threat. The state of South Dakota took the Hutterites to court, alleging that the Hutterites were best understood not as a religious entity but rather as a business. Consequently, Judge Taylor ordered that the South Dakota colonies "dispose of all real estate not devoted to or necessary and proper for its legitimate business, which shall in no event exceed in value the sum of $50,000."[11] This legal action commenced in July 1918, after many colonies had made the decision to sell and escape to Canada. However, the fact that the state itself, not just a hostile mob, was looking for ways to remove the Hutterites from their homes acted as an important catalyst in persuading even the most reluctant leaders to leave. It was clear that "the overt object of this decision was to 'absolutely exterminate' the Hutterians in South Dakota."[12]

To add insult to injury, the draconian and vindictive South Dakota State Council of Defense decreed that each colony that sold its lands should be required to invest 2.25 percent of the proceeds in Liberty Bonds and donate 0.5 percent to the Red Cross: "The council felt that it was unjust that they be permitted to reap the entire benefit of the protection South Dakota had given them at a time when the state's patriotic residents were called upon for world aid."[13] The Hutterites remained adamant that they would not give to "war funds." They arranged for the buyers to pay the imposed taxes. This meant that a typical colony lost a further $4,000 from their hurried land sales.[14] This was a substantial amount, especially as estimates suggest that the colonies received only half of what their lands were worth because speculators took advantage of their weak bargaining position.[15] It was with relief that the Brethren shook the dust of South Dakota off their feet and turned their eyes northward to Canada.[16]

A New Home in Canada

As passions rose against the Hutterites in South Dakota and the colonies found themselves threatened, so a delegation once more hurried northward to confer with Canadian immigration authorities. They met with the minister of citizenship and immigration himself, the Honorable J. A. Calder, who assured them that the exemption from military service promised in 1899 would still apply to them.[17] Calder could hardly do otherwise. Not only were the prairies suffering from a short-term labor shortage because of the war effort, but even more importantly, his mandate was to promote the settlement of the prairies at all costs. This would spur the faltering economy and allow the country to start repaying its wartime debts. Calder explained his vision of the postwar Canadian west to audiences in Moose Jaw and Regina, Saskatchewan. There were, he said, 25 million acres of land awaiting settlers. But one of the problems slowing development was finding interested colonists with enough means to start farming on the prairies.[18] The Hutterites had proved to be excellent farmers and had both the capital and the skills needed to convert unbroken land into prosperous farms. It must have appeared a perfect match: the Hutterites desperately searching for land and the dominion government seeking competent settlers.

How could things go so wrong? Within a year Hutterite immigration would become a cause célèbre. The governor general of Canada was in communication with the U.S. State Department through the British ambassador in Washington to explain his government's intention to close the border to Hutterites and Mennonites. As many of these people were American citizens, the dominion did not want the proposed action to be seen as an unfriendly act.[19] Since Canada attracted one hundred thousand immigrants in each of the three years after the war, how could the inclusion of fifteen hundred Hutterites within that flood threaten to provoke an international incident?

Two interwoven narratives must be unraveled to answer these questions. The first traces the successful efforts of the Hutterites to sell their established colonies in South Dakota and find new homes in Canada. This forced migration once again reduced the Brethren to refugee status as they fled an intolerable situation. It is a story of hardship, pioneering, and family dislocation. Over a period of two years, six Schmiedeleut colonies were established in Manitoba, and eleven Dariusleut and Lehrerleut colonies were founded in Alberta.

The second narrative is a complex story of the Canadian government's efforts to promote the settlement of the prairies while at the same time trying to appease the jingoistic interests that raved against German-speaking "shirkers" who threatened to take up land that they felt rightly belonged to returning war heroes. Passions ran high, and the strident voices of veterans' groups put enormous pressure on the government, which vacillated and finally bowed to their insistent demands. The border was closed to further immigration by Hutterites and Mennonites in May 1919. This left some five hundred Hutterites and six functioning colonies still in South

Dakota. It was by no means a clean break, and it was to be many years before some families were reunited.

The Schmiedeleut in Manitoba

Once assured of their official welcome to Canada, Hutterite leaders lost no time in journeying to Winnipeg, Manitoba, to explore the prospects. It would not be an easy task to find relatively large tracts of land on which to establish colonies. The flood of homestead settlement had flowed through the region a generation before, and almost all the productive land between Winnipeg and Portage la Prairie, Manitoba, had been taken up. They were fortunate to be approached by Senator Aimé Benard.

Benard was born and raised in Quebec but moved west as a young man and worked as a financial agent. In 1907 he was elected as a conservative member of the legislative assembly. He farmed 4,000 to 5,000 acres at Benard and maintained a large dairy herd of 300 purebred cows. He also ranched some 1,000 head of cattle on public land near Lake Winnipeg. In 1917 Benard was appointed to the senate, and this may well have been the reason he was looking for an opportunity to reduce his commitments in Manitoba.

Benard sold the Hutterites 9,300 acres, enough land for three colonies, and also arranged the sale of his son-in-law's holding, which became the site of a fourth colony. This land purchase, in the Elie district of the rural municipality of Cartier, set the pattern for Hutterite settlement in Manitoba. As each colony established daughter colonies, this core area expanded and intensified (see fig. 7). Milltown Colony bought the actual Benard farmstead and the adjoining 3,300 acres for $50 per acre. The site contained two barns and a large house. Twenty-one families totaling one hundred people arrived early in the summer of 1918. The first new building they constructed was a horse barn, which was used as a dwelling until two substantial residences were completed. Each of these housed eight families, while the Benard house accommodated a further three large families. Milltown was close to the train station, and the big horse barn served as a reception center and temporary shelter for other groups of Hutterites as they arrived from South Dakota. Huron Colony bought land

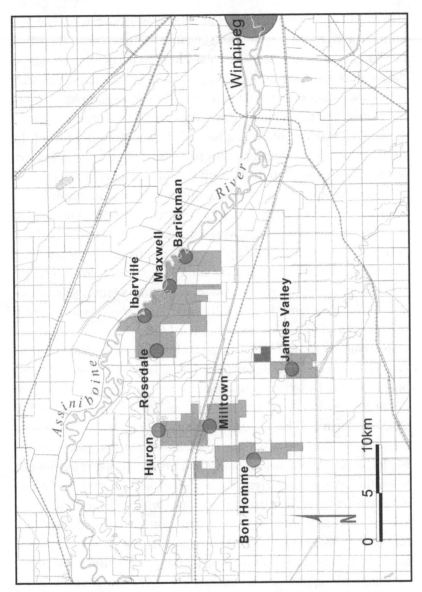

Fig. 7. Map of Manitoba Hutterite colonies, 1920. Colony locations after Ryan, *Agricultural Economy*, and local histories.

adjacent to Milltown northward across the railway tracks. The first families arrived on July 26 and stayed at Milltown until their first dwellings were completed. The colony headquarters was sited just to the south of the Sale (Elm) River, in an area that was almost entirely covered with oak brush. A house and kitchen were completed before Christmas, and the remaining families arrived on December 9.

Maxwell Colony obtained a beautiful tract of land south of the Assiniboine River about 10 miles to the east. The 3,000 acres cost $55 an acre. Existing buildings on the site included a large house and a granary, which provided temporary accommodation for six families. Soon two large residences were completed, housing six families each. These houses were known as *Schtol Hauser*, or barn houses, because of their shape. All the rooms on the upper floor had a dormer window. There was some good timber along the river, and poplar and elm were cut and sawed at the colony's sawmill. In later years men from James Valley and Blumergart would stay at the colony while cutting wood on their lots.

Rosedale Colony was able to dispose of its property in South Dakota for $335,000, a better deal than that obtained by most colonies. It then purchased the Lafleche farm, again through the auspices of Senator Benard. Early in the summer of 1918 an advance party arrived to work the farm and begin construction. They built a 30-by-60-foot house, while cooking was done in a lean-to attached to a preexisting log cabin. Additional housing had been completed by the fall, when the main party arrived. A number of families remained at the old place, however, because of difficulties with immigration. James Valley Colony acquired the Larson farm, some 4 miles south of Elie, Manitoba. The colony bought 3,040 acres for between $50 and $60 an acre. The first families arrived in June and camped out in the existing buildings while they raced to complete the first residence before winter. They were helped by six carpenters from Winnipeg who were on strike and whose services were paid for as part of the land deal. Six more families arrived on December 5, and the minister David Hofer met them at Elie station. It was a pleasant day, and they were bundled up in blankets and conveyed in open sleighs to their new home. The last two families did not arrive until April 1919.

Bon Homme Colony in South Dakota was ready to hive even as the threats against the Hutterites escalated during 1918, and the colony determined to establish a daughter colony in Manitoba. It bought 2,500 acres and established a headquarters site 4 miles south of Benard station. The eleven families selected to move to Canada included ten young men who might have been threatened with conscription if they had stayed in the United States. The planned move from Bon Homme involved only half the population, so the daughter colony of the same name in Manitoba had just eighty souls, which contrasted with the much larger colonies of Rosedale (168) and Maxwell (182). Indeed, as soon as they had established a foothold in Manitoba, the leaders of Rosedale started looking for additional land to establish a daughter colony. They were fortunate to be able to buy land adjacent to their own from farmers Klepper and Clarke, and they laid out a headquarters site on the Assiniboine River. The colony built two residences and during the winter moved several other useful buildings to the site on skids. Eighty people occupied the new site of Iberville Colony during 1919.

Maxwell Colony, also in South Dakota, was in a rather similar position. It had grown to the point where it had acquired a farm, and some families were living there to prepare for a formal split. When the colony was forced to move to Canada, it was unusually large. Even as they dealt with myriad problems associated with building a new place in Manitoba, the leaders had to look for additional land on which to establish a daughter colony. During 1919 they were able to persuade two neighbors, John Sess (Zastre) and a man named Barickman, to sell their properties. This provided a long, narrow rectangular holding, anchored to the north on the Assiniboine River and reaching south across St. François Xavier parish toward the railway. Eleven families and ninety-five people took up residence in Barickman Colony in 1920.

The Schmiedeleut had established a considerable presence in southern Manitoba by 1920. There were eight colonies, which together owned about 23,000 acres. Even as some were building new houses and realigning and refurbishing useful existing buildings, others were starting to burn brush and extend their arable acres. The women were planting large gardens, and the children were helping nurture flocks of geese and ducks. Beehives were often the responsibility of the minister.

The 1921 Census of Canada recorded 787 Hutterites. The forty-three elders, who had been born in Russia and had already experienced a trans-Atlantic migration, were now outnumbered by the 144 youngsters who had been born in Manitoba. The age and gender distribution of the population does not show any marked irregularities (see table 1). For example, the male and female numbers in the twenty-to-twenty-four and twenty-five-to-twenty-nine age cohorts match perfectly, suggesting that few Schmiedeleut young men had been conscripted into the U.S. Army.

Table 1. Population by age group and gender
for all Manitoba colonies, 1921 Census

AGE GROUP	GENDER		TOTAL
	Male	*Female*	
0–4	78	66	144
5–9	69	72	141
10–14	47	65	112
15–19	48	46	94
20–24	35	35	70
25–29	27	27	54
30–34	16	13	29
35–39	16	23	39
40–44	17	16	33
45–49	5	3	8
50–54	13	7	20
55–59	4	13	17
60–64	6	3	9
65–69	5	7	12
70–74	0	2	2
75+	3	0	3
Total	389	398	787

Enough of facts and figures. As one reads the limited accounts available about the first years in Manitoba, one cannot help but be impressed by what the Hutterites had accomplished: the leaders' eye for the country as they chose sites for the colony headquarters, the pragmatic skills of the men who designed and built the houses and barns, and perhaps above all the hardiness of the women. For example, forty-year-old Rachel Stahl, mother of eleven children, her youngest son born the previous year, had to nurture her brood first under canvas, and then in a series of crowded makeshift barns and granaries until the new homes were built. Much of the cooking was done outside, and washing was labor-intensive. Also, as her husband, David, was the minister, the women looked to her to establish their work schedules. It was quite a load to carry, and she managed it with dignity and serenity. As an "English," or non-Hutterite, outsider, one can only speculate that these nascent communities were sustained by their deeply held faith, which was expressed in the way they met the challenges of each day and their knowledge and pride in their long history of martyrdom and forced migration.

The Dariusleut and Lehrerleut in Alberta

In the spring of 1918 a group of leaders from Tschetter and Jamesville Colonies in South Dakota were scouring the country south of Lethbridge for land.[20] They were outbid for one alluring property by the Lehrerleut Milford Colony and returned home disappointed. Later in the summer they returned to Alberta and decided to explore north of Calgary, where there was less competition from other colonies. Paul Stahl, the minister of Tschetter Colony, and his *Wirt*, or colony boss, found a splendid parcel of land along the tiny Rosebud River. The bulk of the land was purchased from the Calgary Colonization Company, while other sections were acquired from homesteaders.[21] After the purchase, the second minister, George Hofer, and a group of young men stayed to prepare the new colony to receive the women and children, the stock, and the machinery. They hauled lumber from Rockyford and started to construct barns and large-frame multifamily dwellings. In the fall tragedy struck. Michael Hofer contracted the deadly Spanish influenza and was dead within a few days. His was the first grave in the Rosebud Colony cemetery.[22]

Early in the spring of 1919 the rest of the colony left South Dakota on a special train bound for the new place. The women and children rode in passenger cars, while the men accompanied the stock and kept an eye on their farm equipment, furniture, and tractors. They crossed into the Dominion of Canada at the Emerson port of entry and were soon in Winnipeg. From there they proceeded westward on the Canadian Pacific Railway to Strathmore, where they unpacked their belongings, hitched up the horses, and moved by wagon to the new colony site, a trek of about 25 miles. They had been traveling for about a week.

It seems highly likely that Jacob Wurz from Jamesville accompanied Stahl westward on his search for land. He purchased adjacent land from the Calgary Colonization Company. This land was designated Farm Number Four and included some barns and buildings. Jim Norstand was the manager and had a crop in the ground. A team of Hutterites soon laid out a new colony site and constructed additional buildings. Before the families arrived, the farm cook, Barbara Senger, cooked for the Hutterite construction crew and forged a bond between her family and the newcomers.[23] The arrival of the main party of colonists must have been a joyful if chaotic occasion. There were almost one hundred souls, scores of horses, wagons, milk cows, 30 or 40 sows, and all kinds of machinery and household items. They named the new place Springvale Colony (fig. 8).

Word soon reached the leaders at Wolf Creek Colony in South Dakota of the success of their neighbors in finding new homes. Soon another deal was made and six men from Wolf Creek were building dormitories a few miles west of Springvale. However, during the long winter months, homesick for their home colony and shaken by the flu epidemic and the death of Michael Hofer, the young men became profoundly discouraged. They decided to leave and made their way to Spring Creek Colony in Montana. This was a daughter colony of Wolf Creek, and the boys were welcomed by numerous family members. The ministers, Joseph and Johann Stahl, reviewed the situation: land had been bought in Canada, the political situation in the United States was threatening, and the first seven years at Spring Creek had been an uphill battle. They decided to take over

Fig. 8. Hutterite women and children at the newly established Springvale Colony, March 1919, with construction activity still evident. Glenbow Museum, Calgary AB, NA-4079-75.

the obligations of their parent colony with respect to the land in Canada. Johann Stahl and six other families moved to Rockyford in the spring of 1919 and founded Stahlville Colony.[24]

The three new colonies formed a compact block along the Rosebud River (fig. 9). The sites had several marked advantages. The first was a reliable source of water. The creek was small but usually flowed year-round, and the water table was relatively high and fed shallow wells. The second advantage was the wide floodplain within which the river meandered. This "misfit channel" had been scoured by postglacial runoff, like many others in southern Alberta, and provided excellent permanent pasture. Fifty feet or so above the floodplain were extensive terraces with well-drained, rich soils. Up from the valley, some of the rolling prairie had already been broken, and the new arrivals were able to get in a crop. Rosebud owned 3,680 acres, while neighboring Springvale occupied 3,360

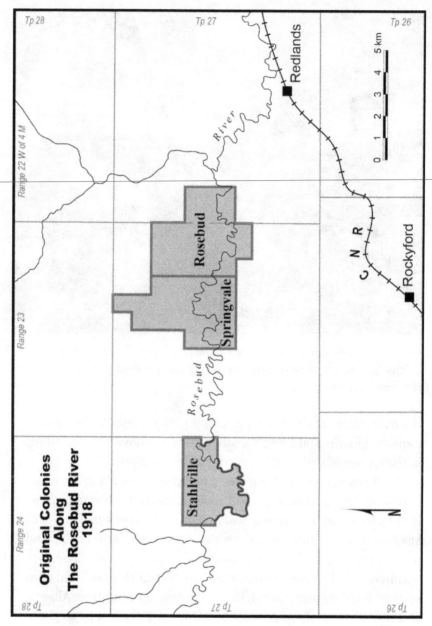

Fig. 9. Map of the original colonies along the Rosebud River, 1918. Drawn from county landownership maps and local histories.

acres. The Stahlville colony was still in the process of finalizing land transactions and had already purchased 2,240 acres.

Larry Anderson suggests that there were broad similarities between the James River valley in South Dakota and the little Rosebud River and that this may have influenced the choice of new sites.[25] I have had the pleasure of visiting both venues, but I found it difficult to imagine either location as it was a century ago. Windbreaks, shelterbelts, orchards, and fences have done much to "domesticate" both sites, and the present landscape bears only a tenuous relationship to that shown in the few historic photographs I have seen. Anderson also points out that both old and new colony sites share the advantage of being secluded. Even today one can drive along Highway 9 from Beiseker to Drumheller and be completely unaware of the Hutterite communities tucked away in the coulee a few kilometers to the south.

Within a couple of years the new colonies were thriving. There were 110 Hutterites at Rosebud, 102 at Springvale, and 52 at Stahlville. Already 35 Alberta Hutterites had been born since the move. In fact, these youngsters outnumbered their twenty grandparents who had been born in Russia.[26] The newly constructed flour mill at Rosebud Colony attracted customers from miles around, as well as grinding grain and preparing feed for the colonies. A small coal mine had been opened on Springvale Colony and produced some 30 tons of coal a day, more than enough to keep homes and barns warm during the winter and to provide steam for the mill.[27]

Much the same process of hurried exploration, speedy purchase, frantic preparation, and excited occupation was repeated again and again in the country south of Lethbridge. By the end of 1918 eight colonies were well on the way to completion there (see fig. 10).[28] The Lehrerleut from Milford, South Dakota, acquired the highly desirable Buck Ranch property and named their new colony after their old place. They had received $230,000 for their land in South Dakota and outbid several other colonies. They were attracted to the property because of its rolling hills and lakes and access to water. Much of the land was already broken, and they were able to get a crop in the ground almost immediately.

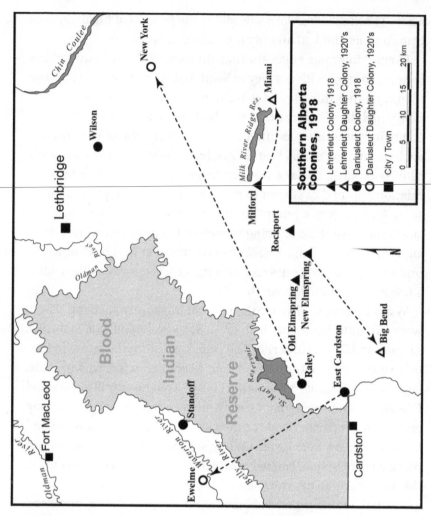

Fig. 10. Map of southern Alberta Hutterite colonies, 1918, showing expansion during the 1920s. Drawn from county landownership maps and local histories.

The biggest single land transaction was the purchase by three Lehrerleut colonies of 27 square miles of the McIntyre Ranch. They were reported to have paid $648,000, which works out to $37.50 an acre.[29] This seems rather a high price for unbroken rangeland. However, there were some great advantages: one deal provided enough land for three new colonies, the huge block of land was on the margin of farm settlement and the Brethren would have no close neighbors, numerous streams running northwestward off the Milk River Ridge provided adequate water supply, and the soils had good potential for arable cropping. Old Elm, New Elm, and Rockport Colonies were established there.

Spink Colony in South Dakota was the first to establish a Dariusleut clan group presence in what was soon to become the southern core of Hutterite settlement in Alberta. The colony purchased the 6,000-acre Pearson Ranch on the Belly River adjacent to the Blood Indian Reserve and called the new place Standoff Colony.[30] They have flourished there ever since in spite of occasional flooding problems. The Richard Colony was not far behind, buying land a few miles northeast of Wilson Siding. Unlike most of the other incoming colonies' sites in coulees or along river valleys, this new place was on the "bald prairie." The land was flat and the nearest water was an irrigation ditch a mile away. The advance party lived under canvas while digging wells, erecting houses, and making preparations to receive the rest of the colony. Much still remained to be done when forty-five men, women, and children and seven train car loads of animals and belongings arrived in the middle of June 1918. The young German Michael Holzach stayed at Wilson Colony for a year during the late 1970s. One of his few complaints was that even then, there was running water only in the kitchen and the communal bathhouse.[31] Warren Ranch Colony, Montana, established East Cardston Colony. This move had two unusual characteristics. First, the land was acquired not through a monetary exchange, but rather by a one-for-one swap of land, stock, and machinery. And second, far from being secluded and inaccessible, the new site was close to the growing Mormon town of Cardston.

The last Dariusleut colony to be founded was Raley Colony. The difficult early years of this community illustrate the problems of managing an emergency migration. Back home in South Dakota, Lake Byron Colony was preparing to establish a daughter colony, having purchased land and started working a farm, but the formal separation of assets had not taken place. When a sudden move became necessary, both parent colony and the farm were sold and the assets pooled. The colony then bought the 5,000-acre Robinson place at Raley.[32] Because of a combination of extremely bad luck—a series of dry years—and less-than-optimal management, the colony fell deep into debt.

The David Hofer family, who had been running the new farm back home, objected to the leadership of the minister, Christian Waldner Sr. The Hofers were disciplined by the community but eventually left to start on their own. They took the matter to "English" outside courts and won a share of the colony assets. In his analysis of the case, Alvin Esau emphasizes that the judge treated the case as a breach of contract concerning the division of a colony. It was not a precedent for private individuals to be compensated when they left a colony.[33] Foster Colony, consisting of the breakaway Hofers, is recorded as a separate entity in the 1921 Nominal Census of Canada.[34] The surprising thing is that there were not more cases of irreconcilable disputes leading to communities breaking up.

Eleven colonies had been established in Alberta by the end of 1919. Seven were Dariusleut and four Lehrerleut. The 1921 census records 1,124 Hutterites in Alberta. Of these the great majority had been born in the United States; there were still 96 robust older folk who had been born in Russia and had made the perilous journey from Ukraine in 1874. Finally, there were already 122 children who had been born since the move to Alberta.[35] Eight of the colonies numbered 100 or more, and the next few years saw several more daughter colonies established, albeit at a more measured and careful pace. Already in 1920 New Elmspring had divided and founded Big Bend Colony. The communities varied widely in size, affluence, and management skills—just as they do today—but they had all survived the trauma of the sudden move, and their existence until the present day bears witness to their successful adaptation to their new home.

The Promised Land?

The end of the war saw massive social dislocation clear across the dominion. Demobilized troops flooded the labor market, while in the factory, the mine, and on the farm, the change from wartime production to the demands of a population at peace caused widespread disruption. On western farms, both patriotism and the lure of opportunity had encouraged a massive extension of the acreage under wheat. However, rising costs of machinery, freight rates, taxes, and above all, labor costs had plunged farmers further into debt. Ordinary families across the West faced inflation too. Costs had risen some 70 percent during the war. It was a struggle to make ends meet, and the prospect of thousands of returning soldiers led to concerns about jobs and employment.[36]

Labor unrest was particularly strong in the West and culminated in the formation of the One Big Union in Calgary on June 4 and the bitter general strike in Winnipeg from May 15 to June 25, 1919. These dramatic and unprecedented events in western Canada played out against a backdrop of the Russian Revolution and terrifying stories reported from eastern Europe. To some extent, the hated "Hun" was being replaced in the public mind by the "Godless communist hordes." The *Calgary Herald* summarized its comments on labor unrest as follows: "In brief, the issue is democracy versus Soviet rule, better known as Bolshevism."[37]

As if these difficulties were not enough, the Spanish flu epidemic brought a real and immediate life-or-death emergency into homes across the prairies. Returning soldiers brought the virus home with them during the fall of 1918, and as they fanned out across the country, so did the flu. Schools were closed and public gatherings forbidden. On Armistice Day in Edmonton the death toll stood at 262, and 100 more died during the following week. Overall, some 35,000 Albertans caught the disease and 3,200 died.[38] It is against this background of "plague," class conflict, and economic uncertainty that the opposition the Hutterite refugees faced can be understood.

As the Hutterites made good their escape from South Dakota, they met with a rhetorical barrage of hostility in the newspapers of their new country. In the provinces of western Canada, the prosecution of the war and the tragic ongoing losses in Flanders dominated public perception. One in four Canadian families had a soldier overseas. The divisive conscription crisis and the election of the Union government in 1917 had whipped up public sentiment against "slackers." Westerners felt that a disproportionate number of prairie boys were being drawn into the war machine, while Que-

Fig. 11. Cartoon from the *Calgary Eyeopener*, September 21, 1918, depicting the perceived flood of undesirable immigrants poised on Alberta's border. In the public mind, there was no difference between Mennonites and Hutterites.

becers were not pulling their weight. In this increasingly jingoistic atmosphere, the arrival of the pacifist Hutterites was greeted with derision (see fig. 11).

One of the strongest statements was that of J. Matheson at a demonstration in Fort Macleod, who stirred up people's feelings with these words:

> This land of ours was a land of brave men . . . from this splendid stock are the thousands of young westerners who are shedding their blood on the fields of France tonight (applause). These brave lads are fighting for the cause of humanity. Not only are the men sacrificing, but the women of the west also. Their splendid work speaks for itself. If these people called Mennonites don't believe in fighting, then tell them to keep away from here. We

don't want them at any price. . . . This fair country of ours is worth fighting for and we don't want any people living and settling here who still possess the German brute in their make up.[39]

Fears of an invasion of German-speaking Mennonites and Hutterites from the United States were fanned by the hyperbolic inflation of the numbers involved. Newspapers talked of twenty-five to thirty thousand potential immigrants massed along the border. These figures were repeated in the House of Commons during a debate on immigration, where the minister of immigration—and sometime acting minister of the interior—James Calder stated that the total number of Hutterites in North America did not exceed twenty-five hundred and that about a thousand had entered Canada during 1918, along with some five hundred Mennonites.[40] But the facts collected from the ports of entry at Emerson, North Portal, and Coutts did nothing to quell the rumors. Bob Edwards remarked in the *Calgary Eye Opener*, "It is said that the particular Brotherhood which has been wished on Alberta has two million members . . . who are coming to Canada."[41]

Apart from their pacifism, another strike against the Hutterites was the "school question." Neither the man in the street in Calgary nor the farmer outside Fort Macleod nor the member of Parliament in Ottawa could grasp the differences among the various branches of the Anabaptist religious tradition. Hutterites were lumped together with Mennonites and were assumed to be demanding their own separate schools in which German was the only language of instruction. In a long speech to the House of Commons, the Honorable William Ashbury Buchanan, member for Lethbridge, said, "They want their own schools and want to teach their own language which is almost wholly German. I object to that because I think that the only way we can develop good citizens in this country is for newcomers to acquire a knowledge of the English language in order that they may mingle with other elements of the population and become good British subjects."[42]

The fact that the Hutterites, like the majority of Mennonites, were perfectly prepared to accept English instruction and the curriculum of the province in which they resided was obscured by the obdurate behavior of the conservative Mennonites. This substantial minority held that their religion and language were so closely linked that any compromise in the language of instruction would inevitably lead to the demise of their spiritual life. After some years of noncompliance with school laws, this group finally left for Mexico and South America.[43]

The armistice in November 1918 did nothing to diminish the hostility toward Hutterite and Mennonite immigration. Indeed, opposition mounted to a crescendo as veterans began to return from overseas. The Great War Veterans' Association (GWVA) grew in numbers and influence. The GWVA was engaged in the "second battle" to secure financial assistance for returning soldiers. In Calgary in February 1919 a delegate remarked, "The men who fought for democracy are not going to go hungry while aliens and slackers get all the jobs."[44] Concern was expressed that undesirable German-speaking aliens were taking up the best land and making it more difficult for veterans to become settled as future farmers.

If the first two accusations leveled at the Hutterites were that they were enemy aliens and "slackers" who wanted their own schools, the third strike against them was that they were involved in a land grab. It was rumored that they were buying up all the good land in southern Alberta and that there would be none left for returning veterans. The *Lethbridge Herald* explained, "The immediate cause of dissatisfaction is the methodical manner in which they are grabbing all desirable land that can be purchased between Lethbridge and the border for a distance east and west of about fifty miles." The paper went on to suggest that the Hutterites were conniving with the government to buy "the Blackfoot Indian reserve." "Whence comes the cash?" the column asked. It went on to express the suspicion that the money came from the German government, "diverted from the huge sums known to have been in German and Austrian hands at the time the United States went to war."[45]

The speed and efficiency with which the Brethren pushed their land purchases to a conclusion was cause for further suspicion. The Hutterites explored a prospective site, asked the price, and promptly put down a cash deposit. There was no haggling, and deals worth hundreds of thousands of dollars were concluded in hours, rather than the months of bidding and counterbidding that was normally the case. On April 11, 1919, a group of ex-soldiers set up pickets at the Emerson port of entry with the objective of preventing Hutterites from entering the country. The threat of violence was real and added to the growing public unease.[46]

The flooding tide of hostility toward Hutterites and Mennonites, orchestrated by the GWVA, was directed at the government as much as the newcomers themselves. The objective was to stop the influx of the "undesirable aliens." Indeed, the most strident calls were to send those already admitted back where they had come from. In the face of this relentless pressure, the government did act, albeit with deliberation and some reluctance. In October 1918 a long-dead order in council was invoked to stop those Hutterites born in Russia, who had not obtained U.S. citizenship, from entering Canada.[47] This would have restricted the movement of many senior ministers and leaders if it had come earlier or been applied ruthlessly.[48] In fact, the Canadian Census of 1921 suggests that many of the Brethren in this category had already moved to Alberta or been admitted as special cases.

This limited measure was not enough to satisfy the vociferous cries of the opposition, and the government gave more ground. On April 8, 1919, five months after the end of the war, the order in council granting Hutterites some degree of military exemption was rescinded, and three weeks later, on May 1, the border was closed to Hutterites, along with Doukhobors and Mennonites. The preamble to the order in council is of interest because it details the basis of public sentiment against these groups:

Owing to conditions prevailing as the result of war, a widespread feeling exists throughout the Dominion, and more especially in Western Canada that steps should be taken to prevent the entry of all persons who may be regarded as undesirable because, owing to their peculiar customs, habits, modes of living and methods of holding property, they are not likely to become readily assimilated or assume the duties and responsibilities of Canadian citizenship within a reasonable time. . . . Hutterites are of the class and character described. On and after the second day of May, 1919, and until further ordered, the entry to Canada of immigrants of the Doukhobor, Hutterite and Mennonite class shall be hereby prohibited.[49]

Interestingly, at this stage the objections were cloaked in the language of citizenship; no mention was made of pacifism, schools, or competition for land with veterans.

The man at the center of the furor over Hutterite immigration was Minister of Immigration James Calder. His performance has been variously interpreted. A. M. Willms suggests that he woefully underestimated the weight of public opinion in the West, while the GWVA proposed a conspiracy theory involving those who sold large blocks of land to Hutterites.[50] On the GWVA's list of suspects were Senator Aimé Benard, who provided enough land for several incoming Schmiedeleut colonies near Elie, Manitoba, as well as Raymond Knight and John McIntyre, who were involved in settling the Lehrerleut along the flanks of the Milk River Ridge in Alberta. A rumor circulated that the minister of the interior, Arthur Meighen, was behind the land deals and stood to profit.[51]

An alternative interpretation portrays Calder as a sophisticated politician, handling his portfolio with aplomb in pursuit of the long-term objectives of his department. Educated at the University of Manitoba, Calder taught at various rural schools until he became a school inspector. Later, he served as deputy minister of education in the Northwest Territories. In 1905 he was elected in the first provincial election of the newly founded province of Saskatchewan and held several portfolios. In 1917 he resigned his seat in the legislature and joined the Borden Unionist government. He represented Moose Jaw and served as minister of immigration and colonization from 1917 to 1921.[52] He knew the issues that faced the West and had worked with Mennonites on the school question when he was a member of the legislative assembly. His reticence in the House of Commons earned him the name "silent James," but he worked tirelessly behind the scenes and enjoyed the confidence of his cabinet colleagues.[53]

He inherited a department of great importance. The war had brought to an end a triumphant period of sustained immigration to the dominion, culminating with the arrival of 400,870 newcomers in 1913.[54] New lands had been apportioned and broken at an unprecedented pace. A cadre of government immigration agents had been active in Europe and the United States for thirty years. They had generated a brand, "Canada, Land of Opportunity," and a drive and momentum that suffered only a temporary slowdown during the war. Canada remained one of the least densely populated parts of the world and was part of the prestigious British Empire, which endowed it with an aura of stability and the rule of law. During a speaking tour of the West in October 1918, Calder stressed that land settlement was essential for the Canadian economy. He asserted that 15 million to 25 million acres awaited settlement.[55] And of course, he was right. For example, the population of the Alberta Dry Belt, where many Hutterite colonies would eventually be located, grew from 374,295 in 1911 to 588,454 in 1921.[56] Calder also explained that the government anticipated a large movement of immigrants toward the dominion after the war, and for that reason, "the Government must keep Canada to the front, now, from a publicity standpoint."[57]

In the short term, too, immigration remained a vital concern. As farm boys left the prairies in droves to enlist, a severe labor shortage developed. Potentially, this could have been as devastating to the production of wheat and meat—and thus to Canada's war effort—as a lack of rain in the growing season or an early frost.[58] The minister of the interior, W. J. Roche, reported to the House of Commons, "There was such great demand for farm help in the west consequent on the heavy enlistments from those provinces that some steps had to be taken to get farm labourers."[59]

Calder and his department did all they could to encourage both Mennonites and Hutterites, eager to escape conscription in the United States, to move north across the border. As the public outcry against this "alien invasion" mounted during the last months of the war and into 1919, Calder gave ground slowly. It was not until five months after the armistice that the border was finally closed, and by that time almost all the Hutterites had moved to new homes on the prairies. Meanwhile, his men on the ground manning the borders and land agencies continued to help small groups of Hutterites with immigration problems. They were able to ensure that Hutterites who already had landed immigrant status could visit family members in South Dakota and that wives and children cut off in the United States could be reunited with their husbands in Canada. Armishaw sums up the situation: "A new pattern quickly emerged whereby immigration and real estate agents, barristers and lower-level immigration officials acted on the Hutterites' behalf, allowing them concessions no top-level person could have offered in the context of the war."[60]

On the one hand, then, the Department of Immigration pandered to the protestations of westerners and put legal impediments in the way of further immigration by Mennonites or Hutterites, while on the other hand, it wanted to preserve Canada's image as a welcoming destination for prospective newcomers. Calder hoped that the passage of time would reduce the tension between these objectives. It did.

As the fall of 1919 gave way to 1920, some of the anti-Hutterite sentiment began to wane. Brave neighbors who were in day-to-day contact with the Brethren spoke out. George Roy, whose farm near Elie, Manitoba was bordered by two colonies, remarked, "They settled last fall . . . and I wish to say from my personal experience in operating with these people as neighbours, I find them quiet, peaceable, law abiding citizens and good neighbours."[61] Moreover, some of the publications of the GWVA printed wild accusations that were patently false. It had overplayed its hand, and Calder admonished the organization that it could not continue to make allegations without evidence.[62] The objective facts spoke for themselves. The "alien hordes" actually amounted to some eighteen hundred Hutterites admitted in 1918, with small additions during the following months. This number was insignificant in light of the fact that the dominion had attracted more than one hundred thousand immigrants in 1919 and 1920.[63] The Hutterites had purchased some 70,000 acres in total, about 35 acres per capita, and much of this land in Alberta was unbroken. There was plenty of land left for veterans.

In the lead-up to the general election of 1921, William Lyon Mackenzie King, the Liberal Party leader, assured his constituency in Waterloo, Ontario, where there was a large Mennonite population, that if he were elected, he would repeal the order restricting immigration of Mennonites, Hutterites, and Doukhobors. He made good on his promise in 1922, and a few hundred Hutterites who had been living in limbo away from their colonies were able to cross the border. The policy of the new government was to encourage immigration, bring new land into production, and exploit Canada's mineral and forest wealth. These were essential priorities in order to tackle the debt incurred during the war. Newspapers like the *Toronto Globe and Mail* and the *Montreal Star* claimed once again that immigration was the fundamental and paramount issue of the day.[64]

This chapter has examined one incident in the long history of the Hutterites in some detail. What does it tell us about the "Hutterite way"? What light does it shed on the beliefs and behaviors of the group during the second decade of the twentieth century? The first, and perhaps the most important, observation is that the Brethren held fast to the basic principles of their faith even under duress. Challenged to be "true patriots" and to support the war effort with men and money, they were consistent and adamant in their refusal. True to their history, there was no hint of compromise nor evidence of individuals or families defecting.[65] Just as their ancestors had refused to defend themselves from enraged neighbors, so too the Brethren of Jamesville Colony looked on while their flocks and herds were stolen and their cellar was broken into.

And yet the Hutterites were not absolutists in their adherence to the principle of pacifism. They were prepared to work hard on their farms to produce food for the general good and to allow their young men to work at alternative service as long as it was not directly related to the war effort or administered by the army. Likewise, they were happy to contribute to charities that were directed toward the poor and disadvantaged. It was only Liberty Bonds and the war effort that they could not countenance. In their eyes, presidents, governors, prime ministers, and other officials were ordained by God to administer the "world" outside their little ark. They tried as far as their consciences would allow to "render unto Caesar the things which are Caesar's." In spite of the unjust treatment they received, they maintained their respect for those in authority.[66]

The Hutterites were equally successful in dealing with the practical problems thrust upon them by their decision to uproot and move. It really was an amazing achievement to move fourteen communities, with some fifteen hundred people, to a new country in the face of bewildered incomprehension or, more often, virulent hostility. It took remarkable leadership on the part of ministers and confident obedience and support from the Hutterite community as a whole. Customarily, important decisions are discussed and mulled over within a colony for months or even years until its members reach a feeling of consensus. In this case, as harassment escalated, the colonies had to make the crucial decision to sell and leave within weeks. Individual ministers had to seek out new colony sites far away in a foreign land. Then they had to shepherd their flocks through the complex bureaucratic obstacle course set up at the border.

It is a tribute to those leaders that none of the new colony sites, acquired under such difficult circumstances, proved untenable. They are all flourishing to the present. Indeed, one of the most pressing problems faced by several of the newly established colonies was the need to look for new sites for daughter colonies almost immediately. These colonies had populations of over 100 when they moved and had not been able to buy as much land as they needed. In Manitoba, Rosedale Colony established Iberville (1919), Maxwell hived to Barrickman (1920), and Milltown founded Blumengart (1922), partly to accommodate an influx of some colonists who had been stranded in South Dakota. The Lehrerleut colonies in southern Alberta also expanded: New Elmspring hived to Big Bend (1920) and Milford to Miami (1924). The need for additional land was not quite so pressing for the Dariusleut, who were able to defer establishing daughter colonies until the mid-1920s, when East Cardston hived to Ewelme (1925), Rosebud to New Rosebud

(1926), and Raley to New York (1924). In total there were twenty-six colonies with 2,622 Hutterites in Alberta in 1922.[67]

A discussion of the effects of the war on the host populations in the United States and Canada is not relevant here. Suffice it to say that the story of the Hutterites illustrates once again the evil contagion of war. Within a few weeks, folk who had been living side by side in relative harmony were riven with bitter hostility. Tolerance became a vice, and truth, in the sense of verifiable facts, was ignored or subverted. The unfamiliar "other" became the scapegoat for the fears and anxieties of the majority. A sad postscript to this narrative is the fact that it was repeated in Alberta only two decades later (discussed in chapter 4).

The Remnant

The closure of the border in May 1919 caught some Hutterite colonies in the midst of their escape from South Dakota. Minister Johann Entz of Milford Colony wrote to the Canadian immigration authorities to explain that his colony had sold all its land in the United States in August 1918 and purchased land near Magrath, Alberta. It had sent 130 of its most able people to build houses and set up a new colony. Eighteen carloads of effects had been forwarded, and three carloads and 54 people had been left behind. This group was to have followed as soon as the new colony was ready, but now they were stranded in the United States.[68] Other colonies were in a similar position, for by this time there were six colonies in Manitoba, which had 625 members in Canada while 247 still languished in South Dakota. The other three big Lehrerleut colonies were in a similar position. They had successfully obtained an extensive tract of land in southern Alberta, and work crews and young families had been dispatched to start building, but the sudden border closure left substantial remnants of the population of Rockport and Old Elm Spring Colonies behind. These groups were not able to rejoin their communities in Alberta until 1929 and 1934, respectively.[69]

Milltown Colony was another community whose plans for an orderly migration were rudely disrupted.[70] Sixty-five people under the leadership of Joseph Kleinsasser had planned to join the rest of their colony in Manitoba, but now they were effectively cut off. When Kleinsasser pleaded his case to Minister Calder, he got a brusque reply.[71] The group settled down to farm the familiar fields for two years. In 1922, when the border had opened again, instead of joining their kin at Milltown, Manitoba, they bought land from Old Order Mennonites in the village of Blumengart, near Plum Coulee, Manitoba, and established Blumengart Colony. The Mennonites had decided to move to Mexico rather than to conform to Canadian school laws.[72]

Some colonies elected to weather the storm of hostility and stay in South Dakota. An example is the original Bon Homme Colony. This community was ready to divide and establish a daughter colony in 1918. As the atmosphere in South Dakota became more threatening, they bought land in Manitoba and sent their young men, who were eligible for conscription, ahead to Canada. They made no moves to sell the home place, and some eighty people remained to maintain the flourishing colony on the banks of the Missouri River. This is the only colony continuously occupied from 1874 to the present.

Wolf Creek, the founding Dariusleut colony in the Dakotas, also stayed. Only a few years previously they had set up Spring Creek and Warren Range Colonies in Montana. They had no pressing need to split again, and perhaps the leadership was reluctant to sell under duress and receive a poor return for all that they had achieved. It was not until 1930 that this last remaining Dariusleut colony joined the others in Alberta, building a new Wolf Creek Colony near Stirling, Alberta.[73]

Thus the forced migration of the Hutterites from South Dakota to Canada in 1918–19 was not a clean break. Michael Scott, a Winnipeg land agent who had handled much business for the Brethren and sometimes acted as their spokesperson, reported that some two-thirds of their people had actually crossed the border by October 1918.[74] The minister of immigration informed the House of Commons that about one thousand Hutterites had entered Canada in 1918.[75] These reports imply that between five and six hundred Hutterites remained in South Dakota, where there were still six functioning colonies.[76] Some were severely depleted in numbers, while others were fully operational with eight to one hundred people. There were some advantages to maintaining a presence in the United States. These colonies provided somewhere for men who had been performing "alternative services" to return to when they were discharged. It also provided an opportunity to conclude unfinished sales of land and equipment.

The Brethren had managed to extricate themselves from the hostile environment in South Dakota. The Schmiedeleut had established themselves in Manitoba and had obtained a measure of acceptance from the host population there. The Dariusleut and Lehrerleut had faced a barrage of hostility on their arrival in Alberta, but they had persevered. By the early 1920s latecomers from South Dakota had arrived and families had been reunited. Now they needed new land for their burgeoning population. Surprisingly, the onset of the Great Depression was to provide them with opportunities to expand.

3

Consolidation and Acceptance

Surviving the Great Depression, 1920–1941

Pierre Berton called it "perhaps the most significant ten years in our history, a watershed era that scarred and transformed the nation."[1] During that decade, from 1929 to 1939, Canada wrestled with the combined effects of devastating drought, a slump in commodity prices, and the complete disruption of world trade. Berton's words echoed those of western Canadian historians R. Douglas Francis and Herman Ganzevoort, who called the Depression decade "possibly the most significant and memorable decade in prairie history."[2] At the personal and family levels, the experience of the "winter years" traumatized a generation of prairie people.[3] However, individuals could grasp only their own local corner of the general disaster. In fact, there were significant differences in the impact of the drought and blowing topsoil in both space and time.

A generation of scientific work has enabled us to set the drought of the 1930s in the cyclic pattern of climate change reaching back millennia.[4] Drought is not an aberration on the Canadian prairies; it is the norm. Indeed, it is one of a complex of factors creating and maintaining grassland ecosystems.[5] The Saskatchewan geographer A. K. Chakravarti used data from sixty-three climate stations over a fifty-year period to produce a series of maps showing where drought struck most severely and which regions enjoyed average precipitation. He concluded that "even during the years of most deficient precipitation, the agricultural areas of the three prairie provinces were affected unequally."[6] This regional variation in precipitation helps one interpret reports from Hutterite colonies that often seem so contradictory.

In 1932 Maxwell Colony in Manitoba established a daughter colony at Alsask, on the border between Alberta and Saskatchewan.

It was close to the epicenter of the dry belt of Palliser's Triangle. Here the droughts started early and were unrelenting. Mary Wipf remembered the blowing dust and a diet that featured blackstrap molasses and *Schreckmuer*, a pudding made with flour and water.[7] After several successive crop failures, the community sold its land and returned to South Dakota, where it bought the old Lehrerleut colony site near Ethan and established New Elmspring Colony in 1936. Huron's daughter colony Roseile, founded near Carmen, Manitoba, suffered much the same fate. Once again, a series of crop failures forced the Hutterites to abandon this colony. In 1936 they repossessed the Dariusleut colony at Jamesville, South Dakota.

In complete contrast, when *Maclean's* magazine correspondent Edna Kells visited Standoff Colony in southern Alberta during March 1937, she wrote, "Western Canada is not all drought and debt ridden. While hundreds of thousands are destitute and on relief, and Ottawa sees a national emergency in the three prairie provinces, there are some western farmers, rich in money, land and cattle to whom debts and relief are unknown. These happy people are the Hutterites."[8] She went on to describe several features of the flourishing community. It owned 8,000 acres and leased a further 2,000, growing 3,000 acres of wheat and 1,000 acres of root vegetables. Almost all the food she relished was grown on the colony: milk, butter, eggs, poultry, meat, and vegetables. She even enjoyed honey from the 50 beehives. Kells backed up her claim that the Hutterites were not hurting for cash by citing the example of Milford Colony, which in 1936 had acquired 15,000 acres, 1,600 sheep, 100 horses, and more than 100 head of cattle for $185,000 cash.

This was by no means a unique case. Lakeside Colony, which split from its parent colony Wolf Creek in 1935, bought 6,462 acres from the Canadian Pacific Railway for $8.25 an acre. "It was almost barren, being leased to a rancher as sheep pasture. Today, the property with its buildings, livestock, farm equipment and other assets is worth $500,000. On this land live twenty-six families, 180 persons in all, and the community is free of debt."[9]

Hutterite communities had several marked advantages compared with family farms. Their relatively large labor force allowed them to carry out a range of agricultural activities. For example, Milltown Colony recorded more than a dozen sources of income during 1935, at the height of the Depression.[10] These ranged from pigs and grain to honey and lamb's wool, as well as lesser amounts for cream, eggs, turkeys, and doves. The colony augmented its income by renting out machinery and labor. Every Hutterite was assured of a warm home and three good meals a day, all supplied by the colony. Above all, the community members could rely on mutual support, cemented by their religious faith. There were cases of real deprivation and belt-tightening, but the self-sufficiency of the colonies shielded them somewhat from the worst effects of the Depression. On many colonies, it was a case of deferring improvements and the purchase of new machinery until better times. Compared with their neighbors, their expectations were humble. Their culture promoted simplicity and a measure of austerity. Some degree of suffering was to be expected as they journeyed through "this vale of tears."

The combination of continuing—if somewhat curtailed—productivity and careful and judicious purchasing allowed many colonies to accumulate capital. Moreover, banks and mortgage companies knew the Hutterites were not going anywhere and regarded them as low risk-clients. All this put them in a good competitive position when they needed to acquire more land for daughter colonies.

The "enemy aliens" of 1919 described in the previous chapter had, over the course of a decade, made the transition to "desirable citizens" by 1929. When Rockport Colony, South Dakota, sought permission to move to Alberta, its agent was able to obtain supporting documents from the premier of Alberta, the Lethbridge Board of Trade, and the mayor of Raymond. Their submissions to the Department of Immigration stressed that "these people have furnished evidence that they will be self sustaining and able to pay their obligations and taxes promptly."[11] In a wire to Prime Minister R. B. Bennett, Joseph Card, an important local landowner, commented, "Owing to prevailing conditions due to several years losses the entry of Rockport Colony would be of great benefit to the vendors, their creditors and other persons concerned in this district (stop) Anything you may do to avoid further delay will be greatly and personally appreciated."[12] The arrival of the colony did indeed bring some benefits to the region. The colony paid the sum of $285,000 for 6,400 acres, and the colonists brought with them $175,000 worth of livestock and machinery. They were reported to have spent $39,000 in the town of Warner during their first year of residence in Alberta at the newly built Hutterville Colony.[13]

South Dakota, too, sought to lure back some of the Hutterite colonies that had been driven out in 1918. Both the state itself and various other loan associations had acquired "so much land they didn't know what to do with it all, with nobody farming and nobody buying, it wasn't any good to them."[14] Agents were sent to Canada to talk to the Brethren. In 1935 the South Dakota Legislature passed a communal corporation law that granted the colonies the same tax benefits already enjoyed by cooperatives.

These overtures received a modest reward. As mentioned earlier, Huron Colony, Manitoba, reoccupied Jamesville by way of Roseile in 1936, and Maxwell acquired New Elmspring, South Dakota, after the failure of Alsask. In addition, Barickman, Manitoba, repossessed the old Dariusleut colony at Tschetter, South Dakota, and Bon Homme, Manitoba, took over the Rockport site when the last group of Lehrerleut left for Alberta in 1934. These long-distance moves were costly and meant that ongoing support from the parent colonies was more difficult. However, familiar tracts of land previously owned and worked by Hutterites were available at reasonable rates. For the bruised and battered communities that had failed to make a go of things in Canada, it was "going home." Nostalgia drew them back to South Dakota. As Paul Gross wrote so lyrically, "Loud lamentations were heard. They longed for the fat catfish and buffalofish which the James River had offered. They longed for the big watermelons and cantaloupes and other fruits which their orchards had provided."[15]

In Manitoba, five Schmiedeleut colonies were established during the 1930s. Bon Homme bought adjacent land to build Waldheim, while Huron's daughter colony Poplar Point was only 8 miles away. Rosedale found land westward, closer to Portage le Prairie, to establish Elm River. Iberville was lured by a good land deal to build Riverside about 80 miles away near Arden, Manitoba. In 1938 Blumengart

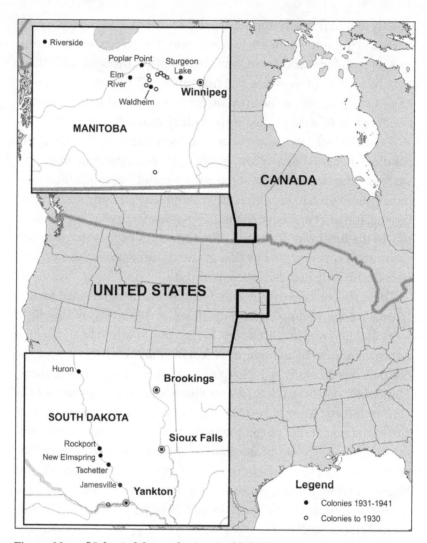

Fig. 12. Map of Schmiedeleut colonies established in Manitoba and South Dakota during the Great Depression, 1930–41. Drawn from county land-ownership maps.

set up the colony of Sturgeon Lake on the northern outskirts of Winnipeg. Figure 12 shows the Schmiedeleut colonies established in Manitoba and South Dakota from 1930 to 1941.

Southern Alberta witnessed a rapid expansion in the number of Hutterite colonies during the 1920s and 1930s. The flight from

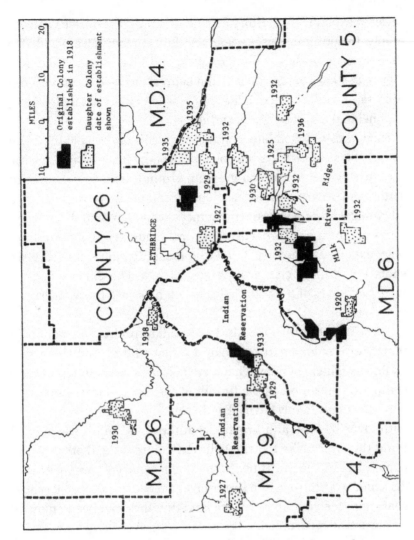

Fig. 13. Map of the original core of Dariusleut and Lehrerleut settlement in southern Alberta, showing colonies established in 1918 and 1920s–30s expansion. Drawn from county landownership maps.

South Dakota had been a financial disaster, and the Brethren were unable to buy the amount of land they required to support their population. Now the Hutterites used their competitive advantage to purchase nearby land for daughter colonies. In southern Alberta, the Lehrerleut established nine new colonies and the Dariusleut seven to expand the territory around their original nucleus considerably. In addition, Beiseker and Sandhills Colonies were added to the Hutterite presence along the Rosebud River north of Calgary. Figure 13 shows the Dariusleut and Lehrerleut colonies in southern Alberta, including the original nucleus of settlement in 1918 and expansion during the 1920s and 1930s.

During this period between the wars, it was possible to obtain blocks of land close to parent colonies in both Manitoba and Alberta. A tightly clustered pattern grew up around the original cores of settlement. Apart from the availability of land, there were marked advantages in moving short distances when horse and cart were the usual means of transport and rural roads were poor. As chapter 6 explores in further detail, the mean distances moved were short for all three clan groups (see table 3). The only exceptions were the moves of the Schmiedeleut colonies back to South Dakota discussed earlier.

The Hutterites throughout the Canadian prairies consolidated their position during this time by acquiring more land and establishing daughter colonies. They were able to take advantage of their competitive position as the tumult of the Great Depression overwhelmed many family farms. For this brief period, they were viewed with favor by local and provincial authorities, and it was a good thing they were able to establish new colonies for their growing population during this time. As the storm clouds of war once again darkened over Europe, the Brethren again became despised scapegoats, and the right to purchase land that they had been enjoying was drastically curtailed.

4

"Enemy Aliens"

World War II and Its Aftermath, 1941–1972

The advent of the Second World War once again changed the public perception of the pacifist, German-speaking Hutterites. Young Canadians were suffering in Japanese prisoner-of-war camps after the loss of Hong Kong in 1941. Londoners were digging out after the blitz, and the United States was girding for war after Pearl Harbor. At home, belt-tightening and rationing were becoming a part of life. As had been the case during the conflict two decades earlier, the bitter passions engendered by war unleashed a barrage of resentment against the Hutterites. They were accused of not being prepared to defend the countries in which they appeared to be thriving. The Canadian Legion and American veterans led the charge to do something about the "Hutterite problem."

In point of fact, the authorities in the United States and Canada were much better prepared to deal with conscientious objectors than they had been in 1918. Most Hutterite young men were deferred from enlisting to continue to do their vital work of producing food on the colonies. Others, judged to be surplus to the needs of the colony farms, were sent to alternative service camps, where they worked in forestry, road construction, and mining and in the paper mills.[1] The Brethren made financial donations to the Red Cross and humanitarian organizations, and these donations were handled by civilian banks. Clearly the Hutterites pulled their weight as far as their consciences would allow, but their efforts were not enough for the zealots.

Farmers also raised their voices in anger and frustration as they entreated the governments to curb further expansion of the colonies. The war had breathed new life into agriculture. As demand rose, so did prices, and as a result there was increasing talk of expansion and mechanization. In such a climate, the Hutterites were perceived as unfair competition. Businessmen in small towns joined the chorus in condemning the Brethren, who they claimed bypassed local stores and bought at wholesale rates in the larger centers. Moreover, because the colonies did not participate in community, church, or school activities, they disrupted the social life of townships in which they settled. A legislator in South Dakota referred to the Hutterites as Russians who lived an un-American existence, people who made huge profits but did nothing to defend their country. He went on to predict that they could take over the whole county if not checked.[2] J. P. Bend of Poplar Point, Manitoba, similarly argued that "the ordinary farmer can't compete with the colony system."[3] The most vociferous anti-Hutterite rhetoric was voiced in rural Alberta, where demands to control the colonies were accompanied by threats to "take matters into our own hands" and engage in civil disobedience, even to burn down colonies.[4]

Even after the end of World War II, agitation against the Hutterites in Manitoba was led by the Community Welfare Association, which pressured the legislature for limits to colony expansion like those being adopted in Alberta. A committee was appointed to investigate the situation, but no action was taken. In 1954 the Union of Manitoba Municipalities took up the cause and maintained annual pleas for restrictive action. But the Hutterites had powerful friends in Manitoba. The two Winnipeg newspapers opposed any efforts to discriminate against the Brethren, and the Manitoba Civil Liberties Association and several of the churches exposed some of the fraudulent claims made against them, pointing out that rural depopulation, increased mobility, and the growth of urban shopping centers could not be blamed on the Hutterites.[5]

Responding to ongoing public pressure, Premier Douglas Campbell met with Hutterite leaders and told them that if they did not reach an agreement with the municipalities, legislation would be enacted.[6] The parties reached a "gentleman's agreement" that met many of the municipalities' demands. The Hutterites agreed to limit the number of colonies in each municipality and their size. Moreover, new colonies were to be sited at least 10 miles from existing ones. The *Winnipeg Tribune* commented, "It is sincerely to be hoped that the agreement will put an end to the essentially undemocratic demands which have surrounded the Hutterite question in Manitoba in recent years." It was clear evidence that the Hutterites were "peace loving people and anxious to maintain friendly relations with their fellow men."[7]

From the Hutterites' point of view, this apparent retreat reflected a realistic appraisal of the likely pattern of future colony expansion. Land values in the core area of settlement west of Winnipeg were becoming prohibitive, and the likelihood of acquiring suitable blocks of land was remote. Colonies were already exploring new venues in their search for sites for daughter colonies. In this endeavor they were assisted by the very factors that were undermining the viability of the smallest service centers: the growing ubiquity of trucks and the marked improvement of rural roads. Proximity to a parent colony had become less of an issue as the friction of distance was reduced. The "gentleman's agreement" may have enhanced a trend that was already developing.

During and immediately after the war, six new colonies were established in Manitoba. Three were located close to their parent colonies and the core, while the others were much more dispersed. Four other colonies in Manitoba elected to establish daughter colonies in South Dakota, where land was available at lower prices. Over the next decade the momentum toward a more dispersed distribution of colonies in Manitoba was maintained. Twelve new colonies were added, and by the end of the 1960s there were thirty-two colonies spread from Brightstone, in the east near Lac du Bonnet, to Deerboine and Spring Valley, close to Brandon in the west.[8]

Yet in South Dakota, beginning in 1949, every session of the state legislature was presented with a bill to revoke the corporate charters of the Hutterites. This constant attrition by the anti-Hutterite clique was ultimately successful. In 1955, after a heated debate, a motion to strip the Hutterites of the privileges they had been granted in 1935 passed by a vote of 40–32. This bill set limits to the size of existing colonies but in no way impinged on the ability of the Brethren to establish new colonies. The new law attracted the attention of news media throughout the United States and brought South Dakota some unfavorable publicity for discriminating against a small religious group.[9]

The James River remained the dominant axis of Hutterite settlement in the state during the postwar period. Five daughter colonies were established from Canadian parent colonies and ten others from within the state. Four of the old colony sites on the river, abandoned in 1918, were reoccupied. But also, for the first time, new sites were acquired in counties farther from the river. Four colonies were founded to the west, from Edmunds County in the north down to Platte County on the Missouri River in the south. They were balanced by four new colonies to the east of the central axis of settlement.[10]

In Alberta, the Social Credit government acted swiftly in response to the hectoring demands of its rural and small-town base. In 1942 it passed the Land Sales Prohibition Act, which prohibited sales of land to "enemy aliens and Hutterites." In April 1947 this temporary measure was replaced by the Communal Property Act, which remained in force—with amendments—until 1973.[11] The act had four main provisions: existing colonies were not allowed to expand their holdings either by purchase or by lease; no new colony could be established within 40 miles of an existing colony; no new colony could contain more than 6,400 acres; and under the Veterans' Land Act of 1942, any land the Hutterites hoped to buy had to be advertised for sixty days so that veterans would have an opportunity to buy it. The implicit objective of the act was to encourage the dispersal of Hutterite colonies and thereby, it was hoped, promote the assimilation of the sect. In fact, the perceived hostility of the outside world only encouraged the solidarity and cohesion of the "little flock." This act had a profound effect on the Hutterite settlement pattern in Alberta, and although much has been written about the Communal Property Act, its spatial and geographic implications have not been evaluated.[12]

A Period of Absolute Legislative Control, 1942–60

With the stroke of a pen, more than a quarter of the agricultural land in the province was placed out-of-bounds to Hutterite settlement.

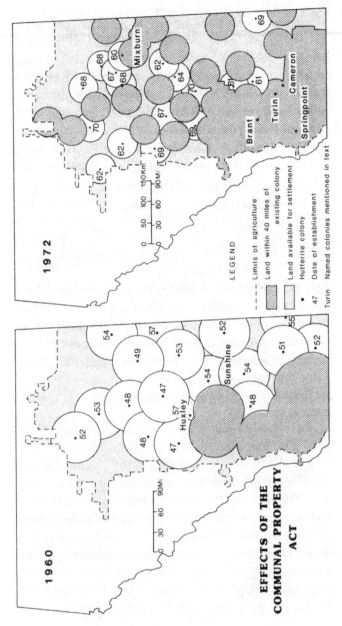

Fig. 14. Map showing the effect of the Communal Property
Act on Hutterite settlement, with the spatial implications of
the original act to 1960 and the revised act to 1972. Drawn
from county landownership maps.

Each new daughter colony drastically reduced the area within which further growth was permitted. For example, 1947 saw the founding of Pinehill Colony more than 40 miles north of Fairview and Red Willow to the east of Red Deer (see fig. 14, where the numbers in the circles denote the colonies' dates of establishment). In 1948 Newdale found a legal site south and east of Calgary, but in general terms, the Hutterites were forced to look farther and farther afield. Only five new colonies were established south of Calgary, while twelve were spread between Calgary and Edmonton and two, Scotford and Pibrock, were located north of Edmonton. As the map in figure 14 shows, toward the end of the 1950s the area in which to look for a legal site within Alberta had become very limited. What had started as a control measure had in fact become an act of banishment.

The relationship between the Hutterites and the governments of the outside world has always been of concern to colony leaders. Peter Rideman, the great Hutterite "prophet," explained, "Governmental authority is appointed by God as the rod of his anger for the discipline and punishment of the evil and profligate nation. Therefore, one should be obedient."[13] The Hutterites respected both the letter and the spirit of Albertan laws. The map shows that only one new colony was established that infringed the provisions of the Communal Property Act. This was Sunshine Colony. The leader of this colony formed a corporation with two non-Hutterites to purchase land after the government had turned down several of his applications to buy land elsewhere.

The location of colonies established during this period of rigidly enforced controls suggests that the 40-mile limit became the prime consideration in the search for a site for a daughter colony. The Hutterites were quick to see the advantage of locating as close to an existing colony as was permitted, for this reduced the area put out-of-bounds to further Hutterite settlement to a minimum. As early as 1948 the sites of Ferrybank, Newdale, and Camrose were within 5 or 6 miles of the permitted limits. The site of Huxley is of particular interest in this context. The possible legal area available was only 15 miles long and narrowed from 6 to 2 miles in width, and the new colony was sited right in the middle of this area.

As land became increasingly hard to acquire in Alberta, a number of colony leaders began to search for sites outside the province. Ten daughter colonies were established in Montana between 1945 and 1951. Land was available there at reasonable rates, and the distance from parent colonies in southern Alberta was well within acceptable limits. Moreover, many heads of families in Alberta colonies still had U.S. citizenship because of their birth or early residence in South Dakota and thus had little difficulty in crossing the border.[14]

The movement of Hutterites from Alberta into Montana was met with hostility. Small towns like Choteau organized citizens committees to fight the "Hutterite menace."[15] However, these intense local feelings did not find legislative expression until 1961, when a Communal Expansion Bill was introduced into the Montana legislature. This elaborate bill, modeled on the Alberta Communal Property Act, passed the house of assembly but was rejected by the senate.[16] Attempts at regulation were revived in 1963 but were unsuccessful.

The Hutterites recognized that continuing migration from Alberta to Montana would intensify hostility toward them. They reached an internal agreement that there should be no additional movement across the international border. Glacier Colony (1950) and Hillside (1951) were the last colonies to be established from outside the state. Hutterite leaders hoped that this agreement would allow expansion to take place within Montana from the newly established nucleus after a period during which tensions diminished.[17]

As expansion south into the United States became more difficult, Hutterite leaders began to look eastward to Saskatchewan. In 1952 the first colonies were established there on the flanks of the Cypress Hills south of Maple Creek.[18] By 1960 there were seven colonies in southwestern Saskatchewan. The Saskatchewan government responded to local unease by initiating a study of the situation that was to be carried out by the Canadian Mental Health Association.[19] A few years later anti-Hutterite sentiment among the general population intensified, and a government committee was established to manage further expansion of colonies and minimize friction. An intensive study of Hutterite-community relations was undertaken, and the Saskatchewan government and the Hutterian

Brethren reached an informal agreement.[20] This memorandum of understanding was designed as a guideline for both the colonies and the provincial government. All Hutterite land purchases were to be approved by a committee, and new colonies were to be located at least 35 miles apart. By and large both sides honored the agreement, and Hutterite expansion in Saskatchewan continued along the lines laid out in the agreement.

A Period of Negotiated Settlement in Alberta, 1960–71

A government inquiry into Hutterite settlement in Alberta was initiated in 1958 and submitted its recommendations in 1959.[21] The tenor of this report was moderate and sympathetic to the Hutterites, although assimilation was still the implicit aim of government policy. It suggested that the inflexible legal restrictions presently in place should be replaced by a "control board" with discretionary powers, which would guide the location of new colonies to the mutual benefit of the Brethren and the farming community.

Parts of the recommendations were incorporated into the Communal Property Act.[22] A three-man board was directed to receive applications from Hutterites who wished to establish a new colony and to decide whether granting their request would be "in the public interest." Then the board was to advise the cabinet, which would make the final decision. Thus the whole question of Hutterite land purchases became a political issue.

The colonies established under the guidance of the Communal Property Control Board filled in the regular but dispersed pattern of the previous period (fig. 14). Growth within the core areas was still strictly limited, but the 40-mile clause was replaced by a guideline suggesting that the colonies should be about 20 miles apart. At once large land areas became available for legal settlement, and twenty-six colonies were founded between those established earlier.

The revised Communal Property Act allowed a wide range of discretion to the board that administered it. The first four colonies established on the board's recommendation were all well within 20 miles of the nearest neighboring colony. In spite of this flexibility, the board was by no means a control in name only. Evidence suggests that only about half of the first-choice locations put forward by Hutterite leaders were allowed.[23]

The smooth operation of the revised act was seriously hindered by the instigation of public hearings for each application. These meetings, which had been envisioned by the 1958 Committee of Inquiry as a means of dispelling misunderstandings between the Hutterites and their neighbors, became confrontations that exacerbated bad feelings.[24] In 1962 the Communal Property Act was further amended to do away with mandatory public hearings.[25]

It is easy to see why many Hutterite elders regarded the Communal Property Control Board with suspicion. Involvement with the board meant delays that were often very costly. It also meant interaction with the outside world for a prolonged period. Sometimes the cabinet turned down expansion plans that had been approved by the board and gave no reason. Many leaders preferred to leave Alberta rather than become involved in prolonged hassles with the government. During the 1960s seventeen daughter colonies were established outside the province from parent colonies in Alberta.

An alternative strategy was to establish a new colony illegally. During the eleven years of the board's operation four colonies were established without its prior approval. Spring Point Colony was established by Granum on land that it had been renting for some years. The move was achieved with a minimum of publicity while the 1942 act was under review in 1960. West Raley Colony had three different sites rejected by the board and was adamant that its new colony should not be as far away as its previous daughter colony. In 1965 it rented land northwest of Taber. Gradually the acreage and the number of people living at "Cameron Ranch" increased. This de facto colony was then officially recognized in 1971.

The most celebrated case of a colony going against the will of the board was Brant Colony, established from Rocklake in 1964.[26] Two other colonies applied to go to this site, but all three were turned down. Nevertheless, Rocklake Colony went ahead and purchased the land through a number of members acting as individuals. Charges were brought against Rocklake by the board, and the colony responded by hiring a lawyer and obtaining an injunction against the board on the grounds that the act was *ultra vires* of provincial jurisdiction. During the following years the case mounted from court to court until it reached the Supreme Court of Canada in 1969. On each case the appeal was dismissed on the grounds that the Communal Property Act was judged to be legislation dealing with land tenure and not with religion, and therefore it was *intra vires* the legislature of Alberta. However, after the final appeal had been rejected by the Supreme Court, no move was made to dispossess the Hutterite community, which by then numbered seventy-five persons collectively owning 7,785 acres. In December 1969 the board approved the existence of the colony. Neighboring Turin Colony was established in almost identical fashion. Four men purchased land from Ewelme Colony, and prosecution was delayed pending the outcome of the Brant case. In 1971 this new colony was formally recognized.

Thus some Hutterite leaders departed from the "Hutterite way" in that they acted illegally and confronted the government, though their actions were not approved by the majority of other leaders. Jacob Walter, minister at Standoff Colony, said at the time of the Brant case, "We are a hundred percent against going against the government. Any colony which goes against the law should be excommunicated."[27] Joseph Hofer of New York Colony expressed similar sentiments: "They did wrong purchasing the land as individuals, and without the government's permission. If they can't get land through the government then they should not move. They bought it the wrong way."[28] However, in 1972 a complete survey of lands owned, leased, or worked by the Hutterites showed that many colonies used land that had never been approved by the board.[29] Thus local action by colonies to increase their land holdings was tacitly supported, while direct confrontation, which often involved adverse publicity, was strongly condemned.

The Geography of Confrontation

Much of the antipathy displayed toward the Hutterites has been based on the nonsectarian population's perception of the inequality of their competitive position.[30] Their basic fear has been that the Hutterites, who own only a small percentage of the agricultural land in the province, are eventually going to take over. The mayor of Drumheller remarked, "We are fighting them on a territorial imperative basis."[31] One scholar observed, "The rapid increase in colonies provides a classic example of the ecological competition for territory, and of population's role in intersocial conflict."[32] What is of interest for the geographer is that this nativism seems to have a spatial dimension.

Most of the serious confrontations that have marred relations between the Hutterites and the larger society since the late 1950s have taken place along the margins of the two core areas of settlement (see fig. 15). Some Hutterite leaders appear to have made a conscious effort to obtain land in these zones, which had been opened to them by the changes in the law described earlier. There were clear advantages to be gained from establishing a daughter colony within 40 or 50 miles of the parent colony. The costs of the move would be reduced, and the new infrastructure could be built from the home colony in an efficient manner. The close ties between parent and daughter colonies could be maintained with a minimum of difficulty. Perhaps most significant was the fact that the new site would be akin to the old one in terms of rainfall, terrain, and soil, and the pragmatic lessons learned in the familiar environment could be applied to the new one. However, these efforts to find land on the margins of the core areas provoked strong resistance from the local population. It is for this reason that the zones roughly encompassing the cores are referred to as "strategic fronts" or areas "of persistent danger or political tension."[33]

Interviews with Hutterite leaders made it clear that they were aware of the hostility of their potential neighbors, though their responses to the situation varied. Some leaders emphasized that they had not even considered these areas simply because they did not want any hassle. They pointed out that trucks and improved roads meant that a distance of 200 miles or more posed few real problems. Others expressed the view that since opposition to their arrival was inevitable, they might as well try to find a new place in the most convenient location and be prepared to ride out the storm

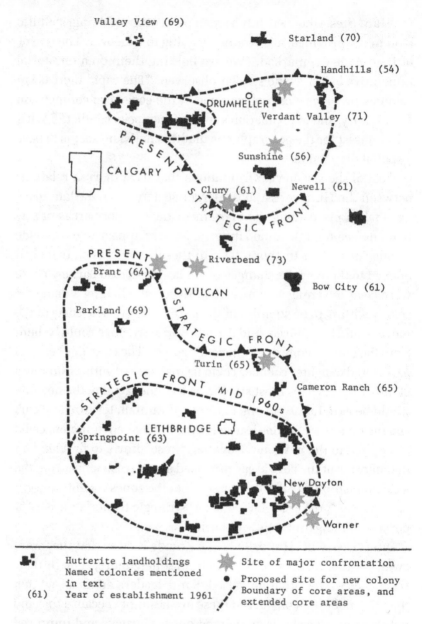

Fig. 15. Hutterite landholdings, confrontations, and expanding core areas during the 1960s and early 1970s, while the Communal Property Act was in force. Drawn from county landownership maps.

of protest that their purchase might provoke. They were confident that they would be able to dispel hostile sentiments within a few years.[34] As to be expected, those who had purchased land in northern Alberta or several hundred miles away in Saskatchewan were highly vocal in deprecating the way in which some "irresponsible colonies" had exacerbated nativism by their choice of a new site or by flouting government regulations.[35]

During the late 1950s the critical section of the strategic front was the southeast sector of the southern core. The New Dayton local of the Farmers' Union exposed what was known as the Duncan land deal, wherein four sections of land some 9 miles south of Lethbridge had been purchased by two Hutterites acting as individuals and as such was in contravention of the Communal Property Act. It is interesting to note that this case involved Felger Colony, which was no longer recognized by the Hutterite Church. Two years later feelings were still running high in the area, and a bitter eruption of hostility followed O.K. Colony's attempt to purchase the Henninger Ranch to the east of Milk River. This property was more than 20 miles from an existing colony, and the land had been on the market for some time.

The Communal Property Control Board met at Milk River to gather evidence concerning this proposed purchase during June 1960. The spokesman for the Warner local of the Farmers' Union warned that farmers were prepared "to break the civil laws of Canada if necessary," and he talked of "seething resentment which could erupt at any time."[36] Mayor Ralph Baird of Milk River predicted that the Hutterites would be driven from Warner County by force if government action did not check their growth. The situation was complicated by the fact that the minister of agriculture, Leonard C. Halmrast, was member of the legislature for the Warner constituency. The hearings reminded lawyer P. G. Davies, who had been retained by the Hutterites, of a "kangaroo court in an uncivilized country," while Rev. Jacob Waldner of O.K. Colony said that the current atmosphere was "repugnant to our sense of values" and that "the threats were very unbecoming of people who stress democracy and goodwill."[37] The option to purchase was not taken up by the colony leaders, who eventually obtained a fine spread near Bassano.[38]

The southeastern sector of the northern core was the scene of more successful efforts by the Hutterites to extend their heartland. In 1960 Tschetter Colony obtained permission from the newly appointed Communal Property Control Board to establish a colony near Cluny on 6,400 acres. Mayor Watson claimed that "the people of the area were threatening to burn as the Hutterites build." Threats were also made against the family selling the land.[39] In spite of this resentment, the colony was built. Thus 1961 saw the foundation of three colonies in this sensitive area, Cluny, Newell, and Bow City, and the tacit recognition of Sunshine Colony, which had been established in 1956 without governmental approval (see fig. 15). The boundary of the northern core now included the county of Wheatland and reached to the Bow River.

Between the two core areas of settlement lie the county of Vulcan and the municipal districts of Foothills and Claresholm. These administrative districts had few colonies in 1942, and from that time until 1960 new colonies had been debarred by the provisions of the Communal Property Act. The mid-1960s saw several attempts to establish colonies on lands that had become available for legal settlement when the law was changed. The strategic locations of Brant, Turin, Cameron Ranch, and Parkland (whose establishment was discussed earlier) on the northern perimeter of the southern core are clear. The rural residents of Vulcan perceived themselves to be threatened by two encroaching fronts of "alien" settlement. The proposal to establish Riverbend Colony near Mossleigh provoked an outburst of derisive bitterness directed toward not only the Hutterites but also local residents who did not share the partisan views of those opposed to the colony.[40]

The area around the town of Drumheller witnessed another series of confrontations. This service center, a few kilometers east of the original northern nucleus of Hutterite settlement, had viewed the amendment of the Communal Property Act with apprehension. The city was suffering from the increasing dominance of Calgary during an era of increasing mobility and from structural changes to its economic base. A study of the possible economic impact of the location of a Hutterite colony within the town's hinterland was commissioned, and it was undertaken by the Calgary firm of Bogehold, Jensen and Lefebve Consultants. Their report compared the spending habits of a colony with those of ten farms that might otherwise have occupied the same area. They reached the conclusion that although the expenditures were totally different, reflecting alternate value systems, the total payoff to the city was very similar in both cases. Mayor E. A. Tosach withdrew municipal opposition to Hutterite expansion, but the proposed purchase of eleven sections by Springvale Colony was vetoed by the Communal Property Control Board.[41]

In 1970 the municipality raised no violent objections to the establishment of Starland Colony, but in February 1971 there were protests to the Board about the "rather secretive and hurried way" in which permission had been granted to the colony to extend their holding to the maximum allowed. Assurances were received from the chairman of the Communal Property Control Board that no further colonies would be located in Municipal District 49. During the summer of 1971 a rumor began to circulate that Hutterites from Hand Hills Colony were interested in acquiring land in Verdant Valley. On September 13 the city of Drumheller protested this expansion. However, on November 24 the new colony was approved by the cabinet, apparently acting on the advice of the board. On December 2 lawyer A. M. Harradence, who had been retained by the Starland Municipality, passed the letter that had been received from the board in February, assuring them that no further expansion would take place, to the minister of municipal affairs, who dismissed the board.[42] A complete moratorium on Hutterite land purchases followed, and this lasted until the repeal of the Communal Property Act in March 1973.

Enough has been said to establish that several of the clashes that took place between the Hutterites and the host society did so along the strategic fronts of the core areas of settlement. Newsworthy protests or even hostile letters to the press were notably absent from towns and villages within the core areas, such as Raymond, Magrath, Lethbridge, Beiseker, and Crossfield. At the same time, colonies such as Warburg, Morinville and Leedale were established in the domain at some distance from the cores and faced little overt nativism.

Scholars studying the Schmiedeleut have made this observation. Paul Conkin notes that it was a representative from Hanson County, the very heart of Hutterite country in South Dakota, who led the defense of the Brethren in the legislature.[43] Victor Peters points out that Jack McDowell, who steadfastly opposed anti-Hutterite legislation in Manitoba, represented the electoral district that had the greatest number of colonies in Manitoba.[44]

The evidence suggests that increased familiarity with Hutterites leads to a decrease in tension and a tendency toward quiescence in a particular area. A spirit of accommodation between the colonists and the larger society has been evident in the core areas. There the passions of the past had burned themselves out, and the school boards and the colonies worked well together. Perhaps harmonious coexistence need not be equated with assimilation. Looking back over several decades to the era of the Communal Property Act, some senior Hutterite leaders point out that the restrictions even had some positive results, since colonies were forced to look farther afield and explore new environments, and this prevented an unhealthy degree of agglomeration of colonies in a few core regions. Nevertheless, as discussed in the next chapter, the Hutterites reacted with caution when the act was eventually repealed. They did everything they could to cooperate with government authorities and actively worked at being "good neighbors" to reduce local hostility.

5

Some Freedom of Locational Choice

Varied Reactions, 1973–1981

The decade of the 1970s was one of change and transition in Canadian society. The implications of the Canadian Bill of Rights—passed in 1960—had been absorbed and debated, and in 1982 the general principles it embraced were made more explicit by the passage of the Canadian Charter of Rights and Freedoms. The perception of Canada as the creation of two founding peoples was challenged by the vision of a country also created by immigrants—a cultural mosaic. The policy of multiculturalism was adopted by the government of Canada under Pierre Trudeau during the 1970s and 1980s.[1] In the United States, two decades of work on civil rights had made some progress in changing attitudes toward the "other." These changes had profound implications for all ethnic minorities.

Throughout the Northern Great Plains, authorities and the media increasingly viewed the Hutterites as a religious group worthy of respect. There were more colonies now, and they were beginning to make a significant contribution to the agricultural productivity of the regions they occupied. For the first time Hutterites were being appointed to advisory marketing boards, and the Brethren could wield considerable political power if their interests were involved. Responding to this more permissive social environment, the number of colonies continued to grow.

In Manitoba eighteen Schmiedeleut colonies were established over the decade 1973–83. Figure 16 shows the distribution of colonies during this period. The concentration in the historic core area is still discernible, but the general impression is of colonies widely dispersed across the fertile southern extent of the province. Three relatively short-distance moves to locations on the periphery of the core extended its area and added to its importance, but the over-

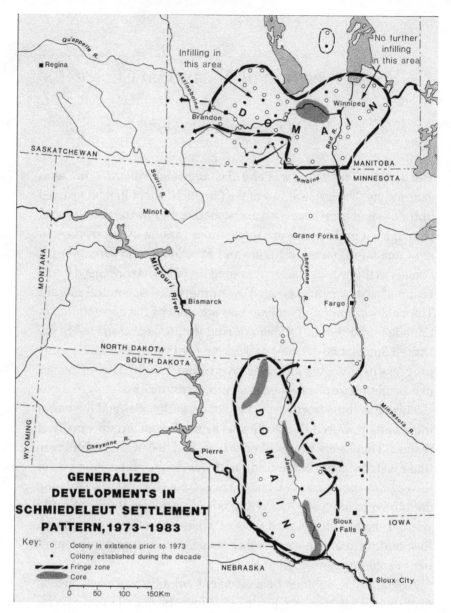

Fig. 16. Map of generalized developments in the Schmiedeleut settlement pattern, 1973–83. Drawn from county landownership maps.

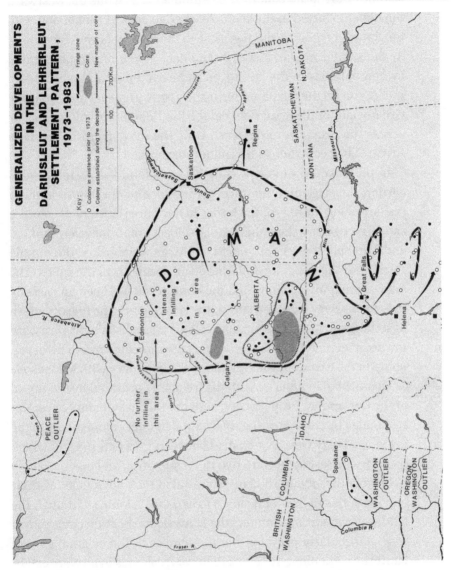

Fig. 17. Map of generalized developments in the Dariusleut and Lehrerleut settlement pattern, 1973–83. Drawn from county landownership maps.

whelming thrust of new settlement was to the west and south. Six colonies were located along the Pembina River, while the westward movement started in the 1950s reached its logical conclusion with the founding of four colonies close to the Saskatchewan boundary. At the same time, areas north and east of Winnipeg, penetrated by new colonies in the late 1950s and early 1960s, did not become nuclei for further expansion in the 1970s. Instead, Brightstone, Greenwald, and Springfield established daughter colonies clear across the province to the west. Only the move from Lakeside to Broad Valley contradicts this generalization.

In the Dakotas, nine new colonies were founded. As mentioned earlier, the settlement pattern here tended to develop in a linear fashion along the axis of the James River. Three clusters of colonies can be recognized along this line: the oldest group, between Yankton and Mitchell; the second, north of Huron, established during the 1950s; and the third, west of Aberdeen, dating from the 1960s. The arrows on figure 16 show that the main trend has been an easterly movement away from the James River, weakening the linear pattern of settlement. Moreover, no new colonies have been built westward toward Pierre. A hint of a new concentration appears to be developing to the east of Brookings, along the boundary with Minnesota.

Meanwhile, in Alberta, with the freedom permitted by the repeal of the Communal Property Act, both the Dariusleut and Lehrerleut responded by concentrating their new daughter colonies within the province. Forty were established between 1973 and 1983, of which five were in Saskatchewan, two in Washington, and one in British Columbia (fig. 17). Both clan groups also took advantage of their opportunities to buy land closer to existing colonies, although the tendency was stronger among the Lehrerleut. Short-distance moves were particularly prevalent on the fringes of the original core of Hutterite settlement in Alberta. Thirteen colonies in all were established there both to the east and north.

A landownership map at a larger scale (fig. 18) illustrates this expansion. Six new colonies were established to the east of the original nucleus of settlement. These colonies, such as Midland and Ponderosa, are shown by vertical lines on the map. All these

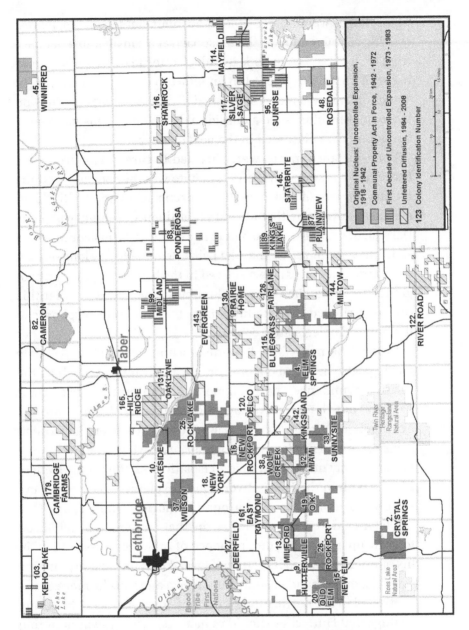

Fig. 18. Map of the southern core of Hutterite settlement in Alberta, showing expansion during various time periods. Drawn from county landownership maps.

new colonies were located at least 20 kilometers from the nearest existing colonies and, for the most part, at a considerable distance from each other. During this decade, Hutterite leaders were working with an advisory board in an effort to defuse controversy. In stark contrast, colonies established after 1984 (diagonal lines on the map) were often sited alongside older colonies. This interesting development is discussed in the next chapter.

Long-distance moves were directed to three main areas: the Peace River Country, Washington State west of Spokane, and the Biggar area west of Saskatoon. The most notable feature of the long-distance moves was that almost all of them were undertaken by Dariusleut colonies. This is not to say that the Dariusleut made no short moves, but rather that the Lehrerleut made few long ones. A similar distinction can be observed in the behavior of the two clan groups in Saskatchewan and Montana, which suggests that this can be attributed to something more than different responses to the removal of legislative controls.

In fact, the motive for long-distance moves is at least partly ideological. There are obvious practical advantages, such as the relative abundance and cheapness of land on the agricultural frontier, but the preservation of *Gemeinschaft* (community) is extremely important too.[2] The long moves represent an explicit decision to find a "place in the wilderness" where the traditional Hutterite way may be pursued in isolation. All the colony leaders I spoke with in the Peace River region explained that there were simply too many Hutterites around Lethbridge and Calgary. One minister said in no uncertain terms that he wanted his children to grow up away from the influence of other colonies, which, in his opinion, were too lax. Others agreed that intercolony visiting could get out of hand in southern Alberta and was far more easily controlled in the north. Along with these concerns were lingering feelings that Hutterites should reduce their visibility by adopting a more dispersed settlement pattern. As one leader said, "Why go where it will cause friction when there is so much good land up here?" Moreover, a tough pioneering role was viewed as positive encouragement to be a good Hutterite. Clearing bush and breaking new land meant that there was more than enough work for every colony member.[3]

These sentiments are not universally shared even among the Dariusleut. Other leaders feel that being a good Hutterite is easiest when colonies are close together. One Dariusleut leader referred to an isolated colony whose crops had been destroyed by a hailstorm. He said it was hard to give help in such a case, whereas if the colony had been within 40 miles, "they would have already forgotten about the hailstorm because their silos would be full." Another minister referred to the fact that several colonies within the Alberta core area were being helped out of critical economic difficulties on the understanding that management decisions would be made jointly until loans were repaid. He explained that this kind of intimate interaction would be difficult with a dispersed pattern of settlement. Others expressed the opinion that the strong sense of community experienced within the colony should be balanced and extended by frequent interaction among colonies.

One of the advantages of relatively short-distance moves cited by leaders is that the colonies may deploy capital more efficiently by sharing equipment. Certainly, a short-distance move causes less disruption in a colony's standard of living, and adults on some colonies are less prepared today to face the rigors of "starting over." These colonies, which occur in all of the Leut, can be identified by their greater expenditures on colony-owned conveniences and, to a limited degree, personal possessions.[4] In one sense, then, the more radical locational decisions are prompted by more conservative ideology. While complacent colonies may stress the material advantages of short-distance moves, strictly traditional colonies will welcome the sacrifices that attend carving a community out of the bush.

The most pertinent consequence of these ideological and behavioral differences with respect to the Hutterite settlement pattern is the tendency toward an increased spatial separation of the Dariusleut and Lehrerleut in Alberta. In 1983 there were no Lehrerleut colonies north of a line drawn from Calgary to the Saskatchewan boundary north of Lloydminster, while there are relatively few

Dariusleut colonies in the southeast of the province. The majority of the Dariusleut moves during the last ten years have been to the north and northwest, while most of the Lehrerleut moves have been to the east and northeast.

As described in chapter 2, the tendency to locate apart dates from the beginnings of Hutterite settlement in Alberta, when the original cluster of Dariusleut colonies was established along the Rosebud River, while the Lehrerleut located along the Milk River Ridge south of Lethbridge. Still, the continued separation is not easy to explain. It is not based on hostility or even antipathy. Yet most social and economic interaction is between colonies of the same clan group, so, other things being equal, daughter colonies prefer to be near other colonies of their own clan.

Separation also reflects slight differences in emphasis in the economic mix of enterprises undertaken by colonies in the two clan groups. All Hutterites make their living from large-scale, diversified agriculture, but there are definite differences of degree among the colonies.[5] On the whole, the Dariusleut colonies emphasize dairy and beef operations, as well as grain, chickens, and pigs. Many also run a flock of sheep. Few Dariusleut leaders would consider seriously a colony site that did not have access to a river or stream and an extensive area of pasture, which helps explain their willingness to locate in the Parkland zones of central Alberta and the Peace River Country.[6] The Lehrerleut, by contrast, tend to specialize in dry farming and grain production, within the general framework of a diversified operation. They have been quite prepared to search for and develop groundwater sources, and most of their colonies are associated with lighter, drier soils of the kind found in southern and southeastern Alberta. Hutterites are pragmatic farmers, whose ability derives from experience rather than theory. There are great advantages to finding a new colony site that mirrors the characteristics of the parent, for lessons learned through the years can be used more readily. Thus the preference for certain environmental conditions is likely to be maintained through several generations and will influence the leaders' perceptions of what constitutes the ideal colony site.

There has been a considerable degree of convergence between the patterns of the Dariusleut and the Lehrerleut in Alberta and the Schmiedeleut in Manitoba. While the former have been able, since the repeal of the Communal Property Act, to locate closer together and to infill the regular dispersed pattern established while the regulations were in force, the Schmiedeleut have been spreading out in search of land at reasonable prices in large blocks. In retrospect, it seems likely that the discriminatory Alberta legislation accelerated a process of dispersal that would have taken place eventually without it. However, a greater degree of homogeneity in aggregate locational patterns masks an increasingly complex range of goals and strategies pursued by leaders within each group. The Schmiedeleut are generally regarded as the most liberal and progressive of the clan groups, yet this is not demonstrated by their diffusion pattern. Perhaps because they have not experienced legislative force, they have not adopted innovative locational behavior, although they have gradually altered the way in which colony division is managed. Their genius for adaptation has been demonstrated more by their willingness to experiment with a variety of new economic activities, ranging from a large-scale alfalfa dehydration plant to an insurance company.[7]

At the other end of the spectrum, the Lehrerleut are the most conservative clan group. They have maintained their regular time periods between divisions and carry out the mechanics of hiving in the traditional manner. Yet their conservatism has found expression in a number of different spatial strategies. When the Communal Property Act was first introduced, they were able to obtain land quite close to parent colonies by expanding into Montana. Later, when increasing hostility barred further expansion in that direction, they pioneered the move into Saskatchewan. Their reluctance to become embroiled with the Communal Property Control Board meant that they maintained long-distance moves throughout the 1960s and early 1970s. Since the repeal of the act in 1973, they have shown a marked desire to reduce the distance moved at colony division.

The relative weakness of the Dariusleut federation of ministers has allowed individual colonies in that Leut more autonomy to make decisions concerning when and where to establish a daughter colony. There have always been maverick colonies in the Dariusleut, which have pursued unconventional courses. The Dariusleut display the widest range of spatial behavior. Some colonies have searched out isolated locations on the agricultural frontier, while others have pursued the economic and social advantages of clustering.

Scholars have concluded that the pace of change in Hutterite culture gathered momentum during the decade under review.[8] Not surprisingly, this trend had a geographic dimension, for the acquisition of land, expansion to new colonies, and the pursuit of large-scale diversified agriculture are all integral parts of the Hutterites' successful adaptation to the North American milieu. Among the Schmiedeleut in Manitoba and South Dakota, a rather more dispersed settlement pattern developed, while in Alberta the Dariusleut and Lehrerleut responded to the repeal of the Communal Property Act with caution and restraint. As discussed in chapter 8, the Hutterites made every effort to cooperate with the liaison officer appointed by the Alberta government. They successfully reduced tension in the rural areas during the decade by avoiding clustering of colonies and pursuing a "good neighbor" policy.

6

Unfettered Diffusion

Expanding Settlement Patterns, 1981–2015

During the thirty-some years bookending the turn of the millennium, the number of Hutterite colonies has doubled. In managers' offices, around kitchen tables, and in Hutterite places of worship, groups of men and women have gathered to make important decisions about their future. When do we have to find a new place? Where might it be? Each of the 223 new colonies built and occupied during this period was the result of years of evaluation, discussion, and consensus building shaped by the experiences described in previous chapters.[1]

Moreover, the ministers and managers leading the discussion, and ultimately responsible for the locational decisions, are a product of their times. They are more confident and assertive in their dealings with outsiders than they were in the past. Many are involved on commodity management boards. Leaders in South Dakota own and manage a nationally significant packing plant, while several Manitoba colonies manufacture products with sales across North America. In Alberta, too, colonies are partnering with the government to develop solar energy and manage the recycling of plastics. How do these gifted and experienced leaders search for new homes in the new millennium? This chapter covers a longer time period and a wider region than the previous ones; it pulls together the narrative of Hutterite diffusion and brings it almost up to the present day. Some familiar themes are reviewed and reinterpreted in the light of recent developments.

Colony Division

The division of a colony into two communities with the establishment of a new autonomous daughter colony is a coping process adopted by the Hutterites to channel their demographic energy in a positive way. If a colony were allowed to grow unchecked, the community would lose the close ties implicit in the word *brotherhood*. Thus hiving is an integral part of Hutterite life. There have been more than 200 splits since 1983. But the fact that colony division is an often-repeated part of the culture should not mask the fact that it is a very significant—not to say traumatic—event in the life of an individual colony. To manage the search for a new place and reach a measure of consensus, to build the new colony, and eventually to manage the equitable division of the community and the move constitute the greatest single challenge faced by colony leaders. The developing patterns of settlement, charted in the maps in this chapter, are the results of the locational decisions made by those leaders.

Though no longer fettered by the same kinds of social and political forces discussed in previous chapters, the founding of a daughter colony is today a long, drawn-out, and complicated business. A normative descriptive model has been used to describe the process.[2] When the population of a colony reaches about one hundred people, leaders start to consider branching seriously. They listen carefully to talk among other colony leaders about land costs and availability. When approached by real estate agents or farmers wanting to sell land, they consider each prospect carefully rather than dismissing it out of hand. Once a short list of possible sites has emerged, the leaders take other colony members to view the land in question. The colony members then debate the strengths and weaknesses of competing sites over a considerable period until a consensus is reached. After the colony has bought a new place, the members farm the land from the parent colony while they erect buildings. Usually, they construct the barns for hogs and chickens and the dairy facilities first, followed by the residences. This building phase may last five years or more.

When the daughter colony is nearing completion, the leaders draw up lists headed by the names of the two ministers and enumerating all the heads of families, taking care to balance age, gender, skills, and experience. No nuclear family will be split up, but extended families almost certainly will be. The Schmiedeleut have a general rule that no more than two brothers should be placed on the same list. The aim is to achieve two balanced groups, not dominated by a particular family or clique, which will ensure that both the spiritual and the economic life of both parent and daughter colonies will continue to flourish. Traditionally, nobody knows which group will go and which will stay. All the colony members pack their things, and the final decision of who stays and who goes is made by drawing lots, thus placing the ultimate decision in the hands of the Almighty.

While this dramatic general scenario may still be played out among Lehrerleut communities, it is much less common among the other clan groups. Each Dariusleut colony is free to make its own locational decisions, and often those who move to the new place are volunteers. Some may have played a major role in farming and building the daughter colony. Splits that do not involve an exact division of people and assets into two equal halves are common. For several generations, Schmiedeleut and Dariusleut colonies have made it a practice to establish a farm as the nucleus of a future colony.[3] This may be home for some families for years as more land is gradually acquired and a building program proceeds. The fragmented land holdings of contemporary colonies stand in contrast to the solid blocks of land covering several townships associated with older colonies. In this important sphere of Hutterite life, there is increasing diversity of behavior within the general uniformity of Hutterite culture.

There are three measures that can help us understand the diffusion of Hutterite colonies and the changing patterns shown on the maps. First, the time period between colony splits provides a measure of the rate at which diffusion is taking place. Second, the distances moved from a parent colony to a newly established daughter colony shape the settlement pattern, as new regions are penetrated and older core regions infilled. And third, the distance between a new daughter colony and its nearest neighboring colony provides a measure of clustering or relative isolation. These three parameters also are a means of evaluating differences among the clan groups.

The Rate of Diffusion

While some differences among the Leut concerning colony division have developed since their arrival in 1874, the colony size upper limit of 120–150 members has remained more or less constant. This means that population growth has straightforwardly determined the length of time between colony divisions. During the first half of the twentieth century the Hutterites displayed one of the fastest rates of population growth ever recorded. The average completed family size of ten children, coupled with a low death rate, meant that the sect was growing at 4 percent and that the Hutterite population doubled every sixteen years. This began to change during the 1960s, and a decline in the birth rate has continued to the present.[4] Today most Hutterite families have three to five children. This change has meant that it has taken longer and longer for a colony to reach a threshold population size. Table 2 shows that the average number of years between colony divisions has risen from fifteen during the decade of 1960–69 to thirty-two during the most recent decade. Thus, as the growth rate of the population has halved, the number of years between splits has doubled (see table 2).

Yet these averages mask quite a range of behavior. For example, among the Schmiedeleut, there were five or six cases where splits took place after only fifteen years, while at the other end of the spectrum, there were colonies that did not divide until after forty or more years. Moreover, it is interesting to note that all clan groups have a number of colonies that have not split for long periods, and these stagnant colonies deserve further investigation.

The implications of longer periods between colony divisions for individual Hutterite lives are considerable. The move to a daughter colony is a milestone comparable to graduation, marriage, or retirement in the outside world. For one thing, it is the only way a Hutterite can relocate. A young Hutterite who is chosen to move to the new place will be faced with exciting new challenges. He or she can expect a number of hard years as the new place is built up and made over, as fields will be drained and enlarged, brush cleared, and reservoirs and settling ponds dug. However, there will also be

Table 2. Mean years between colony
divisions for each Leut, by decade

DECADE	DARIUSLEUT		LEHRERLEUT		SCHMIEDELEUT		ALL LEUT	
	Mean years	N	Mean years	N	Mean years	N	Mean years	N
1930–39	11.7	8	12.4	7	16.4	9	13.7	24
1940–49	16.6	9	19.0	6	14.9	16	16.2	31
1950–59	17.3	12	14.2	12	13.7	18	14.9	42
1960–69	15.6	18	13.5	20	15.5	24	14.9	62
1970–79	16.5	33	15.6	18	16.2	30	16.2	81
1980–89	18.2	23	18.9	26	20.5	24	19.2	73
1990–99	23.7	22	21.7	21	24.1	38	23.3	81
2000–09	28.9	19	25.4	19	30.8	8	27.8	46
2010–19	33.1	19	34.6	18	28.4	16	32.2	53

Note: N refers to the number of colonies. Decade 2010–19 includes Hutterite
farms that will be full colonies by 2019.

new opportunities for more responsibility. Longer periods between
fission can also mean delay and frustration. Hutterite women move
to their husband's colony when they marry. One senior woman
interviewed was about to move for the fourth time. As a child, she
had moved when her birth colony divided. Next, she moved to Saskatchewan to join her husband. Within a decade, that colony divided
and she moved again. Now her colony has more than one hundred
people and is beginning to think about another division.

The doubling of the time between colony divisions also has an
impact on the collective life of the community. There is less urgency
in the drive to accumulate capital for a daughter colony. It takes several years for a new colony to pay off debts incurred during the move

and to reach a plateau of peak production during which funds may be put aside for future expansion. A longer period between divisions means more savings. This has proved to be vitally necessary, as the costs of establishing a new place have escalated. However, the fact that the purchase of a new place is decades away has meant that it is more difficult for colony leaders to impose a regime of austerity and simplicity on their people. Moreover, the obvious differences between the brand-new colony and the aging facilities of the parent colony go against the principle of equality for all. While this situation might be tolerated for a few years, it is not acceptable for decades. For this reason, most parent colonies become involved in a period of extensive remodeling after launching a daughter colony. In many cases this process involves the complete demolition of old buildings and the construction of a new headquarters.

Finally, the longer period between colony divisions has important sociological implications. Hutterites are the first to admit that although they seek to build a heaven on earth, they are all too human. It has long been recognized that splitting provides an opportunity to resolve nagging interpersonal and interfamily difficulties, but with greater time between splits, this potential catharsis might be put off for another decade. So, too, is the opportunity for advancement. The establishment of a new colony demands the creation of a whole new set of leadership roles. Those who have been subservient to a "boss" now have a chance to take over and run things the way they see fit. Bright young men, once they have served their apprenticeship and learned their trade, may become increasingly frustrated by what they perceive as the old-fashioned conservative management of their elders.

Distances Moved at Fission

Just as in previous periods, the distances moved when colonies divide and establish daughter colonies continues to be an important factor affecting the developing pattern of colony locations. Short-distance moves lead to clustering, while buying land farther away produces a more dispersed pattern. There are obvious advantages to establishing a daughter colony close to the parent, not the least of which is the simple fact that the new place can be built more easily and cheaply. One colony I visited during the summer of 2016 was sending a bus full of workers to the new colony site every day. They returned to the parent colony for their evening meal and to sleep. By contrast, Doe River Farm in the Peace River Country is far from its parent colony in southern Alberta.[5] Here a group of young Hutterites were living in trailers while they hacked a new colony site out of the bush. Short-distance moves mean that links with family and friends can be easily maintained. Strategically, too, at a nearby site all is familiar and tested. The lessons learned over the years concerning microclimate and soils do not have to be relearned, and market linkages are already established. Overall, risk is minimized.

On the other hand, some colony leaders insist that daughter colonies can be established too close to parent colonies. They stress that there is a need for some degree of separation so that the autonomy of the new colony can be respected and uncontrolled visiting limited. Purchasing land adjacent to an existing colony may also raise the ire of neighbors and lead to competition between colonies for local markets for produce, eggs, and poultry. Dariusleut leaders, when questioned about their willingness to move long distances to the Peace River Country, answered that they wanted to get away from the core areas of dense Hutterite settlement and welcomed the challenges of pioneering in a new region.

Table 3 shows the mean distances moved between parent and daughter colonies for the different time periods discussed in previous chapters and for the contemporary period. In Alberta the implementation of the Land Sales Prohibition Act in 1942 and the Communal Property Act in 1947 forced the Hutterites to look farther and farther afield for new locations. Since the law did not allow them to buy land within 40 miles of an existing colony, the mean distance moved by the Dariusleut rose tremendously, from 46 to 269 kilometers. The regulations soon led to expansion first into Montana—led by the Lehrerleut—and then into Saskatchewan.[6] The Schmiedeleut in Manitoba were not constrained by legislation, but they were sensitive to the potential problems posed by clustering, and the average distance moved in Manitoba rose from 47 to

103 kilometers. Moreover, as discussed in chapter 3, a change of sentiment in South Dakota during the 1930s allowed them to reoccupy a number of sites there that had been abandoned in haste during 1918, and this led to some additional long-distance moves.

Table 3. Mean distances moved at colony division, by Leut

PERIOD	DARIUSLEUT		LEHRERLEUT		SCHMIEDELEUT	
	Mean distance (km)	N	Mean distance (km)	N	Mean distance (km)	N
1918–41	46	9	47	7	171	11
1942–59	269	21	167	18	127	33
1960–72	184	29	246	26	98	34
1973–83	253	34	73	25	126	27
1984–99	123	33	84	34	68	55
2000–15	250	38	77	37	84	24

Note: These are straight-line distances. N refers to the number of colonies. Period 2000–2015 includes farms.

The distances between parent and daughter colonies since the mid-1980s—the temporal focus of this chapter—illustrate the different locational behavior of the clan groups. The Dariusleut have demonstrated a willingness to look for good land at much greater distances from parent colonies. They pioneered expansion into the Peace River Country during the 1970s and have followed it up with several new colonies there since 2000. Their mean distance move of 250 kilometers during the period 2000–2015 is in marked contrast to that of the Lehrerleut of 77 kilometers and the Schmiedeleut of 84 kilometers. These generalizations are substantiated when the distribution of individual move distances is considered. More than half the Schmiedeleut moves were less than 30 kilometers and involved a drive of only twenty to forty minutes.[7] Among the Lehrerleut 80 percent of their moves were less than 100 kilometers. In contrast, nearly half the Dariusleut moves were over 100 kilometers, and in the most recent period, a quarter of their moves were over 500 kilometers.[8] There were no marked differences in the distances moved by colonies of the same clan group but located in different states or provinces. However, it was interesting to note that there were only five splits in Manitoba during 2000–2015, compared with thirty-five moves in 1984–99.[9] Likewise, only two daughter colonies were established by the Dariusleut in Montana, as compared with sixteen by the Lehrerleut in that state.

Distance is but one of several factors considered by colony leaders as they search for a new place. In some cases the costs of land may be a preeminent consideration, while in others chance may play a role. For example, Fairview Colony bought the site for Shady Lane Colony after the accidental death of the previous owner. More recently, a colony south of Lethbridge obtained more than 7,000 acres and some very valuable machinery and equipment from Miner Creek Farms near Tisdale, Saskatchewan, when the owner wanted to retire.[10] Real estate agents can play a vital role in bringing possible properties to the attention of Hutterites, and the "bush telegraph" between colonies is also well developed. Hutterites can also play a waiting game. In the mid-2000s, Rosedale Colony bid for the huge Baker property in southeastern Alberta close to the Montana border but was unsuccessful. Recently, however, the property came on the market again and was acquired by the colony.[11]

Distances to Nearest Neighbors

If a parent colony is constrained to look for land at a considerable distance away, the existence of other colonies in the prospective region may be a positive factor. The success of an existing community demonstrates that the ecosystem there is productive and that market links are viable. Moreover, the social prospects for visiting and the likelihood of family connections are also enticing. Whenever the Hutterites have been forced or have chosen to expand into new regions, the distance between an incoming daughter colony and its nearest neighbor has increased. Historically, this occurred in Alberta as a result of the provisions of the Communal Property Act, as discussed in chapter 4. Average distance to neighbors jumped from only 21 kilometers during 1918–41 to 73 kilometers in 1942–59. More recently, the voluntary expansion of the Dariusleut into the Peace River Country meant that new colonies were more isolated, and a second surge into the region since 2000 has again increased the distance to nearest neighbor from 24 to 53 kilometers. With more than sixteen colonies being planned in 2015, the nearest-neighbor distance would again decrease. Among the Schmiedeleut, the move of some colonies back to South Dakota and expansion into Minnesota and North Dakota have increased nearest-neighbor distances somewhat. Table 4 summarizes the mean distance to nearest neighbor for each of the three Leut.

Table 4. Mean distance to nearest neighbor
at date founded (same Leut)

PERIOD	DARIUSLEUT		LEHRERLEUT		SCHMIEDELEUT	
	Mean distance (km)	N	Mean distance (km)	N	Mean distance (km)	N
1918–41	38	19	22	14	29	18
1942–59	93	21	91	18	38	32
1960–72	65	29	65	26	28	34
1973–83	67	34	31	25	33	27
1984–99	24	33	37	34	24	55
2000–15	53	38	21	37	20	24

Note: These are straight-line distances. N refers to the number of colonies. Period 2000–2015 includes farms.

However, there are considerable differences among the Leut. The Schmiedeleut in Manitoba and South Dakota occupy a more densely settled region, and the mean distance to nearest neighbor during the most recent decade is 20 kilometers. The Lehrerleut also value a clustered settlement pattern, and their mean is 21 kilometers. The Dariusleut are less concerned with proximity to other colonies and are prepared to search for good land deals wherever they occur. These generalities are confirmed when the distribution of nearest-neighbor distances is graphed. The Schmiedeleut are clustered around a mode of 8 kilometers and a median of 12. There are a few isolated colonies in the southeast corner of the province, such as Haven, Minnesota, and Pineland, Manitoba. The Lehrerleut are rather more dispersed, with a mode of 20 kilometers and median of 23 kilometers. Twin Hills, Montana, and Rose Valley, Saskatchewan, penetrated new areas and were more isolated. The Dariusleut have more than a dozen isolated new colonies, the most extreme being Prairie Elk, at Wolf Point in eastern Montana (141 kilometers from the nearest neighbor), and Crystal Lake, Saskatchewan (190 kilometers from the nearest neighbor).

Schmiedeleut Diffusion: Manitoba

Manitoba can claim the densest concentration of Hutterite settlement in North America. The core region where the refugees from South Dakota settled in 1918 has been referred to often in the foregoing narrative of diffusion. Figure 19 shows the Hutterite landholdings in this core, south of the Assiniboine River between Winnipeg and Portage la Prairie. There were eighteen colonies, and in this relatively small area of the province, their colony farms, while not contiguous, do make a formidable block. Notice the way later arrivals such as Elm River, Summerside, and Brantwood are composed of smaller discrete parcels of land, in contrast to the older colonies, which were able to purchase large blocks of land. As discussed earlier, rising land costs, lack of available land, and a "gentleman's agreement" with the Union of Manitoba Municipalities all led to the establishment of colonies farther from the core during the 1960s and 1970s. The mean distance moved at fission doubled to 143 kilometers from the period 1971–83.

The most obvious characteristic of the distribution of colonies established since 1983 is that almost all of them fall within the areas already colonized (fig. 20). There were no bold thrusts to pioneer new regions, and for the most part, the daughter colonies shown on the map are located well within the existing array of colonies. Thus the addition of forty new colonies has increased the density

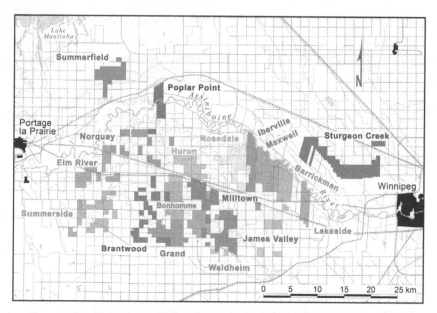

Fig. 19. Map of the core area of Hutterite settlement in Manitoba, 2015.
Drawn from county landownership maps.

of the Hutterite settlement pattern in Manitoba. The mean distance
to the nearest neighboring colony has shrunk to only 14 kilometers, and in ten of thirty-eight splits, the "nearest neighbor" was
the parent colony.

South Dakota and Adjacent States

In 1983 Hutterite colonies in South Dakota were in two linear core
areas along the James River, with a third area of concentration
around Aberdeen. In the decades since, the number of Schmiedeleut
colonies in the United States has nearly doubled, from forty-three
to eighty. A few colonies have chosen to purchase land adjacent to
the parent colony within the old core areas. Examples would be
Rockport to Oak Lane and Long Lake to Grassland. However, the
overwhelming deployment of new colonies has been eastward to
Cook and Lake Counties north and east of Sioux Falls, and farther
north around Brookings. This diffusion involved a number of quite
long-distance moves from the west, such as Spring Valley to Norfield
and Cedar Grove to Golden View. Fourteen daughter colonies have

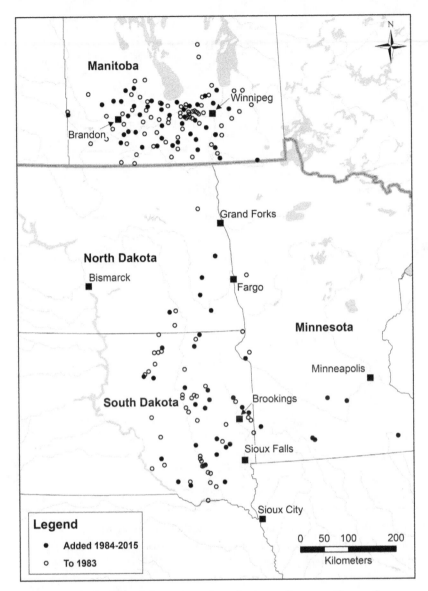

Fig. 20. Map of Schmiedeleut Hutterite colonies, 1983–2015. Drawn from locations in *Hutterite Telephone & Address Directory* and GAMEO.

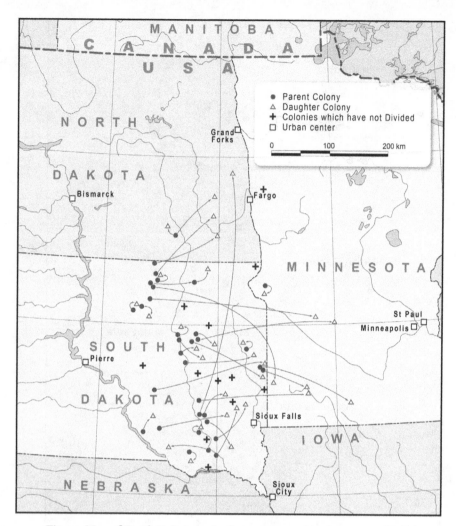

Fig. 21. Map of South Dakota and adjacent states showing moves from parent to daughter colonies, 1984–2015. Drawn from colony branching diagrams.

been located to the east of the James River since 1983. Moreover, seven new colonies have been established in Minnesota, bringing the total there to nine. Again, moves like that from Pembroke to Starland (346 kilometers) and Fordham to Altona (295 kilometers) involved long distances. There have also been a number of moves from the northern core around Aberdeen across the state line into

North Dakota, which is now home to eight colonies. The longest-distance move was from Millbrook in the south to Spruce Lane in North Dakota, north of Fargo, more than 400 kilometers. Figure 21 shows the moves to daughter colonies in South Dakota and adjacent states between 1984 and 2015.

Dariusleut and Lehrerleut Diffusion: Alberta

As we have seen, the two clan groups that originally concentrated in Alberta reacted very differently to the legal restrictions imposed on them by the Alberta government. The Dariusleut looked for new sites within Alberta that complied with the law and were prepared to move long distances and to negotiate with the Communal Property Control Board over individual cases. The Lehrerleut at first postponed any divisions altogether, and then looked for land outside the province. First they located colonies just across the international border in Montana, and later they looked to Saskatchewan for new homes. This movement out of the province ceased when the act was repealed, and for the next decade almost all new colonies of both clan groups were located in Alberta. Thus in 1983 there were two distinct but expanded core areas and a "domain" of more dispersed settlement reaching southward across the border to Great Falls and eastward into Saskatchewan. In addition, the Dariusleut established a few isolated colonies in the Peace River District and in Washington State.

In subsequent decades, the number of colonies in Alberta has nearly doubled, and the settlement pattern has been transformed. As illustrated in figure 22, the southern core has expanded eastward to Foremost and Etzihom, and the northern core has spread out from the Rosebud River south and east to the Bow River through Hussar and Bassano. Most importantly, the two cores have merged as several new colonies have moved in north of Lethbridge and south of Calgary.

The location and timing of colony growth in Vulcan County illustrates this development. The map of the county in figure 23 shows that Brant, Newdale, Bow City, and Turin were widely spaced to abide by the provisions of the act. During the decade after the repeal

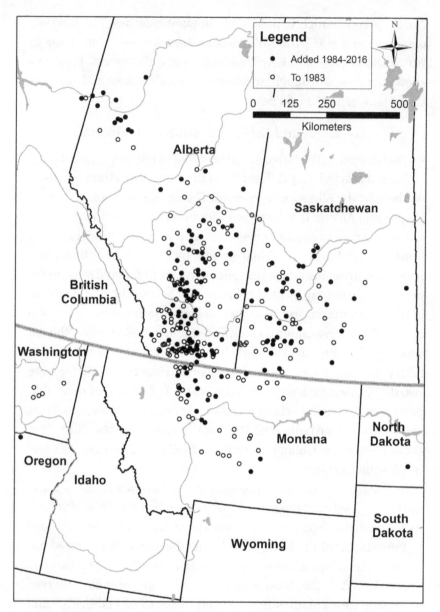

Fig. 22. Map of Dariusleut and Lehrerleut Hutterite colonies, 1983–2016. Drawn from locations in *Hutterite Telephone & Address Directory* and GAMEO.

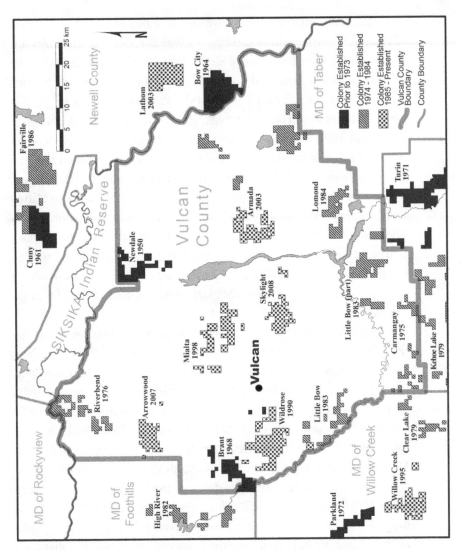

Fig. 23. Map of Vulcan County showing colony expansion. Drawn from county landownership maps.

four colonies were established along the southern margins of the county—Carmangay, Little Bow, Lomond, and Clear Lake—and one at Riverbend to the north. More recently, five colonies have been formed encircling the city of Vulcan: Wildrose, Mialta, Arrowwood, Skylight, and Armada.

Perhaps the most exciting development has been the expansion of Hutterite settlement in the Peace River District (fig. 24). Thirteen new colonies have been added to the four already established there by 1983. Three of these daughter colonies came from parent colonies within the region. South Peace established Peace View in British Columbia north of Dawson Creek, Ridge Valley expanded to Birch Hills, and more recently Twilight Colony, itself a relative newcomer to the Peace region, completed Homeland Colony on land nearby. The others originated from colonies far to the south. The longest move was more than 800 kilometers from Pincher Creek to Hines Lake, but even the move from Warburg, just west of Edmonton, to Codesa was 367 kilometers. These long-distance moves, coupled with a handful of moves from Alberta to Saskatchewan, mean that for the Dariusleut in Alberta, the average distance moved when a colony split rose considerably between 2005 and 2015, from 96 kilometers to 233 kilometers.

In an allied northward thrust, four new colonies were established on the margin of the boreal forest north of Edmonton: Pine Meadows close to Cold Lake, New Pine near Athabasca, Sunny Bend farther west, and Rocfort in the Mayerthorpe area. Interestingly, three of these colonies were linked to parent colonies that already had daughter colonies in the north. Vegreville built Manville in 1988 and New Pine in 2015, while Manville bought a new place at Pine Meadows. Similarly, Sandhills Colony, far to the south, built Morinville in 1971 and then Birch Meadows in the Peace River Country in 2009. Morinville then built Rocfort (now known as Rochfort). Thus only Sunny Bend Colony came from a parent, Cayley Colony, with no prior experience in the north. It seems clear that the obstacles of long-distance moves and the challenge of an unfamiliar agricultural environment can be tempered by successful prior experience. These new colonies have also reduced the relative isolation of Athabasca and Pibroch Colonies.

Equally important, because it involves such an extensive swath of country, has been the increase in density of Hutterite settlement between the margins of the northern core area and Edmonton. Initially, this region was pioneered by colonies forced to look farther

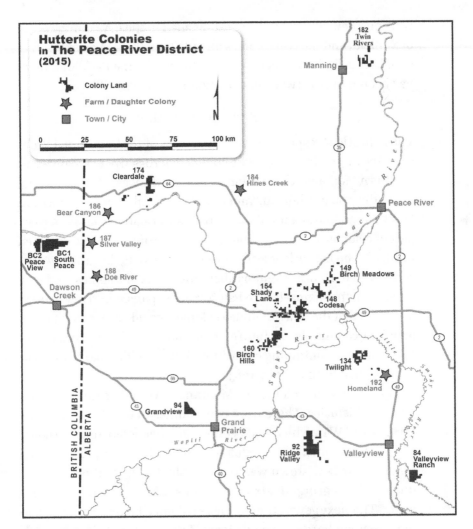

Fig. 24. Map of Hutterite colonies in the Peace River District, 2015. Drawn from county landownership maps.

and farther northward by the provisions of the Communal Property Act. By 1983 there were twenty-five colonies rather evenly spaced over the region. Since that time, 21 more colonies have been added. Many parent colonies have found land nearby for daughter colonies, bearing witness to the fact that they have adapted well to the challenges of a new environment. The axis of settlement has been to the east of Highway 2 along Highway 89 between Stettler and Camrose.

Only one new colony has been established in the dry country north of Suffield, and the two colonies already there have chosen to locate daughter colonies farther west. Northward in the Parkland, there has been more eastward penetration toward Vermillion.

Hutterite Settlement in Montana

The Lehrerleut responded to the strictures of the Communal Property Act by establishing eight colonies across the U.S. border in northern Montana. These colonies were to the west of Interstate 15, along the line of Choteau, Valier, and Cut Bank. They were within less than 30 kilometers of each other and relatively close to their parent colonies in Alberta. The last of this group of moves occurred in 1951.[12] The Lehrerleut leaders were sensitive to the growing concerns voiced in rural Montana about the influx of colonies, and they agreed among themselves to halt further expansion.[13] They wanted to ensure that the newly founded colonies would be able to establish daughter colonies in the future. In this strategy they were successful, in spite of continuing opposition. Fifteen additional Lehrerleut colonies had been built by 1983.

The Dariusleut colonies in Montana have rather different origins and histories. There were two colonies in the state before the First World War, which had been established from South Dakota. In 1918 both joined the exodus to Canada. However, King Ranch Colony near Lewistown was reestablished in 1935. It became the nucleus for a group of six rather idiosyncratic Dariusleut colonies.[14] The next generation of these colonies bought land close to the Canadian border around Havre. Fifteen more Lehrerleut colonies have been established since 1983. Five short-distance moves have bolstered the original core area of settlement west of Interstate 15, while five more colonies have been built to the east of the highway in Toole, Liberty, and Hill Counties. There have been only three Dariusleut splits: Fords Creek built Kilby Butte nearby, Ayers established Heart River in North Dakota, and Surprise Creek went to the northeastern corner of the state to found Prairie Elk at Wolf Point. The map in figure 25 shows the colonies in northwestern Montana as of 2018.

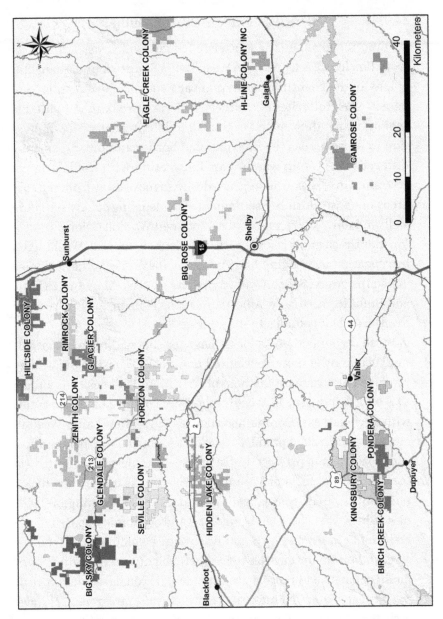

Fig. 25. Map of Hutterite colonies in northwestern Montana, 2018. Montana State Library, MSDI Cadastral, Cadastral parcel shapefiles by county, http://geoinfo.msl.mt.gov/msdi/cadastral/, and Montana Cadastral Base Map Service, https://gisservicemt.gov/arcgis/rest/services/msl/CadastralWebMerc/MapServer.

The Washington-Oregon Outlier

In 1960 the charismatic Hutterite leader Paul Gross led a party from Pincher Creek Colony to Washington State to found a daughter colony in the beautiful countryside at Espanola, just outside Spokane.[15] The Hutterites of southern Alberta were familiar with this region, which they visited in the fall to harvest fruit. The motivation to move across the international border and into an entirely different ecosystem was in part frustration with the legislative restraints in Alberta and in part a desire to move away from the core areas of dense Hutterite settlement. The fledgling colony settled in well, and only twelve years later it founded Warden Colony. In 1974 Pincher Creek endorsed the earlier decision to move to Washington by repeating it, building Marlin Colony there. Two other colonies joined the group: Schoonover from Spring Creek, Montana, in 1979, and Stahl from Huxley, Alberta, in 1980. Thus in 1983 there were five Dariusleut colonies in the state.

By all accounts these colonies have prospered. But their agricultural economy is more specialized than that of most colonies: they produce potatoes with the help of irrigation. Potatoes constitute a $7.4 billion industry in Washington. The colonies enjoy close ties with agribusiness. Companies such as Carnation, Lamb Weston, McCain, and Simplot produce french fries, potato flour, potato chips, and frozen potato products. Most of these products are exported via the deep-water ports of Tacoma and Seattle. At present the major recipient is Japan. Specialization renders these Washington colonies vulnerable to both environmental and economic vagaries. Their investment in machinery and infrastructure amounts to $5,000 per acre, and profit margins are tight. Chris Voight, executive director of the state potato commission, commented, "If you have a decent year, a good year, you might make 4% return on your investment."[16] However, the Hutterites have one advantage over their neighbors: they do all the work themselves and take ownership of their product. As twenty-one-year-old Nick Wollman, the son of the Warden Colony manager, remarked, "These are my spuds. I'm not working for somebody else . . . it's not only my job, it's my responsibility. It's all ours."[17]

By contrast, their neighbors depend on seasonal labor. Only one daughter colony has been established in the region during the decades since. Stahl established Stanfield Colony in Oregon in 2008. The other four colonies are all over forty years old, and further expansion here can be anticipated.

The Hutterites in Saskatchewan

As described in chapter 4, the first Hutterite colonies moved to Saskatchewan during the 1950s. By that time the provisions of the Communal Property Act made further expansion in Alberta difficult, and the move by the Lehrerleut into northern Montana had provoked opposition there. Aware of the hostility to Hutterite expansion in Alberta and Montana, the government of Saskatchewan acted in a proactive manner. A liaison officer was appointed to work with Hutterite leaders to encourage them to adopt a dispersed settlement pattern. The government also did its best to educate the public about the Brethren and to expose the most glaring misinformation that was circulating about them.[18] The fifteen new colonies established during the 1960s were widely dispersed. The repeal of the Communal Property Act in 1973 slowed the movement of colonies across the provincial border to a trickle. However, by that time the local Saskatchewan colonies had begun to hive. By 1983 there were thirty-nine colonies in Saskatchewan, spread evenly across the province as far east as Regina and northward to Battleford.

Between 1983 and 2015 the number of colonies in the province almost doubled. The density of the existing settlement pattern increased, and both eastward and northern "frontiers" were extended. There was also a renewed interest in long-distance moves from Alberta. Two Lehrerleut and two Dariusleut colonies purchased land and built new daughter colonies.[19] As the Hutterites became more confident and assertive and the host population less suspicious, eight new colonies were located close to Swift Current, producing an area of marked concentration. In the north, five new colonies were located along the North Saskatchewan River east of Battleford, while eastward, six colonies found new homes east of a line between Saskatoon and Regina. The map in figure 26 shows

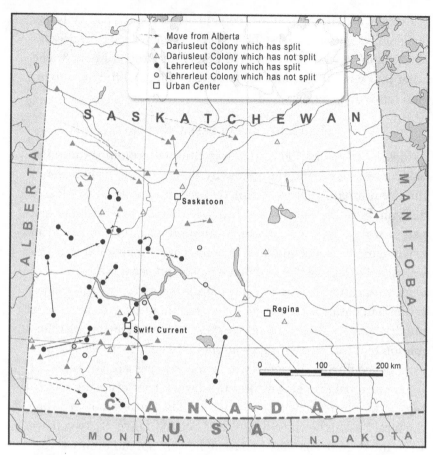

Fig. 26. Map of moves from parent to daughter colonies in Saskatchewan, 1984–2015. Drawn from colony branching diagrams.

the moves from parent to daughter colonies in Saskatchewan from 1984 to 2015.

Here in Saskatchewan, as in Alberta, there is a marked degree of spatial separation between the Dariusleut and the Lehrerleut (fig. 27). Lehrerleut colonies are mostly in the south and west of the province. Wherever possible, they have looked for new sites close to the parent colony. Several of their longer-distance moves have been toward Swift Current, where there were already a number of Lehrerleut colonies. The Dariusleut have been prepared to move longer distances and have embraced more northerly locations in

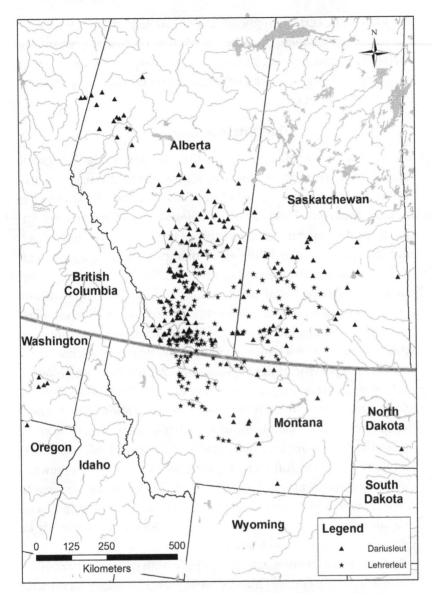

Fig. 27. Map of Dariusleut and Lehrerleut colonies differentiated by clan group, 2015. Drawn from locations in *Hutterite Telephone & Address Directory* and GAMEO.

the Park Belt. Interestingly, all three Dariusleut colonies established on the eastern "frontier" were from Alberta. Perhaps the decision makers felt that as they were moving a long way anyway, they might as well pioneer a new region and perhaps reap the benefits of lower land costs.

The Diffusion Narrative

During the course of research for this chapter, which brings the narrative of Hutterite settlement almost up to the present, two important developments affecting the diffusion of the colonies became apparent. First, many colonies are devoting more attention to, and generating greater returns from, nonfarm activities.[20] Already a majority of Schmiedeleut colonies make a substantial part of their income from manufacturing, including metal buildings and extruded sheet metal, print shops, chemical injection sales and service, kitchen equipment, signage, heat pumps, truck boxes, plastics, ventilation products, and windows and doors.[21] Some question whether one can be a Hutterite without being a farmer, but many who have experienced the evolutionary change have welcomed it and relish the more regular working hours, which allow them to spend more time with their families. The implications for planning the daughter colonies of the future are that less capital will be spent on land and more on machinery and light industrial infrastructure, and there will be a shift from a search for expansive acres toward the locational characteristics sought by light industries—access to raw materials and markets. Of course, no new colony will be located in a suburban industrial estate, but the colonies will certainly be drawn to transportation corridors.

In Canada the costs of acquiring production quotas as part of the national system of supply management present another formidable problem. Colonies that seek to replicate their varied mixed farming activities when they establish daughter colonies are faced with huge initial costs for these quotas. During the summer of 2016 I visited a colony in the southeast corner of Alberta, which had just bought 15,000 acres for a daughter colony. The leader explained that if the daughter colony wanted to establish dairy and egg production on much the same scale as the parent colony, it would be facing a bill of more than $10 million just for the purchase of quotas.[22] This startup cost in addition to the costs of land and construction would leave the big, prosperous colony deep in debt for twenty years and make the colony extremely vulnerable to rising interest rates. It is not surprising that colony leaders listen to debates concerning the future of supply management with deep concern. Some colonies have transferred their dairy quotas to their daughter colonies and closed their own dairy operations.[23] Others plan to concentrate on hogs and beef production, which are not subject to quotas.

A broader question remains: What does our description of Hutterite diffusion tell us about the health of Hutterite culture? Conclusions from our focused investigation mirror those of the more wide-ranging study of Janzen and Stanton.[24] The Hutterite ark is being battered by the winds and waves of change. It is more difficult for the Brethren to insulate their flock from the host society. Computers and cell phones are both a blessing and a curse. The leadership of each colony reacts differently to the challenges and opportunities facing them. Some embrace change, while others stand squarely against it. This has led to an increased range of diversity within each clan group, as well as among the Leut. This diversity is illustrated by the strategies colony leaders use to manage colony division and by the locational decisions that they make.

The slowdown in the rate of colony division and the increasing time between splits is related to the declining birth rate on the colonies. This is a fundamental change reaching to the heart of the culture. It has an important bearing on the balance between the autonomy of the individual family and the collective community. Among the Schmiedeleut there are almost as many thirty- to forty-year-old colonies that have not divided as there are colonies that have successfully split. The Dariusleut in Alberta and Montana also have some very old colonies. This could be related to higher rates of defection, as well as to declines in family size. More youth are leaving and staying away longer. Young women are increasingly joining their brothers in exploring what the outside world has to offer. Evangelical Christian churches have lured whole Hutterite families from their homes on the colonies. Those who leave have become more visible and articulate.[25] Some colonies are experiencing labor shortages because young men age seventeen to twenty-five have left. Moreover, losing children to "the world" casts a dark shadow over the parents and indeed the whole colony.

However, the fact that orderly colony division has gone on regularly during this recent period and that the number of colonies has almost doubled points to the stability and adaptability of the culture. Some colonies have departed from the traditional way in which a colony splits, and there is considerable diversity in the details concerning who goes and who stays and how that decision is made. But the very existence of hundreds of new daughter colonies bears witness to the fact that this complex process has been successfully managed again and again. Few colonies have failed during recent decades. Most leaders exhibit quiet confidence in the future, while the infrastructure of the colonies demonstrates both modernity and innovation. The "Hutterite way" does not appear to be under immediate threat either from external pressures or from internal dissension. There is every reason to believe that for the foreseeable future, the Hutterites will continue to contribute to agricultural outputs and to enhance the cultural landscapes of the prairies and Great Plains.

7

The Driving Force behind Diffusion

Hutterite Demography

The previous chapters have examined the settlement patterns of the Hutterites throughout each of the key periods in their history to the present. With this history as a backdrop, this study now turns to a more detailed look at other aspects of Hutterite life. Perhaps more so than any other factor, demography has played a vital role in maintaining the integrity of Hutterite culture in North America. Hutterites do not proselytize. Over the years, a few brave souls have been welcomed by the Brethren to try to adopt the "Hutterite way," but most have not succeeded. To be a Hutterite, you normally have to be born one. This means that the growth or decline of the sect depends entirely on the size of their families. The Hutterites have demonstrated remarkable demographic vitality. For decade after decade during the twentieth century, average family size exceeded ten children. At the same time, the adoption of the advanced health-care facilities of the host society has promoted low death rates. The result has been rapid population increase.[1]

Over their long history, the Hutterites have developed a way to channel this growth to ensure that it is a strength to the culture rather than a weakness. If a colony were allowed to grow in an uncontrolled manner, it would soon become an unmanageable size, and the daily interaction implied by the term *brotherhood* would be lost. As discussed earlier, throughout their history and independent of Leut, when a colony reaches a threshold size of about 120–150 members, it is divided in two, with half the people remaining at the parent colony and the others moving to the daughter colony.

Chapter 6 demonstrated that the time period between these colony splits is increasing and is linked to the slowing rate of population growth (see table 2). This chapter describes and analyzes the profound and ongoing changes in Hutterite demography and assesses the contributions of scholars from different fields. The approach is chronological and attempts to establish when changes started, how they were set in motion, and why they were instigated. The chapter concludes with some of the implications of population change to the health and vigor of Hutterite culture.

Writing about Hutterite demography is like making a quilt from scraps of cloth that differ in size, shape, color, texture, and age. Material is scarce and precious, and one is reluctant to throw away even the most worn and faded remnant. There is no ongoing sequence of data on the Hutterite population as it has grown during the last one hundred years. This situation is all the more surprising because the enterprise got off to such a splendid start. At the midpoint of the twentieth century Joseph Eaton and Robert Weil embarked on a study of the Hutterites' mental health.[2] A necessary preliminary to this work was a comprehensive assessment of the demography of the sect, conducted by Eaton and Albert Mayer. As they became involved in this endeavor, it assumed an importance and fascination of its own. Here was an isolated population—in the sense that it did not welcome incomers nor lose more than a handful of members to the outside world—growing at a rate that was close to the biological maximum. Moreover, it was a stable population that had maintained its age and sex structure for fifty years, while the total numbers grew steadily.[3]

Eaton and Mayer had established a foundation on which one might have expected ongoing demographic work to be based. Indeed, a number of specialized follow-up studies were published during the ensuing decade.[4] However, it is a remarkable fact that no comprehensive analysis of Hutterite demography has been conducted since 1950. During the last seventy years the total Hutterite population has grown to number more than fifty thousand distributed across four prairie provinces in Canada and five U.S. states. The sect has undertaken a couple of self-censuses, but these provided only an estimate of overall numbers by clan group and location.[5] There were no age and sex data from which a range of vital statistics could be derived. Many scholars who have written about the Hutterites have estimated their total number with varying degrees of sophistication. These scholars have often worked backward from the number of colonies, multiplying this total by the supposed average size of a colony, a practice fraught with difficulties and prone to gross errors.[6]

In the absence of a wholesale updating of Eaton and Mayer's work, a number of researchers have attempted to apply demographic techniques to various samples of the Hutterite population.[7] These researchers have based their work on hard data obtained from national censuses, tax returns, medical fieldwork, or Hutterite archives. Their studies form the building blocks with which this history is written. However, as I compare data derived from a particular clan group in a given jurisdiction with figures from another Leut in another country, I will be careful to define my assumptions. In some cases, studies overlap and provide verification for one another, but there are many gaps, and some duplication is inevitable. The next section describes changes in the total North American Hutterite population since their arrival in 1874, beginning with the 1880 census. Subsequent sections look at family size, crude birth and death rates, and the age and sex structure of the population.

Population of North American Hutterites, 1880–2020

The growth of the North American Hutterite population is illustrated by the graph in figure 28. Starting with the U.S. Census total for 1880, the population has grown exponentially, doubling every sixteen years. Estimates provide checks along the way and involve many of the founding luminaries of Hutterite studies, scholars like A. J. F. Zieglschmid, Bertha Clark, John Horsch, and Lee Emerson Deets.[8]

At midcentury Eaton and Mayer surveyed past growth, analyzed the current situation, and made predictions for the future. The self-census of 1969 (number 10 on the graph) was the first to indicate that there had been a slight diminution in the rate of Hutterite population growth. The total predicted on the basis of Eaton and Mayer's projection was 17,687; the observed total was 16,931.

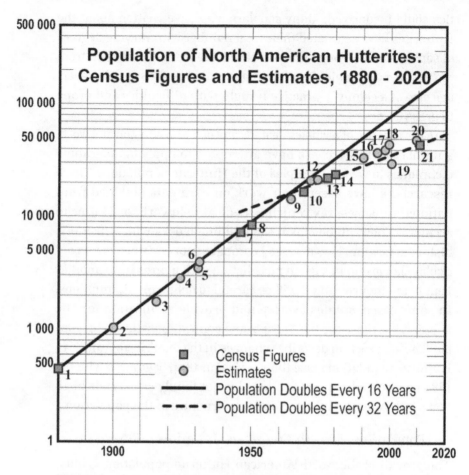

Fig. 28. Population of North American Hutterites: census figures and estimates, 1880–2020. Sources: U.S. Census [1]; Zieglschmid, *Das Klein-Geschichtsbuch* [2, 3, 7]; Clark, "Hutterian Communities" [4]; Horsch, *Hutterian Brethren* [5]; Deets, *Hutterites* [6]; Eaton and Mayer, *Man's Capacity to Reproduce* [7]; Peters, *All Things Common* [9]; Friedmann, "Hutterite Census for 1969" [10]; Government of Alberta, *Report on Communal Property* [11]; Hostetler, *Hutterite Society* [12]; Kraybill, Mennonite World Handbook [13]; John Hofer, *History of the Hutterites* [14]; Friedmann et al., "Hutterian Brethren" [15]; Huntington, "Living in the Ark" [16]; Samuel Hofer, *Hutterites* [17]; Kraybill and Bowman, *On the Backroad to Heaven* [18]; Kephart, *Encyclopedia of Religion* [19]; Janzen and Stanton, *Hutterites in North America* [20]; the author and Peter Peller [21]. For details, see references.

By 1977 the gap between predicted and observed populations had widened to 3,623 persons.[9] Significant change in the rate of growth was taking place.

Since John Hofer's figures for 1980, no censuses of the Hutterite population have been conducted. Estimates vary widely. In an article published in 2010 I remarked, "It is ironic that the Hutterites have been subjected to intense scrutiny by demographers since the 1950s, and yet it is difficult if not impossible to know how many Hutterites there are with any degree of precision."[10] In the last few years confusion has only deepened. In the preface of their masterly 2010 book, *The Hutterites in North America*, Rod Janzen and Max Stanton claim, "Today the Hutterite population exceeds 49,000." Two years later Yossi Katz and John Lehr suggested that the population was only forty thousand.[11] This is a huge difference, and it is high time for an estimate based on hard data.

Peter Peller's patient work with the Canadian and U.S. censuses enables this study to present a more definitive figure. Peller was able to find data on Canadian Hutterites in the 2011 census by combing the tabulation of those living in "Collective Dwellings." For the U.S. colonies, Peller first verified the precise location of each colony using aerial imagery, and then overlaid the census block spatial layer to identify the corresponding census block for each colony.[12] He was then able to find the age-sex breakdown of the occupants of the relevant block. Of course, no system is perfect. The Canadian data contain rounding errors, and some non-Hutterite farmers may have been included in some of the U.S. Census blocks. However, this study presents estimates of Hutterite numbers for 2010–11 with some confidence (table 5). The Canadian Census reported 32,495 Hutterites living in 347 colonies in 2011. The previous year the U.S. Census had enumerated 13,868 Hutterites in 127 colonies. The total number of Hutterites in North America was thus 46,363 in 474 colonies.[13] This total falls very close to the predicted population growth indicated by the broken line on the graph in figure 28.

Table 5. North American Hutterites, 2010–11

2011 Canadian Census	HUTTERITES	COLONIES
Alberta	15,600	170
Saskatchewan	6,110	67
Manitoba	10,355	109
British Columbia	430	2
Canada totals	32,495	348
2010 U.S. Census		
Minnesota	835	9
Montana	5306	49
North Dakota	629	6
Oregon	56	1
South Dakota	6620	57
Washington	422	5
U.S. totals	13,868	127
North American totals	46,363	475

Since this work was completed, new data have become available from two separate sources: the 2016 Census of Canada and 2019 *Hutterite Telephone & Address Directory*.[14] The 2016 Census of Canada records a total of 370 Hutterite colonies, with a population of 35,005. This a 7.7 percent increase in population from the 2011 Canadian Census or an annual increase of 1.54 percent. As the next U.S. Census did not take place until after this study, the Canadian rate has been used to estimate the current American Hutterite population, since the two groups are very similar. Using that rate to extrapolate for both the Canadian (from 2016) and American (from 2010) Hutterite populations would give a total population of 52,414 Hutterites in North America in 2019. The number compiled from the self-enumeration data available in the 2019 Hutterite directory gives a total population of 53,824 Hutterites in North America in 543 colonies. The fact that these figures from two different sources are so similar allows me to say with some confidence that the total Hutterite population in North America was approximately 53,000 in 2019.

Family Size

One of the most straightforward measures of demographic change is family size. What this measure lacks in scientific rigor it more than makes up for in terms of popular accessibility. "How many children do you have?" is a frequent inquiry when my wife and I visit colonies. The fact that Hutterite mothers typically had more than ten children was one of the details from Eaton and Mayer's comprehensive and scientific study that the public embraced. Hutterite family size was among the highest recorded around the world. When coupled with a low death rate, the sect had an annual growth rate of 4 percent, and the population doubled every sixteen years. This growth rate was said to be "startling" and "phenomenal," and the Hutterites were described as "the high fertility champions of the world."[15]

Family size on the colonies has halved since 1950. Studies of Hutterite genealogical records in general, and the *Schmiedeleut Family Record* in particular, have charted this course. The most dramatic decrease seems to have occurred during the 1960s, but the reduction in family size has continued more slowly since then (table 6).[16] Today most Hutterite families have three to five children.

These data sets correspond with anecdotal evidence gathered on colony visits. Family size was discussed while I was having coffee in one living room. The grandparents, in their seventies, had had eleven children. One of their sons was the colony boss. He and his wife had had eight children. Their daughter said of our choice to have but two children, "Right on!" This colony had recently split and had only two youngsters in kindergarten and four in school. The young women who were our guides told us nostalgically about their experiences growing up on the colony when it had as many as twenty teenage girls, riding the ponies and hiding out in the barns.

Crude Birth and Death Rates

Eaton and Mayer's foundational study established that the crude birth rate of the sect—the number of births per thousand of the

Table 6. Family size

DATE OF MARRIAGE	SAMPLE 1: SCHMIEDELEUT (CHILDREN PER FAMILY)	DATE OF MARRIAGE	SAMPLE 2: ALL HUTTERITES (BIRTHS PER WOMAN)
1910–19	10.0		
1920–29	10.4		
1930–39	11.1		
1940–49	10.6		
1950–59	8.8	1954	10.4
1960–69	6.5	1960	8.3
1970–79	5.8	1970	5.8
1980–89	5.5	1980	5.3
1985–95	4.6	1990	4.8

Sources: Sample 1: McCurry, Study of Recent Hutterite Outmigration, 18; Gross, *Schmiedeleut Family Record*. Number of children per family using father's name and date of first marriage. Sample 2: Janzen and Stanton, *Hutterites in North America*, 235.

population—was 45.9 during the five-year period from 1946 to 1950. This was a high rate but not the highest in the world. What made it truly unusual was that it was linked to a crude death rate of 4.4, which reflected a privileged position among those nations that enjoyed the benefits of advanced medicine. This juxtaposition resulted in a growth rate of more than 4 percent. Eaton and Mayer note that "the high fertility and low mortality of this sect combine to produce a rate of increase that may be unique in human experience."[17] Moreover, the growth had been sustained for a prolonged period. The Hutterites, from 1910 to 1950, approximated a statistical model of a stable population in which the total number of persons had changed but the distribution by age and sex had not.

Eaton and Mayer note that their findings should be used with caution as predictive tools, because change may occur in the social factors governing fertility. They point out that in the most recent years of their study, there was already a slight decline in the age-specific birth rates of older women, and in a few more years it would be possible to check whether this was merely a fluctuation or an important new trend.[18]

A group of researchers at the University of Alberta took up this challenge. L. M. Laing used a special enumeration from the 1971 Census of Canada, which gave age and sex data for the Hutterites in Alberta, to calculate the crude birth rate (CBR) of the group. This had fallen from 45.9 per thousand in 1950 to 38.4 in 1971, a decline of 16 percent in twenty-one years.[19] Work with a smaller sample of Dariusleut colonies produced similar outcomes and suggested that the statistical methodology was reliable. With some trepidation, I used Laing's methodology to work out CBRs for the next four Canadian censuses.[20] The figures suggest a period through the 1980s and on into the 1990s when the CBR among Alberta Hutterites stabilized in the mid-thirties. Thereafter, the CBR showed a steady decline to 27.8 in 2011.

Michael McCurry used the Schmiedeleut family records to establish a series of cbrs for the Hutterites in South Dakota from 1950 to 2007.[21] His results show trends broadly similar to those of the Alberta figures. The low CBRs for 2000 and 2007 may reflect the disruption caused by the bitter split in the Schmiedeleut that occurred during the 1990s. This led some five hundred Hutterites, who had married Bruderhof members, to move east and caused a surge of defections of whole families.[22] This short-term disruption led Katz and Lehr to comment, "Over the last few years the number of people leaving the colonies has exceeded the number of births."[23]

Sixty years of change are summarized in table 7. The CBR figures for the various sample populations are not entirely consistent. They include unexpected ups and downs, but the overall trend from forty-six to twenty-eight children per one thousand Hutterites is clearly defined. However, in reviewing this consistent decline in Hutterite fertility, it is important to remember that their CBRs are still more than double those of Canada as a whole. Canadian CBRs have been added to the table in parentheses to keep this in perspective.

Table 7. Crude birth rates of Hutterites, 1950–2011 (various samples)

DATE	CBR	SAMPLE	SOURCE
1950	45.9 (27.2)	North American Hutterites	Eaton and Mayer
1960	46.5 (26.1)	Schm. + Lehr.	Steinberg
	43.0	South Dakota	Goering
1970	35.2	South Dakota	Goering
1971	38.4 (16.1)	Alberta	Laing
1980	42.5	South Dakota	McCurry
1981	35.9 (15.3)	Alberta	Evans
1990	38.1	South Dakota	Satterlee
1991	36.1 (14.9)	Alberta	Evans
2000	27.5	South Dakota	McCurry
2001	31.8 (11.2)	Alberta	Evans
2007	27.3	South Dakota	McCurry
2010	23.2	Montana	Peller
2011	27.8 (10.3)	Canada/Alberta	Peller

Note: Figures in parentheses are cbrs for Canada.

The crude death rates (CDRs) of the Hutterites reflect their age structure and their location in developed countries with access to excellent health care. Eaton and Mayer reported a CDR of 4.4 per 1,000 in 1950.[24] Thirty years later Morgan found that the CDR had fallen slightly, to 4.2 deaths per 1,000. He also demonstrated that there had been a significant drop in infant mortality and a corresponding rise in the number of deaths of old people.[25] The past three decades have seen a continuation of these trends. As family size has decreased, so the life expectancy of women in their middle years has increased. Hutterite CDRs remain below those of the United States (8 per 1,000) and Canada (7.5 per 1,000). The only troubling aspect of Hutterite mortality is that preventable deaths among young people seem to be too common.[26]

Age-Specific Nuptial Birth Rates, 1920–80

Age-specific data on the birth rates of married Hutterite women provide a rare but more sophisticated measure of fertility. Table 8 combines two sets of data in chronological order. The first, from Eaton and Mayer's work, used family records to reach back from 1950 to the 1920s.[27] The second data set—covering only the Dariusleut—came from the Hutterite genetic database at Northwestern University. This project was started in the 1960s by Arthur Steinberg and Hermann Bleibtreu. They saw the possibilities for genetic research in working with an isolated population like the Hutterites, a group who kept excellent records. Carl Peter, Edward Boldt, and Lance Roberts worked for some years with these data during the late 1980s in an attempt to replicate Eaton and Mayer's study. The task proved too cumbersome and time-consuming. Nevertheless, Peter obtained these useful figures on nuptial birth rates and published them in 1987.[28]

My reading of the Eaton and Mayer figures would stress the relative stability of the period from 1920 to 1950. Age-specific rates show fluctuations but no marked decreases. On the other hand, the authors make some prescient comments, which are well worth quoting in full:

> There is also a suggestion of a slight diminution in the rate of growth in the later part of the 1940 to 1950 period, accounted for by a drop in the age-specific birth rate of women aged thirty-five to thirty-nine. In a few more years we shall be able to check whether this is merely a fluctuation round a general trend, or whether it is the beginning of an actual decline in the rate of growth. If and when the decline comes we suspect that it will come despite further improvement in health conditions of both mothers and children. It will be caused by a shift in Hutterite attitudes towards birth control.[29]

Peter's figures allow me to follow up on this suspicion and to establish the timing of the downturn in Hutterite birth rates quite precisely. Before 1970 the age-specific birth rates, for all age groups of mothers, remained high—more or less consistent with previous decades. The figures for 1980 show a series of dramatic declines. The number of babies born to mothers age twenty-five to thirty-

Table 8. Age-specific nuptial birth rates, 1920–80 (per 1,000)

AGES	PETER *Darius* 1920	EATON *All Hutt.* 1926–30	PETER *Darius* 1930	EATON *All Hutt.* 1936–40	PETER *Darius* 1940	EATON *All Hutt.* 1946–50	PETER *Darius* 1950	PETER *Darius* 1960	PETER *Darius* 1970	PETER *Darius* 1980
15–19	—	366.7	—	236.4	—	92.3	—	—	—	—
20–24	391.3	405.9	270.3	389.7	312.5	336.4	377.8	326.9	466.7	180.0
25–29	250.0	451.8	387.1	500.8	519.2	498.2	558.8	551.0	457.6	257.1
30–34	444.4	415.2	451.6	466.7	372.1	442.8	369.2	455.7	370.4	161.3
35–39	416.7	355.0	250.0	435.7	448.3	370.2	320.8	295.8	241.1	118.9
40–44	238.1	238.9	352.9	212.3	142.9	215.1	214.5	242.4	175.0	28.4
45–49	—	23.5	—	47.6	—	43.2	—	—	—	—

Sources: Eaton and Mayer, *Man's Capacity to Reproduce*, 22; Peter, *Dynamics of Hutterite Society*, 169.

nine, in the middle of their reproductive span, was slashed in half. But the most marked reductions occurred at either end of the age spectrum. Birth rates of mothers age twenty to twenty-four dropped from 466.7 to 180.0, while those of older mothers age forty to forty-four plummeted from 175.0 to 28.4. Peter concludes:

> The high birth rate for Hutterite women, which formerly stretched over the whole fertility period of women, has effectively been shortened to ten years, applying now to women from twenty-five to thirty-five years of age. The cause for the population decline of Hutterites must be sought among the twenty-four-year-old women who seem to postpone marriage, and the thirty-five and over women who seem to be able to terminate their reproductive capacity in one way or another.[30]

Two Japanese researchers used Dariusleut church records to review Eaton and Mayer's work and carry it forward up to the mid-1980s.[31] They calculated the total fertility rates (TFRS) for every five-year period from 1901–5 to 1981–85 (see table 9). This is a measure not included in Peter's study. It is of particular interest because the long series of figures suggest that the postwar baby boom experienced in the general North American population was replicated among the Hutterites. TFRS of 9.83, 9.29, and 9.77 were recorded during the periods from 1951 through 1965. This era of elevated TFRS throws the subsequent declines into stark relief.[32] By 1981–85 TFRS had dropped to 6.29, a 36 percent decline in twenty years. Today the inferred total fertility rate for Alberta Hutterites is 3.52 and for South Dakota is 3.85.[33]

Population Pyramids

Where a full range of age and sex data is available, a population pyramid can be drawn to illustrate the population structure. The advantage of this technique is that the data are not subjected to arithmetic manipulation—what you get is what you see. Indeed, the three population pyramids presented in figure 29 boldly and succinctly make the case that the Hutterite population is aging. Eaton and Mayer used eight population pyramids, one for each decade, to

Table 9. Dariusleut total fertility rates, 1901–85 and 2010–11

	TFR		TFR
1901–5	9.84	1951–55	9.83
1906–10	8.84	1956–60	9.29
1911–15	8.45	1961–65	9.77
1916–20	8.10	1966–70	8.13
1921–25	8.67	1971–75	7.22
1926–30	8.25	1976–80	6.39
1931–35	8.78	1981–85	6.29
1936–40	8.43	—	—
1941–45	8.69	2010	3.85a
1946–50	8.80	2011	3.52

Source: Nonaka, Miura, and Peter, "Recent Fertility Decline," 416. Note: For 1941–45, the inferred TFR is calculated from Canadian and U.S. Census data for South Dakota and Alberta by Peter Peller; see text for methodology.

illustrate their contention that the Brethren exhibited the character-istics of a stable population from 1880 to 1950. The total population grew from 443 to 8,543, but the structure of the population remained much the same.[34] Their pyramid for 1950, with its very broad base and tapered top, is typical of a youthful population characterized by large families. It shows that 20 percent of the population was under five years of age and that there were relatively few seniors.

It was Laing's work that first showed marked departures from the "stable population" model. His pyramid showed some constriction in the lower age cohorts and a slight growth in those over sixty-five years of age.[35] Laing's colleagues at the University of Alberta, Kenneth Morgan and T. Mary Holmes, reached much the same conclusion using a larger sample: "If one compares the age-sex distribution of Canadian Hutterites in 1971 with that of North American Hutterites at the end of 1950, it is obvious that the population has aged."[36] A decade later, Boldt used data based on tax returns from colonies to present a picture of the Manitoba Schmiedeleut population, which demonstrated that the trends detected by Laing in 1971 had been

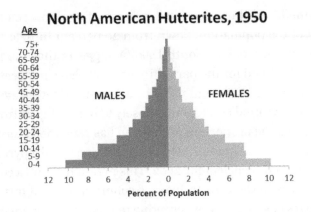

North American Hutterites, 1950

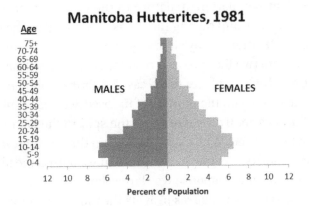

Manitoba Hutterites, 1981

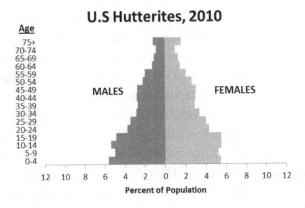

U.S Hutterites, 2010

Fig. 29. Pyramids illustrating the aging of the Hutterite population. Eaton and Mayer, *Man's Capacity to Reproduce*; Boldt, "Recent Development"; U.S. Census.

maintained.[37] Children under five years of age now made up 11 percent of the population, down from 20 percent in 1950.

More recent work in South Dakota suggests that the marked changes identified for the period 1950 to 1980 have not been maintained into the new millennium. The fifteen-to-nineteen age cohort in the 2000 pyramid corresponds closely to Boldt's figure from 1981, showing that the proportion of children has remained more or less stable since the millenium.[38] McCurry also presented a pyramid for Manitoba's Schmiedeleut for 2002. This pyramid shows a considerable increase in the zero-to-five age cohort, a surge of births after some years of stability. It is tempting to relate these changes in the Schmiedeleut population structure to the turmoil that occurred within this clan group during the 1990s. Described as the greatest threat to the "Hutterite way" in modern times, the dispute split the clan group into two factions and resulted in the outmigration of at least five hundred Hutterites to the east.[39] This disruption must have had an impact both on the number of married Schmiedeleut women and on family size. By the late 1990s the split in the Schmiedeleut had been formalized. While some looked on this division with sadness, the majority accepted it and were more optimistic about the future. Perhaps one response was larger families.

The 2010–11 census figures provide the most recent insight into ongoing changes in the Hutterite population structure. Peter Peller has produced a population pyramid for all the Hutterites in the United States. Broadly speaking, it also shows that the number of young people under nineteen years of age continued to remain more or less constant into the new millennium. Certainly, there has not been any marked decrease, as is so clearly illustrated in the 1981 pyramid. The relatively small size of the twenty-to-twenty-four age cohort may reflect increased defection rates at this age.[40]

It is not practical to reproduce all the population pyramids to which we have referred, but Table 10 shows the percentages of the population in the zero-to-fourteen and sixty-five-plus age cohorts. The table summarizes the trend toward aging being discussed but also illustrates the variations among samples. The figures show that the population maintained a youthful age profile from 1950 through the early 1960s but changed considerably during the later years of that decade. This aging process continued until the 1981 census, but the rate of change slowed through the 1990s. This more gradual trend toward aging has continued to the present. Overall, the younger cohorts have declined from more than 50 percent to about 33 percent, while seniors have increased from nearly 2 percent to 7 percent.

Table 10. Population percentages of age
cohorts 0–14 and 65+, 1950–2011

DATE	0–14 AGE COHORT (%)	65+ AGE COHORT (%)	SOURCE
1950	51.3	1.7	Eaton and Mayer (N. Amer. Hutterites)
1960	49.2	1.76	Steinberg (Schmiedeleut and Lehrerleut)
1971	44.4	2.5	Laing, Canada Census Special (Alberta)
1981	40.3	3.2	Canada Census (Alberta)
1981	37.3	3.8	Boldt (Manitoba)
1990	42	3.0	Goering (South Dakota)
1991	40.4	4.3	Canada Census (Alberta)
2000	36.8	4.1	McCurry (South Dakota)
2001	36.8	5.2	Canada Census (Alberta)
2010	35.4	5.8	U.S. Census (South Dakota)
2011	33.4	7.4	Canada Census (Alberta)

This study of population change among the Hutterites over the past sixty years raises three intriguing and closely interrelated questions: How has the slowdown in population growth been achieved? Why has limiting family size become the preferred option? What are the implications of this change for the continuing health of Hutterite culture?

The Declining Birth Rate

Over two or three generations, Hutterites have adopted the full range of family planning options employed by Canadian society. That this has been a prolonged process should not be a surprise. The Hutterites have historically viewed having large families as being in accordance with the will of God and have strictly forbidden any human attempts to limit or meddle with procreation.[41] Moreover, the process is far from complete. Diversity within conformity is a characteristic of the "Hutterite way" in the new millennium. Each Leut interprets Hutterite culture and tradition in slightly different ways, and within each clan group there is a range of attitudes toward modernity, from very conservative colonies to those that are much more progressive and innovative. Family planning has been commonplace in some colonies for a generation or more, while it has made more limited headway in others.

Some researchers, steeped in Hutterite culture and respectful of their beliefs, have been reluctant to recognize that the Brethren have made concessions in the area of family planning, as in so many other areas. Others have tried to explain decreasing Hutterite family size by citing later marriage and the rising number of unmarried women on the colonies. It was not until an explicit and unequivocal article by Bron Ingoldsby and Max Stanton was published in 1988 that what had been hinted at earlier was openly discussed. Their work interviewing doctors and health-care workers in southern Alberta demonstrated that more than one-third of Hutterite women over thirty-five had had a tubal ligation or hysterectomy, while a similar proportion of younger women had used the pill, condoms, or an IUD. They concluded, "A great many Hutterites are now using artificial means of birth control."[42]

Katherine White's in-depth interviews with a small group of Dariusleut women threw additional light on the subject. She, too, found that surgical sterilization was the most common form of birth control used on the colonies. Indeed, her respondents did not include medical termination in what they understood as birth control. They confined the use of this term to IUDs, pills, and condoms. Interestingly, White found that traditional techniques, like the rhythm method and prolonged breastfeeding, were still widespread among Hutterite women as they sought to control the timing of their pregnancies. They employed a number of strategies to use birth control "on the sly." In some cases women requested the pill to mitigate severe cramps, which allowed it to be charged to the colony account as a medicine. Other women used the free services of family planning clinics.[43]

Other factors have also played a part in reducing Hutterite birth rates. The age at which Hutterite men and women get baptized and then married has risen gradually decade by decade. Eaton and Mayer report that the median age of marriage for females had risen from 19.5 during the period 1880–1905 to twenty-two years of age in 1950. By the 1980s most Hutterites married at age twenty-six to twenty-seven for women and twenty-nine to thirty for men. Based on my own experience, my feeling is that these figures have not changed appreciably during the last forty years.

Defection rates from the colonies have risen. As many as 15 percent of Hutterites choose to leave permanently, while many more leave for one to five years to experience "the world."[44] This outmigration clearly has ramifications for Hutterite demography. Most obviously, it affects the total Hutterite population. More subtly, the absence of young males—either temporarily or permanently—might be expected to lead to an imbalance between men and women of marriageable age. In our Alberta sample for 2011 for the three age cohorts twenty to thirty-four, women outnumbered men by 1,955 to 1,630. In Montana comparable figures were 630 females to 475 males. One Dariusleut colony I visited had 116 people and was looking for a new place. The colony had twenty girls of marriageable age. This imbalance would mean that young women are forced to postpone marriage until the young men return to the fold and get baptized. Alternatively, it might mean that young women leave the colonies because their prospects of marriage appear poor. Certainly, the assumption that most defectors are young men is no longer tenable. Young women are almost as likely as young men to leave the colony to pursue their education or other dreams. Moreover, there has been an increase in the defection of whole families, often lured by the attractions of evangelical Christianity.[45]

A 2013 book by nine young people who left their Schmiedeleut colonies reveals the profound impact that "spirit led" and "born again" Christianity has been having on the colonies.[46] The authors convey the turmoil roiling beneath the apparently placid surface of life in some colonies. Part of this internal strife is due to the lingering effects of the split in the Schmiedeleut over relations with the Bruderhof. But this in itself was closely linked to differing, and emotionally charged, visions of salvation. While some of the authors left to answer a personal spiritual call, others left because parents or siblings were excommunicated and had to leave the colony. Many of the leaders who pronounced judgment and saw to its implementation were close members of the family. Several of those who tell their stories were sons or daughters of ministers or German teachers. Often they aspired to pursue their education or had gifts that could not flourish under the strict rules governing behavior on the colony. There is some danger that outmigration might involve the best and brightest of the young Hutterites.

The book describes "English" evangelical ministries on both sides of the international border that see it as part of their mandate to reach out to Hutterites who have left, or are hoping to leave, the colonies. At the same time, Hutterites who have made the transition to the outside world see it as their duty to try to "rescue" those still on the colonies. It is abundantly clear that evangelical Christianity will continue to be an important catalyst spurring defection.

The Population Growth Rate Slowdown

A major reason for the slowdown in Hutterite population growth is the influence of the larger culture in which they find themselves. The Brethren try hard to maintain their distance from "the sinful world." However, the boundaries they establish are permeable, and they are acutely aware of what is going on in the host society. I have never forgotten a Hutterite minister in 1971 explaining to me that "God said 'Be fruitful and multiply,' he did not say overpopulate!" This was at a time when Canadians were very much concerned with the global population explosion, and Hutterite leaders had clearly absorbed and to some extent shared these concerns.[47]

Laing points out that the CBR in Canada declined from 26.1 to 16.2 per 1,000 between 1961 and 1971. He goes on to say, "This remarkable coincidence of Hutterite fertility decline and Canadian fertility decline is unexplainable at present. The decline occurred in different groups for possibly entirely different reasons."[48] In Canada small families were acclaimed, and there was widespread convergence among Canadians with respect to having only one or two children. While I agree that the two groups were very different, I can't help thinking that the behavior of the larger society had a gradual and indirect influence on the Hutterites. White shares this view, observing that "Hutterites interact with outsiders almost daily, whether such interaction entails face to face contact, listening to the radio, or perusing the newspapers. They are a well informed group, and such access to mainstream information may plausibly impact their views."[49]

Others have framed the slowing of Hutterite population growth as a pragmatic response to economic pressures. Karl Peter argues that because of mechanization in all facets of agricultural production, rapidly expanding population had become a problem rather than an asset. Unemployable and idle young men "became a source of social problems undermining the social order of the community." This, he thought, might translate very slowly into a drop in the rate of reproduction.[50] Sam Hofer recounts a Hutterite man explaining the decline in family size in a lighthearted manner, which nevertheless goes to the heart of the matter:

Here's how it works, it has to do with economics. Today, with all the big equipment we use, having too many people on the colony just isn't good. People need jobs. If people don't have work, they get into the wrong kind of work—for their own pocket. With all the land required these days for farming, the capital needed to build the modern houses, barns and operations, it can cost up to fourteen million dollars to establish a new colony. These days there are fewer resources for purchasing land for new colony expansion and this somehow indirectly affects fertility.[51]

Certainly, slower population growth means longer periods between fission. Colonies have more time to build up capital savings for the eventual purchase of a daughter colony. The mean years between fission have increased from 15, during the 1960s, to 27 in 2010.[52] This is clearly a great advantage in times of rapidly increasing prices for agricultural land and decreasing profit margins in many agricultural enterprises. On the other hand, if the ever-present pressure to save and work for the welfare of the next generation is relieved somewhat, the motivation to live lives of simplicity and austerity is also reduced, opening the way for frivolous consumption and competition among the colonies.

Today it may be that the pendulum has swung too far. A combination of smaller families and increased defection rates has led to a shortage of young men on some colonies. On colony visits in 2015 I came across anecdotal evidence of critical labor shortages. One minister admitted that his colony could use five or six more hands immediately. Another talked of hiring some extra non-Hutterite workers and even of exploring the possibility of getting some temporary immigrant laborers.

Some Implications of Demographic Change

This chapter has described how a slowdown in Hutterite population growth has been achieved, at first through surgical means, but more recently by the adoption of the full range of family planning techniques. This is in spite of scriptural encouragement to multiply and a cultural prohibition of birth control. What are the implications of this contradiction for the future of the Brethren?

Some observers have suggested that these changes will have far-reaching effects on Hutterite culture and its continuing ability to withstand assimilation. They picture the structurally tight Hutterite society, in which norms are imposed from above, shattering as individuals make fundamental life choices for themselves.[53]

Those who have focused their attention specifically on the Hutterite family have reported a shift in balance between the power and influence of the community on the one hand and the family on the other. Ingoldsby observes, "The center of life now seems to be the family, with the colony as a shared business extended family. . . . But the family is now psychologically over the community, which has become a support rather than the center."[54] The use of birth control by Hutterite women is both an indicator of this trend and a contributor to the autonomy of the family.

When I visit colonies as a geographer, the conversation tends to focus on "worldly matters" such as milk quotas, supply management, capital accumulation, and land acquisition. But my wife often accompanies me, and as we sit and chat over coffee or go on a tour guided by young women, the conversation ranges widely. I find it hard to accept that the gradual adoption of birth control is a major threat to Hutterite continuity. The manner in which this change has occurred is but another example of "controlled acculturation," where new ideas are slowly accepted by the group with a minimum of fanfare.[55]

The Hutterites are, if nothing else, a patriarchal society. Having babies and child-rearing are considered "women's work." Innovations have been introduced under the guise of medical necessities.[56] Men are well aware of the physical toll on their wives from multiple births, and all Hutterites share a huge respect for the medical profession. As one leader said, "I have eight children. If you know much about Hutterites, you'll know that is not a really large family. But if you look in the cemetery on the hill here in the colony, you'll see the names of too many young women and their babies."[57] When a beloved wife tells her husband that the doctor has informed her that another pregnancy will endanger her health, and ultimately her life, he will accept the diagnosis without question. The fact that large families and rapid population increase are perceived as something of a problem, rather than a strength, by today's Hutterites may encourage thoughtfulness and consideration for the well-being of a partner. While tubal ligation and hysterectomies may be the means by which women avoid further pregnancies, they are invasive techniques. Is it really a sin to take the pill to ensure continuing good health? After all, the men take their heart and cholesterol medications.

Young Hutterite mothers express the opinion that women of their generation are not as strong as were their parents and grandparents. They are not as capable of surviving serial pregnancies and large families. One woman from a Lehrerleut colony said that "today, after a few births [women] suffer from high blood pressure, heart conditions, etc. and thus they receive certificates of approval from the doctors, presented to the ministers, in which they are ordered not to get pregnant any more. . . . In the past, when the doctor used to warn them against giving birth again, they wouldn't listen to him. Today, they do."[58] Thus women are using medical counsel as a way to gain more control over their lives in a patriarchal society. This has far-reaching implications. Women also express the idea that with smaller families, they can devote more care and attention to each child.

In some Dariusleut colonies, kindergarten has been abandoned. This may be partly because there are few children under five, but as one minister remarked, "The women simply don't want it." The transition from "house child" to kindergarten has always been one of the most abrupt and traumatic steps for both mother and child.[59] Without kindergarten, the family stays intact until the child starts school at five. But this is a significant departure, since kindergarten has played a vital role in Hutterite socialization for hundreds of years. It is here that the child is molded to the requirements of the community. The youngsters are drilled in obedience, sharing, and conformity, while selfishness and individuality are firmly suppressed. If this trend to abandon an age-old practice becomes widespread, it is hard to avoid the conclusion that it will have a negative effect on the social cohesion of the colonies.

The changes in Hutterite demography over the past sixty years have been profound, and it would be a mistake to downplay their importance. Smaller families and slower population growth, combined with higher defection rates, could lead to a period of no-growth stagnation for the Hutterites. Already there are a number of colonies that have not branched for more than fifty years. The model of diversified agriculture, which has proved so successful, could be stalled by a labor shortage. Fewer young men in the fifteen-to-twenty-five age cohorts could result in their being overworked and resentful, and this might lead to further outmigration. Widespread adoption of family planning may indicate a marked swing toward individualism and away from collective values.

But demographic change must be evaluated in context. The waves of modernity are clearly battering the Hutterite ark. Their primary tenet of pacifism is repudiated when one colony takes another to the worldly courts. Their traditional forms of worship are challenged by evangelical Christians, who have divided some colonies into "born again" and "born against" factions. The principle of simplicity and asceticism is challenged by increasing affluence and by competition among the colonies. The widespread adoption of nonagricultural activities tends to break down isolation and draws Hutterites into closer interaction with the host society. Smart phones and burgeoning technology are both a blessing and a curse. The flowering of romantic love and more liberal attitudes toward dating have had far-reaching effects. Change is everywhere, and evolving attitudes toward procreation are but a part of this turmoil.

What does it all mean? Is Hutterite culture on the brink of demise, as predicted as far back as 1965?[60] In July 2013 I visited eleven of the twelve colonies in the Peace River area. Everywhere, I witnessed vigor, optimism, and confidence. Four new farms were being readied to become fully fledged colonies in the near future. On existing colonies, new infrastructure, including schools and churches, was being completed. Some of the new colony housing complexes would grace an Edmonton suburb. There was a spirit of innovation and risk-taking as colonies embraced nonagricultural opportunities. Some were undertaking contract work for the government or for oil companies. One colony was preparing for a visit from Japanese buyers who were interested in their organic honey. Another had just completed a state-of-the-art slaughterhouse facility. It seems safe to say we can look forward to at least another generation of Hutterite expansion. As we learn more about the Brethren, we may benefit from the example of a society that provides radically alternative ways of dealing with aging, youthful alienation, child-rearing, loneliness, and materialism.

8

Bones of Contention

Factors Shaping Diffusion

As described in chapter 4, the outbreak of the Second World War had far-reaching implications for the Hutterites, especially in Alberta.[1] From 1942 to 1947 "Hutterites and enemy aliens" were forbidden to buy land in the province, and it was an offense to sell or lease land to the Brethren.[2] With the cessation of hostilities, it became a priority to make sure that land was available to returning veterans.[3] In 1947 the Communal Property Act was passed, which sought to promote the assimilation of the sect by ensuring that new colonies were sited at least 40 miles from existing ones.[4] The Hutterites' every locational decision in Alberta was subject to time-consuming evaluation, often accompanied by local outbursts of nativism, and soon they were forced to look to Montana and Saskatchewan for new locations for colonies. This unflattering story has been told from a number of different viewpoints,[5] and the resulting changes in settlement patterns have been described earlier in this book. It needs no further embellishment.

On March 1, 1973, the newly elected Lougheed Conservative government repealed the Communal Property Act on the grounds that it was incompatible with the Alberta Bill of Rights. This action ended a dark chapter in the province's history. For thirty years the rights of a specific ethnic group of Canadian citizens had been seriously restricted. The repeal of the act might have been hailed as demonstrating "a new level of maturity, tolerance and reasonability in the conduct of Alberta's affairs."[6] However, it did nothing to calm the fears of rural people or to discourage their tendency to blame all the ills facing farmers and small-town businesses on the Hutterites. Indeed, the government's avowed intent to get rid of the act provoked a desperate last-ditch attempt to keep it in place.

The years since the repeal have seen a complex dance played out between the Brethren and the host population among whom they live. In some areas and over some periods of time, the populations worked out a measure of accommodation and mutual respect. In other areas, stereotyping continued and resentment still simmered just below the surface. There have been outbreaks of bitter anti-Hutterite sentiment, which have continued right up to the present. For example, at the beginning of the new millennium, the Conservative member of the legislative assembly (MLA) for Little Bow, Barry McFarland, proposed a private member's bill to limit the amount of land in any county or municipality that could be owned by "any individual, corporation, or religious group."[7] His avowed aim was to protect the family farm, for he feared that "a religious group or corporation could eventually acquire all the land in a county or municipal district."[8] His words echoed those of several generations of rural Albertans who have remonstrated against a perceived Hutterite takeover.[9]

Hostility, whether overt or muted, has done little to curb Hutterite expansion in the province. The Brethren have used their freedom from the constraints of the Communal Property Act to find new colony sites within Alberta, while the flow of colonies to Montana and Saskatchewan has slowed to a trickle.[10] In 1972, just before the act was repealed, there were 82 colonies in Alberta and 6,732 Hutterites.[11] The 2016 Census of Canada reported 16,935 Hutterites living in 175 colonies.[12] More colonies have been established since the act was repealed than existed while it was in force. In the context of declining rural populations across Canada, this is a remarkable record that has implications both for its cultural landscapes and for its agricultural economy. However, it is important to note that, as described in the previous chapter, the rate of Hutterite expansion has declined substantially during the past decades.

Chapters 5 and 6 discussed the changes in settlement pattern that have come about among the various Leut since the repeal of the act. The object of this chapter is to shift from settlement patterns to focus on the story of the changing relationships between the Hutterites and the people of Alberta during the same period.[13] The fact that expansion has occurred throughout the province, with only limited and sporadic opposition, suggests that far-reaching shifts have taken place both in the host society and among the Brethren. The first four sections of this chapter review the attitudes and attributes of the main actors. The main protagonists involved in guiding the pattern of Hutterite expansion have been the government, the Hutterites themselves, and the rural and urban populations of Alberta, and each of these groups is examined in detail.

While the party name of the government remained unchanged for forty years, until its defeat by the New Democratic Party in 2015, the balance between progressive and conservative has oscillated. Overall, as the heft of the oil industry and its contribution to the economy has grown, this has led to a decrease in the relative political significance of rural concerns. At the same time, the process of urbanization has progressed to the point where almost 80 percent of Albertans live in towns and cities. There has been a growing divide between the worldviews of the urban majority and the dwindling rural minority.

As the number of Hutterites has doubled, the "Hutterite way" has broadened and diversified. Generalizations about Hutterite perceptions or behavior are increasingly problematic. The Brethren have been drawn into contact with the host society through marketing boards, school boards, and the courts, and as their knowledge and familiarity with the ways of the outside world have increased, so, too, has their self-confidence. The last four sections of the chapter briefly discuss some of the issues that have continued to act as irritants between the Hutterites and their neighbors: fear of a Hutterite "land grab," education of Hutterite children, purchasing patterns, and environmental concerns.

Actors 1: The Government of Alberta

The Progressive Conservative government of Premier Peter Lougheed ousted the Socreds in 1971. The new government wanted to project an image of vigor and modernity.[14] It passed a total of 243 bills during its first two years in power. The Communal Property Act was repealed along with the odious eugenics law, while the Individual's Rights Protection Act and the Alberta Bill of Rights were among the flood of new legislation put in place. But Lougheed was a pragmatist. He realized that his rural constituents continued to fear Hutterite expansion and favored continued government controls.

Lougheed determined to follow up on the suggestions put forward in the *Report on Communal Property*, which was published soon after he came to power.[15] The report emphasized that much of the hostility toward the Brethren was based on misinformation. The commissioners proposed that a committee composed of both Hutterite elders and representatives of the municipalities be formed to help guide the Hutterites in their choice of locations for new colonies and to educate the public about the sect. Arnold Platt, a highly respected and experienced member of the farming establishment, was appointed to chair the Special Advisory Committee on Communal Property and Land Use. Platt was under no illusion that the repeal of the act had miraculously dispersed the cloud of anti-Hutterite sentiment. He described his role as being the government's "lightning rod."[16] Nevertheless, he determined to pursue a policy of openness and to promote frank discussion of differences. He hoped that rational dialogue would lead to peace. He stressed that his committee was to help and advise, not to direct or coerce, and that its role was to be temporary.

Even before the committee was formally in place, it was in trouble. The Hutterite elders were suspicious that the legal controls of the act had been replaced by morally binding guidelines, like those in force in Saskatchewan. Bishop John M. Wurz of Wilson Siding Colony admitted that he had been asked to keep silent about the repeal of the act "so that we don't arouse the public."[17] Minister Robert Dowling did little to clarify matters when he remarked enigmatically that "there are certain responsibilities Hutterites must assume if they expect to have total rights."[18] To the rural farm population, the Special Advisory Committee looked like the Communal Property Control Board in a new guise—they expected it to hold public hearings and to listen sympathetically to their views.

The center for opposition to the repeal of the Communal Property Act was the county of Vulcan. Community leaders there organized a protest motorcade to Edmonton, and they were joined by delegations from Hussar, Rockyford, Drumheller, and Hanna. Some three hundred people met with the premier on the steps of the legislature. They were told that the act had been repealed by a vote of 60–4, and that the matter was settled.[19]

Rumors of extensive Hutterite land purchases in Vulcan County led to increasing tension. Meetings between Hutterites and locals, designed to air the fears and grievances of both sides, did little to dissipate the bad feeling. After the second meeting, David Mitchell, president of the Vulcan Chamber of Commerce, stated his uncompromising position: "At this time, we are not prepared to welcome this group into our midst, and in fact will do whatever we can to prevent their establishment in this or any other area of Alberta."[20] Things came to a head during a meeting at Mossleigh Community Hall on May 9. Speakers from the floor repeatedly stated that if the government would not control Hutterite land purchases, they would have to take matters into their own hands. "We'll burn them out" was a common threat. Before the meeting, Arnold Platt had received a number of threatening phone calls; these were followed up by a note delivered to him at the hall. After the meeting, he sped away in a darkened car to foil those bent on harming him.[21]

This confrontation forced Platt to change his policy of openness. He admitted that "some conflicts cannot be resolved by discussion or negotiation and under such circumstances the best course is to proceed quickly and decisively with what is allowed by law."[22] Platt generously took responsibility for the atmosphere of distrust that had arisen in Vulcan. "I thought we could discuss Hutterite land buying with their neighbours and everybody would be reasonable, but I should have known better. . . . Vulcan, as a community, kind of got destroyed . . . everybody is watching their neighbours, they're suspicious of who might sell next. It really wasn't the Hutterites fault, mine perhaps because I thought we could be open."[23]

Thereafter, meetings of the Special Advisory Committee were strictly confidential. Each proposal to establish a new colony was evaluated according to its merits. Sites at some distance from existing colonies and made up of a coherent block of land were favored, although no formal guidelines were adopted. Several new colonies were established without any overt opposition.[24] Platt published an interim report in 1973 and followed it with annual reports in 1974 and 1975.[25] He was able to show that the rate of land acquisition by the Hutterites had not accelerated after the repeal of the act. Thirteen colonies had been established during the period 1971–75, compared with twelve colonies in the previous five years. The Special Advisory Committee's job was completed, and it was disbanded in 1976. Platt put his talents to work writing the report of the Alberta Land Use Forum.

The government retained the services of Kenneth Hoeppner, who had been Platt's right-hand man. His position was consultant on communal farms, and his mandate was to keep abreast of Hutterite expansion and to act as an impartial chairperson for the committee of Hutterite elders who were to continue to evaluate all requests from colonies to buy land or to establish colonies. This committee was completely different from the cumbersome Special Advisory Committee, which had included several non-Hutterite members. For the next decade Hoeppner worked with colony leaders to guide the land purchases of both the Dariusleut and Lehrerleut. Between 1976 and 1986 some thirty colonies were established without prolonged or bitter outbursts of hostility. Jake Waldner of O.K. Colony commented, "There are some colonies that haven't adhered to the board's decision. But overall the committee has worked wonderfully."[26] One of the objectives of the committee was to ensure that colonies did not concentrate too much in areas where there were already many colonies. They achieved this aim.

Figure 30 shows that only two colonies moved 20 kilometers or less to establish a daughter colony, while most moved at least 40 kilometers. Indeed, a flourishing group of colonies had been established far away in the Peace River Country. It seemed that the Brethren had gained a measure of acceptance. Jacob Stahl, leader of a colony near Calgary, said that local townspeople now greeted him with "smiles from ear to ear. It wasn't always like that. In the bad old days, the Hutterites were widely resented, but they're very happy with us now."[27]

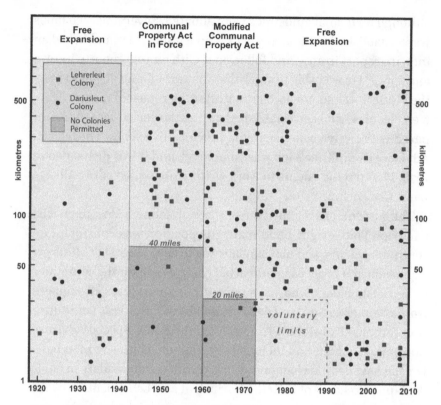

Fig. 30. Distances moved from parent to daughter colonies in Alberta, 1918–2010. This graph illustrates the impact of the Communal Property Act. It shows that few colonies broke the law and almost all respected the self-imposed voluntary limits even after the law had been rescinded. Only since 1990 have many colonies opted for short-distance moves. Graph drawn by Simon M. Evans.

However, hostility toward Hutterite expansion remained. Plans to develop a new colony south of Staveley and rumors of similar action east of Coutts led to the formation of protest committees and letters to the minister of municipal affairs. Minister Julian Koziak replied that there were no grounds for the provincial government to become involved. He suggested that it might be up to the municipal councils to take up the matter.[28] This recourse had already been adopted in Saskatchewan, where zoning bylaws had been used in an attempt to check Hutterite expansion.[29]

A few years later there was another flare-up concerning Hutterite expansion. This time it was north of Calgary in the Stettler area.
Erskine Colony was putting together land for a daughter colony. It
was opposed by a group of local farmers.[30] Premier Don Getty was
running in a by-election in the area and was petitioned to intervene. The Council of Elders of the Hutterian Brethren Church discouraged the land purchase because the land in question was made
up of a number of isolated parcels. They urged Erskine Colony to
continue its search for a new home. This was entirely in keeping
with precedent and practice.[31]

However, politics and personality intruded, and this case became
another, albeit subtle, turning point in the relationship between the
government and the Hutterites. In 1989 Hoeppner's contract was
not renewed.[32] At the behest of the Alberta Association of Municipal Districts and Counties, Helmut Entrup, who had been farmers'
advocate for Alberta agriculture, replaced him. From the Hutterites' point of view, a diplomatic and neutral academic had been
replaced by a spokesman for the farm lobby. Nor was Entrup long
in demonstrating that a new broom was in use. He announced that
although the guidelines hadn't been enforced in the past, "since I'm
in charge now [they] are going to be enforced. There is no question
of it, they're going to be enforced."[33]

This bombastic utterance indicated a change to a more dictato-
rial and high-handed approach on the part of the liaison officer. It
reflected his confidence in the support he would receive from the
new minister of municipal affairs, Ray Speaker. Speaker, the MLA
for Bow Island, was a longtime opponent of the Hutterites and had
voted against the repeal of the Communal Property Act. It also sig-
nified a misunderstanding of his role, which was limited to acting
as a neutral chairperson for meetings of Hutterite elders. Entrup's
job was not to set an agenda or impose unwritten guidelines.

Joe Hofer of Clearview Colony near Bassano, a member of the
Council of Elders, admitted that he was unaware of these guidelines.[34] This was not surprising, since there were none. Arnold
Platt had argued against written rules: "Guidelines tend to become
regulations, protecting Bureaucrats and the Hutterites from imag-

inative thinking or tough decisions by vesting responsibility for decisions in a set of rules instead of individuals."[35] Nevertheless, this unwieldy committee, made up as it was of six non-Hutterites and eight elders, needed some general principles to guide their discussions and decision-making. Some guidelines were published in the annual reports of the Special Advisory Committee. The committee carefully avoided mentioning any specifics and included the following caveat: "Care must be taken so that such inquiries [about the attitudes of a community] do not reveal the plans of the potential vendors that might well jeopardize their chances to dispose of property or subject them to difficulties of any kind."[36] In other words, there should be no public meetings to discuss particular purchases by the Hutterites. When the Special Advisory Committee was disbanded in 1977, even these working principles formulated by that committee disappeared too. However, perhaps some of the ideas implicit in them have helped guide the locational decisions made by the elders during the next decade of quiet expansion.

Now Entrup was boldly claiming that guidelines existed that colonies were required to give notice of their intention to expand, that they should not locate within 15 miles of another colony, and that they should not own more than eight sections in any county or municipal district. These provisions closely resembled those of the Communal Property Act. Entrup admitted that his guidelines had no legal basis. "They can tell me to go to hell if they want to . . . but it would not make any sense. They want to live peacefully. . . . I would say it's more a gentlemen's agreement strictly on the basis of good common sense, not to offend their neighbours. [It's] for their own good and the good of all."[37] The press was quick to defend the Hutterites. An editorial pointed out that "aims formerly accomplished by law are now gained by quiet coercion. The result is a restriction that no socially responsible group in Alberta should be required to bear."[38]

Since the repeal of the Communal Property Act in March 1973, Hutterite elders had cooperated with the government and done all in their power to live up to their principle of pacifism. They had frequently turned the other cheek to maintain peace. Now it seemed that their efforts had been in vain. For nearly two decades they had been going well beyond the letter of the law to gain acceptance, only to be faced with the prospect of tighter restrictions and further "inquiries" into communal property.[39] Enough was enough. The elders determined to use the freedom—which everybody else in the province enjoyed—to buy land wherever and whenever they desired. Since 1990 nearly half (46 percent) of new colonies were established within 30 kilometers of their parent colonies. Indeed, many actually bought land adjacent to the lands of the old colony. The core areas of Hutterite settlement grew rapidly. This development was as dramatic a change to the Hutterite settlement pattern as that witnessed when the Communal Property Act was imposed in 1942. This time it was driven by a behavioral change on the part of the Hutterite leadership.

Actors 2: The Hutterites

As the number of Hutterite colonies has multiplied and their geographic dispersal has increased, so it has become less and less useful to use a single descriptive model to attempt to encompass the "Hutterite way."[40] In the new millennium, dynamic change and diversity are emerging characteristics of the Brethren.[41] The 1990s saw a major split occur in the Schmiedeleut, and there are now four clan groups.[42] Moreover, the behavioral and linguistic traits separating the Leut have been intensifying.[43] Even within a clan group there is likely to be a wide range of attitudes toward modernity. For example, the conservative Dariusleut leaders of Wilson and Three Hills Colonies took their case against having photographs on their driver's licenses all the way to the Supreme Court of Canada. Meanwhile, the Wipf brothers of Viking Colony were happy to act as "poster boys" for the Alberta Dairy Producers.[44] Some leaders still regard personal photographs as "graven images" to be shunned, but many Hutterite households have scrapbooks to record weddings and birthdays.[45]

More significantly, perhaps, there is an increasing range in the way Hutterites make a living. Of course, agriculture remains the focus of their endeavors, but there are important general differences among the Leut. The Schmiedeleut colonies in Manitoba and South Dakota are smaller, concentrate on hogs, have the most nonagricultural enterprises, and make the most use of computers and information technology. The Lehrerleut, by contrast, focus on grain growing and dairy farming and have not embraced industrial enterprises or computers. Meanwhile, the Dariusleut display the widest range of economic activities—in part because of their diffuse settlement pattern.[46] In Washington State, they concentrate on producing potatoes; in the Peace River Country, their colonies are true mixed farms; and farther south, they tend to feed their grain to beef herds, as well as to pigs and chickens, and they prize rangeland highly.

The two clan groups that have made Alberta home—the Dariusleut and the Lehrerleut—have rather different perspectives as to the role and importance of intercolony relations. The Lehrerleut have a well-organized and authoritative council, which approves the appointment of ministers and all decisions about when and where to establish new colonies. The Dariusleut are less willing to cede autonomy from individual colonies to their council. They are more likely to go it alone and consequently exhibit a wider range of spatial behavior.[47]

Most Lehrerleut colonies manage the process of colony division in the traditional manner described above. When, after some twenty to thirty years, the population grows to a critical size, the colony purchases a block of land for a daughter colony. In a sustained burst of frenetic activity, members construct buildings and farm new fields. Within a few years, the formal split between parent and daughter colonies is arranged. The population is divided into two groups, balanced carefully with regard to skills and experience on the one hand and demographic structure on the other. The final decision of who goes to the new place and who stays is made by drawing lots, as described in chapter 6.[48]

As one example, the split of Hutterville Colony and the establishment of its daughter colony, Deer Field, followed this model closely. The colony bought land in 1988 and took crops off the 6,000 acres during the next two years. Members constructed three hog barns and an elaborate reservoir and pumping station, which drew water from the St. Mary's River. The minister, Jake Wipf, said that the objective was to make Deer Field as equal to Hutterville as humanly possible. If the colony had eight combines, four would move to the new place. He explained that "nobody knows who will move . . . they will be picked like a baseball team."[49] The parent colony had about 140 people, so the new colony started with a population of 70. The final split occurred in 1992 after a five-year building period.

The Dariusleut display a wider range of behavior in the manner in which they arrange branching out. They are more likely to buy land piecemeal as it becomes available or when they hear of a good deal. Often the new place will be worked as a farm separate from the parent colony for a protracted period while the new place is being constructed.[50] In many case, those who eventually go to the daughter colony are volunteers, and efforts are made not to divide families. Sometimes splits are not exactly half and half.

Under the provisions of the Communal Property Act, Hutterites were encouraged to buy a single block of land at one time. The Council of Elders also pursued this ideal from 1976 to 1988. However, the fragmented land patterns of some colonies established during the past three decades suggests that this is no longer a priority. Today a new place may be put together a section at a time over a period of years.[51]

During the same time period, the Hutterite leadership has become more confident and assertive in their dealings with the power structure of the host society. In the late 1970s the Dariusleut challenged the way in which they were assessed for tax. They sought continued exemption as a religious organization, although Revenue Canada regarded each colony as a corporate farm. Litigation went back and forth over a five-year period, but the Supreme Court of Canada finally ruled against them.[52] A decade later the Schmiedeleut sought the help of the courts when a dispute erupted over intellectual property rights.[53] Once again litigation was messy and protracted, and it resulted in the split in the Schmiedeleut group. More recently, some Dariusleut elders protested against the use of photographs on their driver's licenses. The Supreme Court ruled against them in 2009.[54] Lawyer Alvin Esau has discussed these cases with both sympathy and insight. He would, I think, draw a distinction between the taxes and licenses cases, which both involved disputes with worldly authorities, and the Schmiedeleut case, which did not. Here the courts were asked to make a judgment on an internal matter between Hutterites. Esau asks how a pacifist, nonresistant group, based on brotherhood, can "request court adjudication enforced by state violence to settle an inside issue." He suggests that fundamental values of their belief system must be questioned.[55]

The Hutterites have become increasingly visible to members of the host society. This is partly due to their increase in numbers and ubiquity, but it is also a result of changed behavior. The Brethren are increasingly ready to interact with the urban public. Several colonies participate at each of the farmers' markets in Calgary, while others set up their stalls in small towns around the province.[56] Moreover, Hutterite families are frequently encountered in Value Village thrift stores, in the Real Canadian Superstore supermarket, and even at hockey games.[57] School boards have played a significant role in ensuring that no children in Alberta complete the social science curriculum without at least a superficial understanding of who the Hutterites are.[58] Books and films have made the polka dot headscarves and long black skirts of Hutterite women and the black work clothes of men instantly recognizable to most Albertans. To mention but a few recent examples, Mary-Ann Kirkby's *I Am Hutterite* has been a best seller, while Sam Hofer's *Born Hutterite* was made into a widely viewed film.[59] Hutterites have also been featured in large-circulation magazines, such as *National Geographic* and *Equinox*.[60]

The authors of the influential 1972 *Report on Communal Property* stressed that attitudes toward Hutterites "have been influenced in some instances by much mis-information and emotionalism." They continued, "Local residents sometimes develop stereotypical images of the Hutterites . . . and many of the characteristics often ascribed to them are not accurate, and some are only partly correct."[61] They went on to express the hope that more careful education of Albertans about the Brethren, and a conscious effort on the part of the

Hutterites to be more forthcoming about their way of life, would lead in the long term to better relations.

Actors 3: The Rural Population

As one reads the accounts of confrontations between the farmers and the occupants of small towns across Alberta, on the one hand, and the peace-seeking, communal-living Hutterites, on the other, one is struck by the bitterness and passion exhibited. These rural people have often been described as "the salt of the earth" and "the backbone of the province." They are the sons and daughters of the "brave pioneers" who feature so largely in our collective history. Hardworking, conservative, and pious, these are not—at least at first glance—folk from whom one would expect hatred and threats against their neighbors. Yet a moment's reflection reminds one that anger is an immediate human response to a perceived threat, and what is threatened here is their whole way of life and their place in the world. In the past, the homesteaders blamed the government, the banks, and the Canadian Pacific Railway for drought, grasshoppers, and fluctuating commodity prices.

Today the Hutterites are handy scapegoats. Ever since the end of the Second World War, farm and ranch families have been caught in a squeeze between ever-rising input costs and relatively low prices for their products. As the size, power, and cost of complex agricultural machinery have grown, the pressure to enlarge the size of the farm to obtain economies of scale has inevitably followed. Rural people feel themselves oppressed by economic and social forces that they can hardly understand, let alone control. Roger Epp has described the vast provincial hinterland away from the Fort McMurray to Lethbridge corridor as "outer Alberta," its population stable or declining, older, less educated, whiter, and with a lower per capita income. A region more reliant on government transfers, including pensions, "its communities live on the defensive, struggling to maintain schools, hospitals and other public services in the face of population losses and government cuts."[62] These people have seen their political heft decline and their ability to have a say in health-care decisions and what goes on in their schools abrogated by superboards and government ministries.

Rural people feel left behind when the frenetic pace of change in attitudes and lifestyle experienced in urban Alberta is brought home to them through television and interactions with their children and grandchildren. As the verities of the past are swept away, they feel increasingly alienated, and their voices are marginalized.

These are the deeply rooted causes of antipathy toward Hutterites that has sometimes found expression in ugly outbursts. For the Hutterites are perceived as being more or less invulnerable to the economic storms that threaten to engulf rural folk. They farm large acreages; they have an enviably large labor force, which allows them to diversify their outputs; they purchase goods for sixty or one hundred people and can claim substantial discounts; their austere lifestyle allows them to build up capital relatively quickly; and when they are struck by fire or tempest, they come to each other's aid. It is a striking contrast to the lonely struggle of an isolated farm family to make ends meet.

Actors 4: The Urban Majority

The face of Alberta in the twenty-first century is an urban one.[63] Political and economic power is concentrated in Calgary and Edmonton and in the busy corridor between Fort McMurray and Lethbridge. These conurbations are the magnet that continues to draw immigrants from across Canada and abroad. The province has always been ethnically diverse, but the influx of Asian immigrants during the past several decades has been directed toward the metropolitan centers and has changed their complexions and textures. The urban host society is younger, better educated, and more diverse than the Hutterites' rural neighbours.[64] They are more concerned with the Super Bowl and *Dancing with the Stars* than they are with branding parties and church fairs, with Facebook rather than political party memberships, and with tee times rather than the café on Main Street.

The focus of these urbanites is on the health of the oil patch and the free-market economy. The prices of hogs or canola futures matter less to them than the uncomfortable lurches in the values of urban real estate or the prospects for investment in recreational property in Salmon Arm or Phoenix. Nevertheless, their worldview tends to be "small-l liberal." They espouse the charter of rights nationally and human rights internationally. While many are not drawn to organized religion, they favor religious toleration and support ethnic and social minorities.

The implications for the Hutterites are obvious. Concerns over communal property have paled into insignificance in this context. Urban Albertans are intrigued when Hutterites, from time to time, impose on their consciousness. The Brethren are a link to the mythic rural past from which urbanites have become increasingly disconnected. It is difficult to imagine a government discriminating against the Hutterites, given this supportive atmosphere among the urban majority. However, old-order societies like the Hutterites present a challenge to a modern-day culture that glorifies personal fulfillment.[65] The Brethren impose definite limits on individual behavior for the betterment of the community. In particular, the Hutterites curtail and structure the education of their young people and circumscribe the role of women.[66] *Fundamentalist* is not a term of endearment in our relativistic society, and public sentiment could once more turn against the Hutterites.

Newspaper editorials both reflect the changes in the larger society in their attitudes toward Hutterites and play a role in promoting those changes. In 1972 the *Calgary Herald* welcomed the report from a select committee of the assembly with the headline "Hutterite Freedom: A First-Class Report."[67] The editorial board supported the repeal of the Communal Property Act and thereafter was quick to criticize the government for any attempt to appease rural voters by softening its stand.[68] Small-town newspapers, which had much more to lose, nevertheless were unflinching in their support for the Hutterites. For example, the *Lethbridge (AB) Herald* had this to say, under the headline "This Is Democracy?"

When attacks are mounted on the Hutterites in the name of democracy and protecting democratic institutions, they should not be left unchallenged. One of the briefs presented to the [land use] forum bordered on the barbaric, suggesting enforced dissolution of the colonies, distribution of their property throughout the province and even limitation of the size of families. This is not democracy. . . . Perhaps the Protective Associations should give a little more thought to what they are protecting.[69]

The *Medicine Hat News* quoted Hutterite minister Jacob Kleinsasser in its headline "Hutterite Control Is Racism and Envy." The article reported on a resolution to the Annual Meeting of Manitoba Municipalities, which had proposed introducing limits to Hutterite expansion.[70] The motion was soon quashed, but the article provided an opportunity for Kleinsasser to explain that the colonies did buy goods locally and were often a major contributor to the success of rural businesses. It concluded by quoting the conclusions of geographer John Ryan that the Hutterites made a far greater contribution to the agricultural economy of Manitoba than the extent of their land holdings warranted. Ryan cautioned against any future attempt by municipalities to control Hutterite growth, saying, "Democracies are judged by the way they treat their minorities."[71]

The *Edmonton Journal* was quick to point out the hypocrisy of the government when it started to revisit the idea of guidelines to control Hutterite settlement in the late 1980s. An editorial noted, "Hutterites are frequently reassured that they have the legal right to buy land anywhere. Invariably, they are also warned not to exercise that right. . . . The old law died but its spirit lingered. The legal restrictions became 'guidelines' that Hutterite elders voluntarily accept to keep the peace."[72] A decade later editors were both consistent and forceful in their rejection of a new attempt to limit Hutterite expansion. The headlines "Religious Persecution" and "Stop This Attack on Hutterites" need no elaboration.[73]

Major newspapers across the country have shown an interest in the controversy over Hutterite land expansion because of the light it throws on the working out of multiculturalism and on politics and culture in Alberta. In a series of thoughtful and balanced articles in the *Toronto Globe and Mail*, Suzanne Zwarun laid out the essentials of the "Hutterite way" and the reasons for opposition to expansion of the colonies.[74] The *Vancouver Sun* used a private member's bill in the Alberta Assembly as the basis for a general article on the Brethren.[75] Its tone was sympathetic, and it quoted two knowledgeable informants, an accountant and an agricultural reporter, at length.

The support of the print media for the beleaguered Hutterites has had a profound effect on opponents of the sect. Anyone brave enough to voice disquiet about Hutterite expansion risks being branded as a redneck bigot. For example, when the reeve of Oakland, Manitoba, proposed restrictions on Hutterites at a convention of Manitoba municipalities, he was roundly condemned. "That's precisely the sort of thing that will make Manitoba look bad in the East," the Canadian human rights commissioner for Manitoba remarked.[76] Two decades later Barry McFarland prefaced his introduction to a private member's bill aimed at restricting Hutterite expansion by saying that he was prepared to be branded "rednecked and bigoted and discriminatory."[77] He was not disappointed. The *National Post* commented, "Blaming a reclusive and peaceful sect for this demographic shift is foolish scapegoating, nothing more. . . . The hardy people who survived four hundred years of oppression by Europe's warring empires should be able to fend off this attack by a political bumpkin with a shaky grasp of economics and property rights."[78] Nevertheless, in spite of these shifts in the balance of power between Hutterites and the host society, confrontations have continued. These flare-ups have been provoked by a variety of issues.

Issue 1: A Hutterite "Land Grab"?

In 1973 petitioners explained their fears to the premier of Alberta:

> Our fear is that the repeal of the Communal Property Act will precipitate unlimited expansion of these [communal] groups to the detriment of the citizens of rural Alberta. . . . [W]e fear that the removal of restrictions on land purchase by communal groups will quickly lead to a monopoly ownership of the agricultural land in Alberta. . . . [T]here is a very real expectation

of their being able over time to possess almost total ownership of agricultural land in Alberta.[79]

This dramatic claim summarizes the pervasive, almost subliminal, fear among rural people of a Hutterite "land grab." At the time this brief was presented, there were eighty-two Hutterite colonies in Alberta. Their population represented less than half of 1 percent of the provincial population, and their landholdings amounted to about 1 percent of the arable land in Alberta. However, the cold facts and rational discussion have done nothing to dissipate the fear of a potential Hutterite takeover. Almost all those who have voiced their disquiet over Hutterite expansion during the past several decades have echoed the sentiments expressed above. In January 2000 conservative MLA Barry McFarland proposed a private member's bill to limit the amount of land in any county that could be owned by an individual, corporation, or religious group. His objective was to support the threatened family farm, for he claimed that the province's best farmland was being monopolized by communal and corporate farm operators, and that they could eventually acquire all the land in a county or municipal district. "I think it is a definite possibility," he said. "It may take the next two generations but it is a possibility."[80] His words echoed the Vulcan brief quoted above.

These scenarios of Hutterite expansion, which are so unsettling for rural people, are based on projecting growth trends into the future without careful analysis. Even by 1973 it was apparent that Hutterite population growth was slowing down. An average Hutterite family now may have three or four children rather than ten. The age of marriage has risen, and the number of unmarried women has also grown. The population growth rate is less than 2 percent, much the same rate as that of the Canadian population as a whole during the 1970s. The period between colony divisions has increased, and some colonies have not established daughter colonies for thirty or forty years.[81] One reason for this may be increased defection rates. While many young Hutterite males have always left the colonies for a spell in the world, today young women and whole families have been leaving, and these people seldom return. The split of the Schmiedeleut posed many problems to Hutterites who had married partners from the Bruderhof. As many as five hundred Hutterites of all ages are thought to have moved to the east.[82] The evidence does not support the assumption that the Hutterites are a homogeneous group with a constant growth rate. Nevertheless, the number of Hutterite colonies has increased, albeit at a slower rate.

It is hard not to be sympathetic with energetic and relatively successful farm families that wish to expand their land base or to set up a son or daughter on their own place, only to find that they are in competition with the Hutterites. A farm family's operating space is limited to a few townships, for if land is not available within a few kilometers, it will not be economical for them to share equipment and labor. As one looks at maps of Hutterite landholdings in the core areas, one can well imagine that the opportunities for non-Hutterite farmers are severely circumscribed. It is not helpful to tell a farmer along the St. Mary's River that the Hutterites own less than 2 percent of the arable land in the province, since in his immediate vicinity, they own almost everything. Francis Van Herk, of Fort Macleod, poses a real dilemma when she remarks, "We have a big family. We have 11 boys, where are they going to go when they decide to start their own farms?"[83] Likewise, one can appreciate the way in which Vernon Henry's life was affected by the purchase of Alix Colony west of Stettler. Henry owned 640 acres and had rented 800 acres for two decades. The rental land was sold to the Brethren. He commented, "That tips my world upside down. But for me to buy more land, I'm going to have to go outside the area because I can't compete with the Hutterites. Single family farms can't compete with them. We don't have financial backing. They get cuts for volume buying, we don't."[84]

On the other hand, one can well imagine the relief of an older farmer, well past retirement age, at finding a buyer for his place, and moreover, a buyer willing to pay a fair price in one lump sum. Much of the land in Fort Macleod mentioned earlier had been on sale for several years. Yet the sellers faced hostility and resentment when they sold to the Hutterites. Ted Skene, a longtime resident in the area, said, "We'd like to sell our land in peace and still be friends. . . . I've worked hard to get this land. It's mine and I'm ready to sell. I feel I have the right to sell it for whatever money I want to and to whoever I want to."[85] Dave Rigel pointed out that his land had been up for sale for three years and not one of his neighbors had made an offer. He was delighted to sell and to get out from under his mortgage so that he could concentrate his attention on a cattle operation.[86]

As one ponders these opposing views, a number of hard questions come to mind. In the world of agriculture in the new millennium, the past is a poor template for the future. The status quo is not a realistic option. One has to ask how many young people want to become farmers. Many have seen their parents put in a lifetime of hard work for somewhat uncertain material rewards. Is the real obstacle standing in the way of a young person considering establishing a farm a shortage of available land or a lack of capital? In those few cases where capital is available, one must wonder whether the traditional extensive grain growing operation would be the best investment. Perhaps an innovative and intensive specialized venture, aimed at a niche market, might offer better returns from less land.

Issue 2: The School Question

In 1899 the dominion government agreed not to interfere with the Hutterites' religious beliefs and conceded, "They will also be allowed to establish independent schools for teaching their children if they desire to do so, but they will have to be responsible for their maintenance themselves. The children will not be compelled to attend other schools if their education is properly provided for."[87] The Brethren have staunchly resisted any attempts to infringe on this right ever since. Today most colonies in Alberta have "colony schools" administered by local school boards. These schools are unusual faith-based public entities that are attended only by Hutterite students.[88] For their part, the colonies provide a schoolroom and maintain it. In former times, this space also served as the community church, and this was a source of frustration to the teachers. Nowadays, most colonies I have visited have custom-built schools, often with several classrooms and sometimes with spacious gyms.

The Hutterites believe that to maintain their way of life, it is absolutely essential that they keep their children on the colony and do not allow them to be bused to local public schools. They want to wrap their young people in their culture and protect them from the "evils" of the outside world. Fundamentally, the Hutterites espouse different aims and outcomes. For them, all education should contribute to salvation and demonstrate obedience to God's way. They believe God has commanded them to live together in brotherly love, and therefore, education should promote relevant characteristics: unselfishness, obedience, consensus, and conformity. There is no room for individualism, competition, and self-realization, so often featured in the mission statements of public schools.

To achieve their objectives, the Hutterites start schooling early. At two or three years old, children start to spend a good portion of their day in kindergarten, which is run by the older colony women. Here they learn to conform to a routine and to play and eat with other youngsters. Prayer and singing are introduced. Joseph Hofer of Erskine Colony explained the role of kindergarten using words that would make modern educational theorists blanch: "We've got to get them at three to break them, break their will. When they are young you can teach them to forget about themselves. You know how kids are, 'I want to do this, I want to do that.' They want everything their own way. They've got to forget about 'I.' Any older and it's too late, too hard to teach them."[89] The transition to "young Hutterite in training" can be very hard on both mothers and children. However, I hasten to add that—in spite of Hofer's gruff words—young children are much loved and carefully nurtured on the colonies.[90]

In recent years, some Dariusleut colonies have not organized kindergartens, usually claiming that they have too few children to justify doing so. One elderly Hutterite remarked, "The women just don't want it."[91] This is a significant change and will surely have a far-reaching impact on the socialization of future generations. It represents a marked swing away from the communal ideal and toward a more individualized family orientation.

Hutterite children start primary school at six years old. On most colonies, classes are held in a school building built by the Brethren adjacent to, but separated from, the residential area of the settlement. A typical colony school might have twenty students and two classrooms. The teacher is a non-Hutterite or "English" individual who holds relevant teaching credentials from a university. The teacher's appointment is made by the school board but approved by colony elders. When I started visiting colonies over forty years ago, it was common for teachers to live on the colony, at least during the school week. This seems to be the exception today. In the past it was sometimes argued that colony schools were refuges for the least able or ambitious teachers or those with personal problems.[92] However, I have met teachers who have taught in colony schools for decades and who have a deep understanding and respect for Hutterite culture. Those who teach in Hutterite schools have periodic conferences to share common experiences and new ideas.[93]

It is only natural that there may be mutual suspicion between a new "English" teacher and the colony leadership. The teacher represents perhaps the most pervasive outside influence on the colony and is entrusted to instruct the children who will make up the next generation of Hutterites. On the one hand, Hutterite elders deprecate any emphasis on competitiveness or pride in individual achievement, and they are sensitive to any notes of strident patriotism or militarism. On the other hand, they admit that the teacher can be a useful window on the outside world for colony youth.

The German school mitigates the influence of the "English" teacher. Children attend this school for an hour or so before and after regular school. The German teacher instructs pupils in reading and writing High German and introduces them to Hutterite history and culture. The effect is to balance the secular and worldly influence of the English school and to emphasize Hutterian community and spiritual values. Young adults continue to attend German school on Sundays until they are baptized.

Although the schools use the Alberta curriculum, sensitive topics like evolutionary biology and sex education are dealt with, for the most part, in accordance with Hutterite beliefs. Often Hutterites have a hand in reviewing and approving textbooks. Many Hutterite leaders are mellowing in their attitudes toward education. As the host society becomes ever more complex and interconnected, and as technology evolves, the Hutterites are coming to see the advantages of their young people knowing more about language, history, science, and current events. It is the young people who are most confident and competent at using the new technology, whether it is the GPS system on the combine harvesters or the computer system used to grade eggs or record milk yields. Some progressive Dariusleut colonies have computer labs in their schools, and laptops are becoming more common.

Education is one of several areas where change is taking place in Hutterite society. On many progressive colonies, gifted students are encouraged to finish their high school education by correspondence. This is most common among liberal Schmiedeleut colonies and Dariusleut colonies, and this new option seems to appeal more to girls than to boys.[94] Other colonies send young people to technical colleges to receive advanced training in operating and maintaining complex machines.[95] Perhaps the most radical departure from tradition is taking place among colonies in Manitoba, where increasing numbers of young Hutterites are attending institutions of postsecondary education with a view to gaining teaching certificates. Although not all these individuals elect to return to their colonies, many do, and it is now common for progressive colonies to employ Hutterite teachers to teach in the English school.[96] This trend has sparked a lively debate between those who fear these Hutterite teachers will introduce too many worldly ideas into the colonies and those who suggest that better-educated Hutterites will be better equipped to make a living in the modern world. Some also believe that a broader exposure to history and culture can give the Brethren a deeper understanding of their own beliefs and practices.

Most young Hutterites in Alberta finish their formal schooling at the end of the year in which they turn 15. At that time they are regarded as adults and become a vital part of the colony labor force. However, it would be wrong to think that their education was truncated at this early age, as they spend the next few years in an informal apprenticeship. Young men will work where they are needed. Some may work with the colony electrician as he wires a barn; others may lay an irrigation pipe or repair something in the machine shop. Over a period of years, they will have the opportunity to learn a variety of skills, and then their preferences and aptitudes will draw them to specialize in a particular area. It is no wonder that it is not hard for "runaway" young Hutterites to find jobs in rural Alberta. They have a variety of skills, they are used to hard work, and they accept responsibility with confidence and cheerfulness. Similarly, young women from the colonies have both the temperament and the skills to work in nursing homes and elder-care facilities. If the role of education is to prepare youth for their working life, then one must reckon the extended colony system a success. The young Hutterites I have met impressed me with their robust self-confidence and the cheerful and natural way they interacted with adults, both Hutterites and strangers.

Opposition to Hutterite schools on the part of rural communities and their representatives has been consistent since the Brethren arrived in Alberta in 1918. For several decades the focus of complaints was the perception that Hutterite schooling did little to foster patriotism and Canadian citizenship.[97] Implicit in this criticism was the understanding that schools should be used as tools to achieve assimilation of this alien culture. This view is illustrated by a plea from the United Farmers of Alberta for the government to take decisive action "to cause the Hutterite people to conform to Canadian ways, at least to the extent of compelling their children to take the same educational training as Canadian children of surrounding districts, with a view to their ultimate assimilation as Canadian citizens, speaking our common language."[98]

Since the repeal of the Communal Property Act, hostility toward Hutterite education has been more focused and pragmatic. A combination of rural depopulation, better country roads, and the aspirations of educators has led to the inexorable process of school consolidation. The hope has been that fewer but larger schools can offer a wider range of programs and take advantage of modern technology in an economically viable manner. But like the Hutterites, rural people see their local schools as vital to the survival of their communities They bitterly oppose any proposals to close "their" schools and often blame newly established colonies for such actions. Steve Dixon of the Southern Alberta Development and Protective Association led the opposition to the establishment of a colony school at Brant Colony during the 1960s. He asked the question that has been reiterated again and again: "Why should Hutterite Schools be allowed to exist while other schools are closed?" Dixon went on to explain that school busing had become a growing grievance in rural areas.[99]

Two decades later Barry McFarland, then a Vulcan county councilor, echoed Dixon's words. He explained that Mossleigh School, about 35 kilometers north of Vulcan, had been closed when enrollment fell below twenty-eight students. "There are two colonies within 20 miles that have 14 and 22 students," he said. "Bussing the Hutterite kids would have saved the school."[100] Hutterite expansion in Stettler County provoked a similar reaction, and many of the same arguments were voiced. Gadsby and Botha Schools were amalgamated, one taking grades 1–6 and the other grades 7–9. Larry Derr commented that displacement of farm families by Hutterites had to be a factor in this decision: "You can't blame it all on the Hutterites because it is mostly older farmers that are left now. But you keep farmers out and it's bound to have an effect. I don't know what's going to happen to the schools and communities if they keep getting thicker."[101] Gloria Diegel, who farmed close to Red Willow Colony, complained bitterly: "They tell me what school to send my kids to. They told me this year I had to send two to Gadsby and one to Botha, because they had put amalgamation in. Why can't they tell the Hutterites they have to send their kids to our schools? Anybody can hide behind religion. I don't believe for a minute anybody should get away with hiding behind their religion."[102]

In 1996 Gillian Bushrod, superintendent of the Clearview School Division, provided a broader perspective when she explained, "In the last 35 years, Stettler County has gone from 1580 students in 8 schools to 980 students in 7 schools. It is about the same number of schools but 600 less children. We've got less and less children in our schools." Bushrod did not blame the Hutterites for declining enrollment. The trend toward smaller families, rural residents moving to urban areas, and fewer families with school-age children were all contributing factors. "I see the main issue in this decline as a general transfer of population," she said. "That's a natural progression in rural Alberta."[103]

I have looked in vain for evidence of outbursts of overt hostility toward Hutterite schools since the turn of the millennium.[104] Unfortunately, I don't believe this means that envy and resentment of the Hutterites have disappeared. Rather, it may reflect the fact that the painful process of school consolidation has slowed, that some of the larger rural communities with high schools are actually growing, or that morale in rural regions is so low that they are immobilized by a sense of powerlessness.

Having, for the present, won the battle to keep their unusual public-private colony schools, the Hutterites may face subtler and broad-based criticism in the future. Some people among the urban majority might question whether the human rights of Hutterite children are being trampled on. Why should they be forced to leave school at 15? Why should they be deprived of the full range of programs and the progressive technologies offered in public high schools? And, at a deeper level, does the colony have the right to restrict the creativity and individuality of their children? There can be no doubt that the educational developments in "the world" are rocking the hitherto stable ark of Hutterite culture.[105]

Issue 3: Purchasing Patterns

"We continue to view the increase of their [Hutterite] holdings with concern and alarm. . . . [If unchecked,] towns and communities would disintegrate from disuse and lack of support, and services would disappear."[106] Businessmen in small service communities have viewed the replacement of family farms by a new Hutterite colony with apprehension. They have established common cause with farmers in opposing Hutterite expansion. They argue that the Brethren bypass local retailers to take advantage of lower prices offered by stores in larger cities. Moreover, they point out that the Hutterites are self-sufficient in ways that farm families are not and do not support local groceries, restaurants, fast-food outlets, and bars. These complaints have been a consistent theme in anti-Hutterite rhetoric. The fate of "withering small towns" is bleak, and this is thought to be due to the increasing number of colonies.[107]

Objective studies of the economic impact of new colonies on business activity in small towns have demonstrated again and again that these negative assumptions are wrong. Even before the repeal of the Communal Property Act, the mayor of Drumheller commissioned a study that compared the spending patterns of a colony with those of the farms that it replaced. The study concluded that although the expenditures were different, the total payoff to the city was very similar.[108] The 1972 *Report on Communal Property* surveyed the sales policies of major companies that sold agricultural machinery, fertilizers, and seed. It found that there were no advantages in bypassing local suppliers, although the head office of a company would often assist a local dealer in making a sale.[109] John Bennett carried out a precise accounting of the purchases of four colonies in southwestern Saskatchewan during the 1960s. He demonstrated that local businesses handling agricultural machinery, vehicles, fertilizers, and building supplies had all benefited from the advent of the Brethren. The Hutterite operations were more diversified and aggressive than those of the farmers and ranchers they replaced. Their local purchases were greater in volume and frequency. For example, their fuel bills were far higher, and they replaced machinery more often. One dealer reported a 15 percent increase in his turnover.[110]

During the past three decades Hutterite leaders have shown an increased willingness to respond to complaints that the colonies do not support local communities. In 1989 Sam Hofer, boss of Donalda Colony, wrote a letter to his local newspaper in response to one such accusation. He pointed out that his colony spent $200,000 a year buying supplies from Bashaw businesses. He went on to explain that nearby Red Willow Colony had spent $1 million replacing all its housing units and that most of the materials, including $150,000 worth of concrete, came from Bashaw.[111] Hand Hills Colony's manager, Sam Kleinsasser, said in 1996, "We try to do business in our own towns as much as we can. We try to give them first chance. In the last thirty years, every Hand Hills truck has been purchased from Hanna dealers."[112] Colony members patronize local drug, fabric, grocery, and hardware stores, as well as lumberyards and banks. They also interact with local grain and livestock dealers, insurance companies, lawyers, accountants, and veterinarians.[113]

Nevertheless, Hutterites, like other rural dwellers, do come to major centers for both business and pleasure. I see groups of Hutterites quite frequently at my suburban Walmart store and coming in and out of nearby Value Village. Colony women have always sought out the best possible deal for yard goods, from which they make clothes. It seems likely that both the frequency of visits to town and the volume and value of personal purchases have increased. However, the Brethren cannot be blamed for the seismic shift that has occurred both in rural population density and in buying patterns throughout the prairies.[114]

Issue 4: Environmental Concerns

During the 1990s the expansion of Hutterite colonies was challenged on new grounds. Rural people argued that the intensity of colony farming operations posed threats to the environment. In particular, the disposal of manure from hog barns, dairy barns, and chicken facilities could contaminate groundwater and produced odors that were impossible to live with. The articulation of these concerns reflected a growing sophistication among country people about "green" issues. They now could invoke existing municipal bylaws before the appropriate planning committee to challenge proposed developments by the Hutterites. This provided a politically correct way to block a new colony without merely arguing that the Hutterites were "taking over" or were adversely affecting local businesses.

The Municipal District of Willow Creek denied permission for a hog and dairy operation on the newly purchased Willow Creek Colony. The proposed development was within 2 miles of the hamlet of Staveley, and it was feared that "prevailing winds in the area would have brought odours from the operation in the direction of Staveley." The Hutterites' application was turned down as not being in the public interest. Staveley's mayor, John Burns, was pleased with the decision but expressed concern lest the decision be seen as "Hutterite bashing."[115] After the ruling, the facility was located farther south on the Hutterites' 7,400-acre property. This case became a precedent when Big Bend Colony applied to establish Greenwood Colony within the same municipality in 1995, but this time the development appeal board allowed the intensive livestock operation to be built.[116]

A more serious disruption of Hutterite expansion plans occurred in Starland County in 1991. After more than a year of back-and-forth negotiation, the Municipal District of Starland's development appeal board rejected plans for a new colony on the grounds that the planned hog operation would pose environmental problems. Neighboring farmers Kevin Boon and Arnold Shand maintained that fertilizer-enriched runoff could threaten the area's water supply. Ric Smith, a regional engineer for Alberta Agriculture, argued that the farmers' concerns were overstated. "What they are actually doing is not creating pollution, but in fact improving the soil and benefiting both crops and plants."[117] Arthur Grenville, reeve of the municipal district, said that the greater public interest had to be protected. He went on to point out that the municipality had a number of colonies already and that any proposal that met planning concerns and lawful requirements would be upheld. For their part, the Hutterites felt that the verdict was the result of prejudice and religious persecution. They filed a complaint with the Alberta Human Rights Commission and promised to look for expansion somewhere else with different lawyers.[118] They obtained land in the same region and established Blue Sky Colony in 1995.

More recently, the villagers of Carmangay used environmental issues concerning confined animal feeding operations to justify their passionate opposition to Clear Lake Colony's establishment of a daughter colony, to be called Summerland. The headline of a CBC news report says it all: "Alberta Village Fights Plan for 'Horrible' Animal Feeding Operation on Nearby Hutterite Colony."[119] In fact, the story goes back to 2014, when Clear Lake Colony, which had been buying land for some years, applied to the Municipal Planning Commission to build a new colony. After the colony made three attempts to gain planning permission, the commission finally allowed development to go ahead in 2016. However, when the colony applied for permission to build barns for chickens, hogs, geese, and ducks, it was refused because of fears of smells and pollution. This long, drawn-out battle shows how close to the surface hostility to Hutterite expansion remains in some areas. The colony initially obtained the land and permission to build its headquarters, but not the barns necessary to make a living.[120] At the time of this writing, the new colony has secured permission and is building various agricultural buildings. However, according to David Waldner, one of the managers at Clear Lake Colony, they have not yet been given permission to build homes on their own land.[121]

It is clear that Hutterite leaders are well aware of the need to conform to strict antipollution bylaws. The new hog barn at Erskine Colony, which houses 400 sows, boasts a retractable subfloor that drains waste into a 1.6 million gallon stainless steel container. The colony boss explained, "We had a meeting for all the colony members to decide what to do [about the effluent]. . . . We thought this would be the most environmentally friendly. But it was hard to think of spending $230,000 for shit!"[122]

While the disposal of sewage poses an environmental problem to new colonies, water supply may become an increasingly pressing concern. Hutterite colonies are heavy water users. To the domestic needs of a community of one hundred or more people must be added the demands of pigs, chickens, and cattle, as well as irrigated crops. Of course, a good water supply has always been a consideration as leaders search for a site for a daughter colony. Many colonies are aligned along the banks of rivers, such as the Waterton, Oldman, Bow, and South Saskatchewan. One cannot help but be impressed with the six huge diesel pumps that provide water for Cameron Farms Colony on the Oldman River.[123] As we are facing a drier and warmer future, and demand for water is going to increase dramatically, some colonies are buying water rights to ensure future supplies.[124] Here and there, colonies have been fined for illegal water abstraction or for violations that disrupted fish habitat.[125] There seems little doubt that while all farmers in southern Alberta will have to adapt to scarce water supply, the Hutterites, with their extraordinary demands, will be particularly vulnerable. Opposition to the application of Lone Pine Colony to draw 6.2 million gallons of water from two wells is but the first of many cases that are likely to arise.[126]

Looking to the Future

Over the past several decades the number of Hutterite colonies in Alberta has continued to increase, although at a much slower rate than was feared by those who opposed the repeal of the Communal Property Act in 1973.[127] In spite of this increase, overt expressions of hostility toward the sect have become less and less frequent. This points to far-reaching changes in Albertan society.

The provincial government has remained adamant in its determination not to reopen any discussion about limiting Hutterite expansion.[128] This firm stance reflects both the diminishing power of rural voters and the perception that the urban majority would have little patience with any discriminatory initiative based on religion or ethnicity.

On the farms and in the communities of "outer Alberta," attitudes toward the Brethren remain unchanged. Every new colony is a perceived threat to the small, the local, and the familiar, for the Hutterites are regarded as large corporate entities tied to metropolitan and even global trading systems. However, voices are less strident than they once were. Rural folk acknowledge their weak position and look forward with some trepidation to a future dominated by agribusiness.

Alberta's urbanites are largely indifferent to the Hutterites. At the same time, they probably know more about, and have more contact with, the colonies than any previous generation. They are predisposed to favor minority rights, but which minority and whose rights? While it is hard to imagine them supporting a move to control Hutterite expansion, public opinion is fickle. In the future the Brethren could be challenged to explain the constraints that their culture imposes on women and children.

Hutterite leaders have viewed with some concern the periods of their history when they were not threatened by outsiders. Resolute defense of their culture in the face of a hostile world has proved a powerful uniting and stabilizing force. The new millennium has seen another golden age dawn for the Hutterites in North America, but it has spawned its share of internal problems. One can point to instances where the fundamental tenets of the "Hutterite way" have been compromised. The family has gained ground at the expense of the community. Pacifism has been set aside in a search for justice (or revenge) in "English" courts. And separation from "the world" has been challenged by the demands of corporate agriculture and internet technology.

Nevertheless, most colonies in Alberta are flourishing. They retain at least 80 percent of their young people and welcome home many who have spent some lonely years working on isolated oilfields. The size and diversity of their enterprises have enabled them to remain competitive in a sector where profit margins have shrunk, and their contribution to Alberta's agricultural output has steadily increased. By 2025 there will likely be between 225 and 250 of their farm villages spread throughout the province, all adding a significant element to the cultural landscape.[129]

9

The Legacy of Diffusion

Cultural Landscapes

Flying low from Calgary to Lethbridge, Alberta, and on to Great Falls, Montana, one can easily pick out the Hutterite colonies.[1] Their relatively large and complex footprints stand in marked contrast to those of neighboring family farms. Colonies even show up clearly when viewed from the cruising altitude of a jet airliner. Their extensive bare work yards between machine shops, the barns, and the grain stores stand out as white parcels in a textured sea of green agricultural land (see fig. 31). It is ironic that their colonies, with their uniform geometric layouts, resemble small military establishments, considering the passionate pacifism of the sect. Descending closer, one can distinguish banks of gleaming grain storage silos, neat gardens, and long low barns (see fig. 32). Many colonies are surrounded by extensive feed corrals and lagoons to contain effluent from pig and chicken barns. Harder to see, because it is often partially obscured by trees and shrubs, is the residential heart of the colony. This is the zone of nurture, where children play and adults sit and chat at the end of the day. As illustrated in figure 33, the world of work, commerce, and contact with the "English" outsiders is discreetly excluded from this central core. Figure 34 shows several long multifamily dwellings framing a spacious court. Concrete pathways link these dwellings to the kitchen–dining room complex in which the community meets for meals three times a day. The kitchen plays an important role as a central meeting place on a colony. The coffeepot is always on, and workers and visitors come and go. The communal dining room is attached, as are storerooms, a bakery, and a small room for children to eat in. Hereafter, this multiuse building is referred to simply as the kitchen.

Fig. 31. Satellite image of three Hutterite colonies in the Milk River Reservoir area of Alberta. Google Earth, 2019.

The two main objectives of this chapter are closely allied. The first is to use aerial imagery to make an inventory of selected site characteristics of Hutterite colonies in general. As the tide of rural settlement continues to recede on the prairies and Great Plains, the growing number of Hutterite colonies constitute an increasingly important element in the cultural landscape. Earlier chapters have charted the diffusion of colonies; this chapter provides systematic analysis of the morphology of these agricultural villages, examining their physical and visual makeup. The second aim is to describe the built environment of individual Hutterite colonies and evaluate contrasts among them over time, space, and clan group affiliation. The next section describes the methodology; this is followed by a discussion of the context and rationale for pursuing these themes. This foundation provides a basis for comments on the relationship between the form and function of the settlements and the pace and direction of change in Hutterite society in the last part of the chapter.

Fig. 32. Beiseker Colony, Alberta, Dariusleut, founded in 1926. The residential core is in the foreground, with barns and grain storage behind, kitchen on the left, and three six-unit residences with extensions. Photograph by Simon M. Evans, 2014.

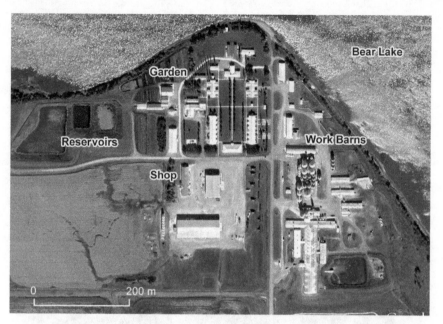

Fig. 33. Layout, orientation, and residential core of Grandview Colony, Alberta, Dariusleut, founded in 1977. Orientation is north-south, with work-related buildings east of range road. Google Earth, 2010, County of Grande Prairie No. 1.

Methods

To use Google Earth for colony classification, it was necessary to create a layer of georeferenced points for all North American Hutterite colonies (494 colonies at the time of this writing). This was accomplished by obtaining the geographic coordinates (latitude and longitude) for each colony, along with information on its parent colony, date founded, and Leut.[2] A colony shapefile containing this information was created with ArcGIS software and then converted to a Keyhole Markup Language (KML) file. The resulting KML file was used in Google Earth to do an audit of the following characteristics of each colony's residential area: geographic orientation, geometric layout, and housing types. For a small number of colonies, the Google Earth images were a bit dated (in the case of very new colonies), obscured by cloud or snow cover, or had too low a resolution.

Fig. 34. Two views of Grandview Colony. *Top*: Looking past the kitchen on right to older housing with extensions. *Bottom*: Newer row housing, six units and landscaped court. Photographs by Simon M. Evans, 2013.

The ArcGIS web map service served as a secondary imagery source for these cases. With the two imagery sources, 487 colonies (98.6 percent) were successfully classified.

The geographic orientation was usually assessed from the direction of the long axis of the residential buildings; however, in cases where buildings were aligned in different directions, the long axis of the geometric layout of the whole residential area was used. Where the buildings were equally oriented both north-south and east-west and the layout of the residential area was square, the orientation was categorized as "north-south." When there was more than a 5-degree deviation from a north-south or east-west orientation, the orientation was classified as "other cardinal."

Three categories were used to evaluate the geometric layout of the buildings in the residential area. "Rectangular" included rectangular, square, L-shaped and linear layouts. "Innovative" included the following shaped layouts: curved, horseshoe, semicircle, circle/oval, diamond, triangle, hexagon, fishbone, and star. When no discernible order was visible, the layout was classified as "nongeometric." The number of detached single-family dwelling units was also recorded, and a ratio of detached to multifamily units was calculated for each colony. The category "other" was used where the detached single-family units exceeded 50 percent of the housing on a colony.

It is important to note that the use of remote sensing tools such as Google Earth does not preclude colony visits; in fact, touring colonies and talking to Hutterite leaders is an essential prerequisite for interpreting what is seen on the aerial imagery. I visited communities along the Rosebud River and in Vulcan County in 2017 and colonies in Manitoba and South Dakota during the summer of 2018.[3]

The Growing Significance of Hutterite Colonies

The cycle of gradual population increase over decades, followed by colony fission, has profound implications for the colony site. As population increases, the existing housing units become overcrowded. The remedy may be to add a further multifamily dwelling, to build a number of smaller temporary units, or even to bring in some mobile homes. After the division has occurred, there is surplus space. Large families may be permitted to occupy additional units, while some smaller buildings may be moved to the daughter colony where this is practical. This process of colony division has led to considerable growth in the number of colonies and diffusion from the original cores of settlement: there were 230 colonies in 1974, 300 a decade later, and 515 recorded by the Canadian census in 2016.[4]

In contrast, a dominant theme in the human geography of the plains has been rural depopulation. Indeed, an extreme view has been to envision a "rewilding" of the grasslands.[5] Certainly, away from urban growth poles and transportation corridors, the tide of rural settlement has continued to recede.[6] These are counties where the population is stable or declining, and they are home to older, less educated folk with lower per capita income. Entire regions are more reliant on government transfers, including pensions, and communities live on the defensive, struggling to maintain schools, hospitals, and other public services in the face of population losses and government cutbacks.[7] While some rural towns have emerged as "winners," with hospitals, high schools, and a solid range of retail and service outlets, smaller "minimum convenience" centers have disappeared, and the future of many other villages, which are not on major transport arteries, is in question.[8] To this extent, the visual human-made landscape of the Canadian prairies and northern Great Plains has been diminished.

However, the number of Hutterite colonies has continued to grow during the same period. The time between colony divisions has lengthened as the rate of population increase has slowed, but these farm villages have proved that they can flourish in spite of the challenges faced by the agricultural sector of the economy. A decade hence, another generation of colonies will have been established, bringing the total to more than seven hundred.[9] This growth will do something to mitigate rural depopulation and balance the loss of the smallest central places. In 2011 in Alberta, for example, there were already nearly two colonies for every census village, and Hutterites made up 12 percent of the farm population.[10]

Characteristics, Diversity, and Change in Colonies

This inquiry focuses on the residential heart of the colony: the orientation, the plan of the settlement, and the nature of the housing. This constitutes an important part of the whole colony footprint; it is easily identified and is amenable to interpretation. The characteristics of Hutterite colonies are described in this section, which explores the range of contrasts among colonies over time, space, and clan group. Most of the existing research on the layout of colonies dates back to the 1980s, and there have been significant changes since then. Moreover, previous work was based on a sample of colonies used to establish a typical model.[11] Presently, using the publicly available sources of imagery described earlier, it is possible to glean a considerable amount of information about almost all colonies in different jurisdictions. These data demonstrate both the broad uniformity among colonies and the emerging variations in design that are becoming more commonplace.

Any evaluation of the appearance of Hutterite colonies and their contribution to the cultural landscape must take into account not only the diffusion of new colonies but also the renewal of older parent colonies. The evolution of the colony headquarters site does not cease when division has taken place. The newly established daughter colony reflects the state of the art with respect to new residences, kitchen and laundry appliances, and church and school buildings. In contrast, the parent colony has housing stock that is at least twenty-five to thirty years old and probably forty to fifty years old. As soon as the parent colony has recovered from the huge investment it has made in establishing a new colony, the leaders address the problem of inequality between living conditions at the new place and the old. In some cases these plans may only involve modernizing the kitchen or building a new school. Frequently, however, all the accommodations at the parent colony are replaced, and the look of the settlement is transformed.

In the early 1970s colonies along the Rosebud River were made up of the original two-story frame houses built in 1918, complete with outhouses. Now these colonies have been completely rebuilt.

Fig. 35. Site transformation along the Rosebud River. *Top*: Sandhills Colony in 1972. Four multifamily frame houses built in 1936, with outhouses. Photograph by Simon M. Evans. *Bottom*: Sandhills Colony in 2018. Four Brant-style buildings with extensions (no outhouses). Google Earth, 2018.

Brant Colony was established in 1968 not far from High River. It was among the first colonies to incorporate an indoor bathroom and partial basement. Indeed, for a time during the 1970s and 1980s Brant-style housing was widely adopted among the colonies. Today Brant Colony boasts four sleek, modern row houses, each divided into seven units. Fashions have changed, and so has the look of this flourishing colony.[12] Older colonies established in the 1920s and 1930s may well have gone through this process of renewal more than once. To take one example, Sandhills Colony (founded in 1936 and shown in fig. 35) has undergone considerable change between 1972 and 2018.

Geographic Orientation

John Hostetler's 1974 account of colony organization is an outgrowth of his analysis of the Hutterite worldview. He observes, "The Hutterite world view leads to the creation of an earthly environment that is ordered spatially, temporally, socially, and symbolically."[13] Because they are sojourners and have been forced to move frequently, the Brethren create their own uniform physical environment, in which everyone knows his or her place and socialization of the young can proceed uninterrupted. With respect to orientation, Hostetler quotes a preacher who explained why the long houses of the headquarters sites run due north and south: "They are squared with the compass. You don't walk crooked to the earth, you walk straight, that is how our buildings should be, straight with the compass and not askew."[14]

Our inventory found that three-quarters of all the colonies were indeed oriented north-south. Among the Lehrerleut, this figure approaches 100 percent. Interestingly, quite a number of the older colonies are laid out just a few degrees off north. Today's township roads, laid out more recently with more sophisticated technology, bring this discrepancy to light.[15] A growing number of Dariusleut colonies are aligned east-west. Many of the colonies aligned between the major cardinal points of the compass reflect the unique characteristics of their locations: some are aligned along riverbanks, while others nestle within the curves of meanders, like Bloomfield

Colony, Manitoba. Table 11 summarizes the geographic orientation of the colonies studied.

Table 11. Geographic orientation

ORIENTATION		ALL COLONIES	DARIUSLEUT	LEHRERLEUT	SCHMIEDELEUT
North-south	n	370	116	139	115
	%	76	73	98	62
East-west	n	72	25	1	46
	%	15	16	0.7	25
Other cardinal	n	30	12	2	16
	%	6	7	1	7
No obvious orientation	n	15	6	0	9
	%	3	4	0	5
Totals	n	487	159	142	186

Note: In the Schmiedeleut there were no obvious differences between Schmiedeleut One and Two colonies, partly because so many colonies were established before the split, so all Schmiedeleut are amalgamated in this and the other tables.

Geometric Layout

The majority of Hutterite colonies were laid out in a rectangular grid conformation. However, the details of this geometry vary among the clan groups. The Lehrerleut colonies display long, narrow rectangular plans, defined by their multifamily row housing. Their common buildings are in a parallel line between the residences. The Dariusleut colonies tend to have a shorter primary axis, and in many cases the kitchen and church may be built at right angles across the top and bottom of the rectangle to enclose it. The Schmiedeleut colonies tend to be square, primarily because they have opted for smaller residential housing. This group leads the way with respect to innovative designs for their colonies, with 18 percent of their colonies breaking new ground. Eleven colonies are harder to interpret; the buildings appear to be grouped around the kitchen in a random fashion. While some of these sites have become more complex over time, others chose a less structured form for their living space from the beginning. Table 12 summarizes these geometric layouts.

Table 12. Geometric layout

LAYOUT		ALL COLONIES	DARIUSLEUT	LEHRERLEUT	SCHMIEDELEUT
Rectangular	n	428	142	139	147
	%	88	89	98	79
Innovative	n	48	12	3	33
	%	10	8	2	18
Nongeometric	n	11	5	0	6
	%	2	3	0	3
Totals	n	487	159	142	186

House Types

This inventory of sites and house types on Hutterite colonies comes at the end of a forty-five-year period of change and experimentation. In their 2012 book Yossi Katz and John Lehr comment, "Only a few decades ago, they used to draw water from wells in the yards, bathrooms were outside the house, there were no kitchens in the houses . . . and houses in general were much smaller. A house in James Valley Colony [Manitoba] that today is occupied by a family of four might have been home to 17 people only 40 years ago."[16] John Ryan and Sibylle Becker describe the transition in Manitoba from the first generation of frame multistory houses to smaller, more modern housing, as well as the widespread adoption of duplexes among the Schmiedeleut during the 1970s and 1980s.[17] The figures in table 13 suggest that this process has, for the most part, run its course. Today most colonies in Manitoba and the Dakotas have a nucleus of duplexes and some additional row housing.

Table 13. House types

HOUSING		ALL COLONIES	DARIUSLEUT	LEHRERLEUT	SCHMIEDELEUT
Row	n	231	77	127	27
	%	47	48	89	14
Ls	n	28	23	5	0
	%	6	15	3	0
Mixed row & Ls	n	57	46	9	2
	%	12	29	6	1
Duplex	n	29	0	1	28
	%	6	0	1	15
Mixed row & duplex	n	123	1	0	122
	%	25	1	0	66
Other	n	19	12	0	7
Trailers and bungalows	%	4	8	0	4
Totals	n	487	159	142	186

Note: Ls = houses with extensions to house bathrooms.

In 1985 John Melland described the incremental process by which modernization was achieved on Lehrerleut and Dariusleut colonies. The first stage involved building extensions onto existing multifamily houses. This new space was used for a bathroom, and a partial basement was excavated for the water heater and furnace. These Brant-style houses, providing homes for four or six families, spread widely during the 1980s. However, it was not long before new daughter colonies began to appear, with long, low row houses in which six to eight family units were aligned side by side. Typically, these dwellings had full basements. They were thought to be cheaper and easier to construct and had the aesthetic appeal of simple clean lines.[18]

The Lehrerleut have completed the transition to this design, and only nine colonies still have some residences with extensions. As is so often the case, the Dariusleut display more diversity. While many colonies have adopted row housing, many others have a mix of the older design and the new. Indeed, some colonies that have recently completed major rebuilding projects have elected to stay with the familiar house type. Although all row houses present a uniform footprint from the air, styles vary considerably on the ground. In most cases residents reach the main floor by ascending steps either outside or in the hallway. Some colonies have walk-out basements with lots of windows, while others have basements that are used only for storage and perhaps a bedroom for boys.

Single-Family Dwellings

One of the unexpected findings of this research was the prevalence of single-family dwellings on several colonies of this communal group. The average number of residential units on all colonies was 22.[19] Among the Schmiedeleut, 16 percent of their units were designed for single families, while the corresponding figure on Dariusleut colonies was 12 percent. There were very few single-family units on Lehrerleut colonies (0.3 percent).

The averages mask great differences among colonies within each clan group. There are many colonies without any single-family dwellings. On other colonies, old farmhouses, trailers, and bungalows make up more than half of the available accommodations. This is particularly true of the Schmiedeleut as a whole and of colonies in the Dakotas in particular. For example, Grassland, in South Dakota, a Schmiedeleut Two colony founded in 1990, has eight trailers in addition to two duplexes and four multifamily row houses.

Fig. 36. A typical Lehrerleut colony. Brant Colony, Alberta, founded in 1968. Orientation north-south, with seven-unit residences giving rise to a typical rectangular plan. Common buildings in the middle. Google Earth 2012.

The use of mobile homes and existing houses during the construction phase of establishing a new colony is a well-established practice. For example, Vauxhall Farms, a Dariusleut colony in Alberta, had a neat row of mobile homes to provide temporary accommodations while the full complement of multifamily houses was being constructed to the west. In contrast, on the group of Dariusleut colonies surrounding Lewistown, Montana, single-family units make up a large proportion of the available living space and seem to be the preferred option.

Lehrerleut Colony Characteristics

The Lehrerleut exhibit a remarkable degree of uniformity in the way they organize their living space. Whether old or new, located in Alberta, Saskatchewan, or Montana, Lehrerleut colonies look almost identical from the air. With few exceptions, colonies are aligned north-south. Typically, a rectangular plan is framed by four row houses, each divided into seven or eight units. In the middle

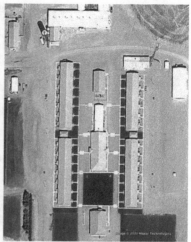
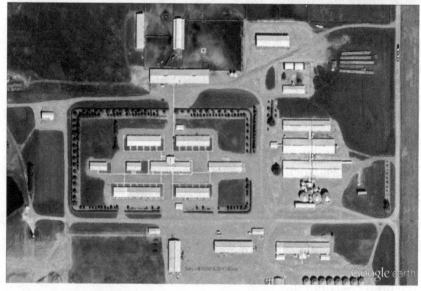

Fig. 37. Layout shared by almost all Lehrerleut colonies, regardless of the time of establishment or location. *Top left*: Milford, Montana, founded in 1947. *Top right*: Haven, Saskatchewan, founded in 1967. *Bottom*: Butte, Saskatchewan, founded in 1991. This is the only Lehrerleut colony oriented east-west. Note the elaborate windbreaks. Google Earth, 2012.

stands the kitchen complex, which in many of the more recently remodeled colonies contains a church. Two smaller buildings in this central row of communal buildings house the laundry and the kindergarten. These features are illustrated in figure 36. Milford Colony in Montana, originally founded in 1947, has been rebuilt to exemplify this model. The layout can be compared with that of Haven Colony in Saskatchewan (1967) and with the more recently built Butte Colony in Saskatchewan (1991). All three colonies are shown in figure 37.

Lehrerleut colonies are meticulously neat and rather austere looking. Landscaping is usually limited to tiny patches of grass around the houses and functional shelterbelts. Much of the open space between the residences and the work buildings is covered with gravel or left as bare earth. At first glance this presents a rather unattractive and cold impression, but it has some pragmatic advantages. Gravel between the buildings drains well, requires a minimum of maintenance, allows occasional access to vehicles, and encourages the use of concrete walkways, which are cleared of snow during the winter. Even among the Lehrerleut there are slight differences in ambience between one colony and another. Some have rather more green space, mature trees, and even flower gardens, while others are bereft of any softening touches. These differences reflect both the age of the colony and the attitudes of the leadership.

The aerial imagery of these colonies freezes the buildings at one moment in time. In reality, these Lehrerleut colonies—indeed most Hutterite colonies—are undergoing almost constant change. Among a handful of Alberta colonies I visited during 2015, Riverbend was in the process of replacing its kitchen complex with a sleek new building that will include a church, Brant had just completed a multiclassroom state-of-the-art school building with a large attached gymnasium, and neighboring Wild Rose Colony had almost completed the long process of remodeling all its residences. Everywhere, infrastructure is being updated and construction is underway. This means work for colony plumbers, electricians, carpenters, sheet metal fabricators, and machine shops. Almost all the physical construction work on a colony is done in-house. Only

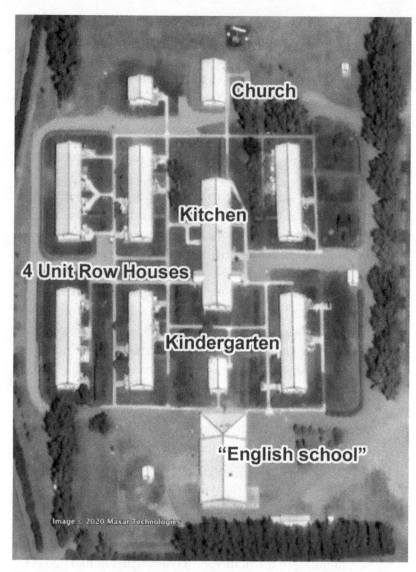

Fig. 38. A typical Dariusleut colony. Swift Current Colony, Saskatchewan, founded in 1978. Orientation north-south. The adoption of four-unit row housing means the plan is roughly square. Google Earth, 2018.

where bylaws and building codes are involved do colonies enlist the help of outside specialists to develop plans and guide them through the bureaucratic hoops. Nor should the plain outward appearance of colonies be allowed to tell the whole story. Many contemporary colonies enjoy a level of comfort—not to say luxury—quite foreign to many households in the suburbs of major cities. Residences and common buildings have under-floor hot water heating pumped from a central boiler house. Built-in cupboards and linen closets are designed to meet the needs of the homemakers, and a kitchen nook equipped with a refrigerator and microwave allows the preparation of snacks between meals in the communal dining room. Family units contain two bathrooms, and toilets are fitted with elaborate bidet systems.

Dariusleut Colony Characteristics

Dariusleut colonies exhibit much more diversity in their layout and conformation. All colonies have much in common, however, and differences are merely variations on a familiar theme rather than wholesale departures from tradition. A Hutterite family transported from Rock Lake Colony, depicted in a map by Hostetler as it was in 1965, would have no difficulty finding their bearings and feeling at home in a modern colony like Arrowwood, Alberta, or Big Sky, Montana.[20] Most Dariusleut colonies are laid out in precise geometric patterns, and their multifamily housing units display many of the characteristics already described. Figure 38 shows a typical Dariusleut colony.

Three-quarters of the Dariusleut colonies in Alberta are laid out with a north-south axis. But this means that one-quarter of the colonies are aligned differently. Thirteen colonies are oriented east-west. In some cases this may reflect a conscious effort to benefit from passive solar energy. Thirty-five years ago, when I visited the newly established Berry Creek Colony, the boss explained that they had decided to build row housing and to align it east-west. He boasted that they were already benefiting from lower heating costs. Eight other colonies, such as Beiseker, Alberta, are aligned between the

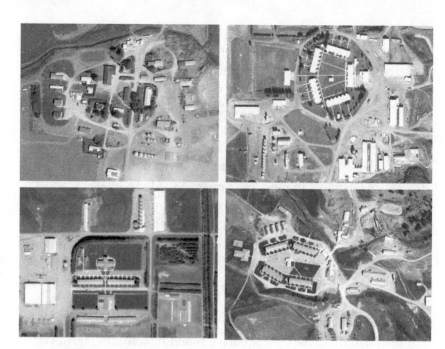

Fig. 39. Four Dariusleut colonies with different layouts. *Top left*: Ayers Ranch, Montana, founded in 1945. Unplanned, with houses and trailers. *Top right*: Red Willow, Alberta, founded in 1949. Rough circle, with six-unit longhouses. *Bottom left*: Belle Plaine, Saskatchewan, founded in 1990. Linear, with church to north, kitchen to south. *Bottom right*: East Cardston, Alberta, founded in 1918. Arc layout, still developing. Google Earth, 2014, 2007, 2016, and 2015.

cardinal points of the compass. In addition, a handful of colonies have evolved with no obvious plan or orientation.

The majority of Dariusleut plans are geometric and rectangular, and yet there is a marked difference from Lehrerleut layouts. In many cases the north-south axis is shorter and is matched by an east-west dimension to create a square shape rather than an obvious rectangle. Unlike the Lehrerleut, the Dariusleut have opted to build freestanding churches set apart from the other communal buildings. Thus in a newer colony like Arrowwood, Alberta, the residences are flanked to the east by the kitchen and to the west by the imposing church building. Several colonies have modified the rigid rectangular layout by angling some residences to form an

Fig. 40. Original Standoff Colony, Alberta, Dariusleut, under construction in 1920. Note the use of the existing farm and residential buildings. The new frame residences were half the usual size, with four units rather than eight. Glenbow Museum, Calgary AB, NA-2635-52.

open diamond shape, while a few colonies have experimented with more radical plans. Red Willow aligned its four residential units to form a loose circle focused on the kitchen–dining room complex. Vauxhall Farms, established in 2008, built three residences in an arc. East Cardston, too, rebuilt its housing on an oval plan. Finally, a handful of colonies do not have a geometric plan. Thomson and Ribstone both have a variety of nonuniform residential buildings apparently situated at random. Figure 39 shows several different Dariusleut colony layouts.

Multifamily row homes are the most common housing type adopted by the Dariusleut. But unlike the Lehrerleut, they have retained many more older homes with extensions. The Dariusleut have been less eager to rebuild and modernize their housing on a wholesale basis. They have preferred a more piecemeal approach, so the older and the new often stand side by side. A number of Alberta Dariusleut colonies display anomalous housing characteristics. Standoff Colony, established in 1918, is an interesting example.

Fig. 41. Standoff Colony in 2019. The row of six original houses, much modified, can be seen running northeast-southwest. Several of the structures built in 1918 can be identified, although they were altered and adapted over the years. Google Earth, 2020.

The original frame housing units were half the size of those built elsewhere, and they provided homes for four families rather than eight. Through the decades since, the colony has transported some buildings to the colony and built some nontraditional houses, and the present site is complex. Figures 40 and 41 show Standoff Colony as it looked in 1920 and at present.

Dariusleut colonies in Montana present a marked contrast to those elsewhere, representing a group of colonies that display consistent departures from the norms. Eight of the fifteen Dariusleut colonies in the state have no obvious plan. The sprawling King Ranch has eight houses—some clearly multifamily—and five trailers. The site is masked with trees, and it is hard to distinguish the communal kitchen. Ayers Ranch, too, has eight or nine houses, as well as a row house with four units and two custom-built single-family units. They are neatly arranged but lack a geometric plan. The eight colonies that share this apparent lack of concern for rigid planning are all related. The original colonies came directly from South Dakota rather than from Alberta. In contrast, Deerfield Colony (1947) and the colonies derived from it display a range of more traditional plans and housing types. Deerfield itself has a somewhat loose plan but has four multifamily row houses. Its daughter colony, North Harlem (1963), has a neat geometric plan comparable to many Dariusleut colonies in Alberta. Gildford (1974) and Loring (1981) are also carefully laid out and feature row housing. These colonies are in the Havre region of northern Montana.

Schmiedeleut Colony Characteristics

The Schmiedeleut are often described as the most liberal of the Hutterite clan groups.[21] Certainly, their colonies have a rather different feel to them. They are smaller and more compact. This is partly due to the denser settlement pattern in Manitoba, but it is also explained by crucial collective decisions made during the 1960s and 1970s.

When the Schmiedeleut arrived in Manitoba following their exodus from South Dakota in 1918, they built colonies that mirrored the homes they had been forced to abandon. Long, two-story wood-frame houses were constructed, each providing space for eight families. Forty years later, these structures had to be replaced, and by then the sensibilities of the Hutterites had changed. They were less threatened by the host society and had enjoyed decades of material prosperity. They were now ready to consider more modern homes with more space for each family and with inside bathrooms. The postwar housing boom influenced those responsible for planning daughter colonies and renovating older ones. They saw the houses being built in "the world" outside the colonies and learned from designs promoted in *Manitoba Farm Life* and other journals.[22] Some colonies abandoned the longhouse and experimented with semi-

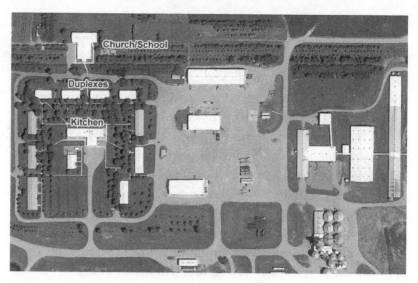

Fig. 42. Brentwood Colony, South Dakota, founded in 1987, a typical Schmiedeleut colony. Duplexes form a square around the kitchen. The church/school complex is a more recent addition. Google Earth, 2014.

detached houses, single-family bungalows, and three- or four-unit row houses. Other colonies were quick to follow suit. Over the years, the duplex emerged as the most ubiquitous choice (fig. 42), although many colonies have a mixture of duplexes and row housing.[23]

The adoption of these smaller houses had far-reaching implications for the layout of colonies, for the units could be arranged in a variety of ways. The majority of Schmiedeleut colonies are laid out in a simple geometric grid. But these sites tend to be square rather than rectangular, as is so often the case among the Dariusleut and Lehrerleut. Typically, a ring road demarcates a square, and houses are spread around the edges backing onto the road, while the kitchen commands the center. Brentwood, South Dakota, and Aspernam, Manitoba, are good examples. Each unit has access to the road and a parking space, which suggests that the Schmiedeleut have significantly increased the number of vehicles on the colony.[24]

Maxwell Colony, on the banks of the James River in South Dakota, was established in 1949 and provides an example of a rather complex site where several eras have contributed to the present plan

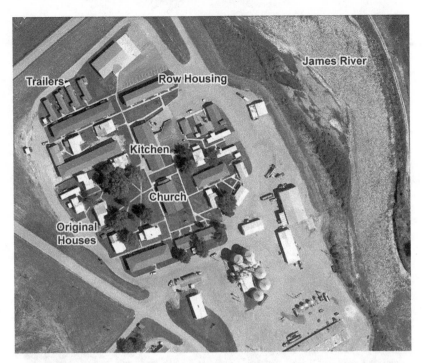

Fig. 43. Maxwell Colony, South Dakota, Schmiedeleut Two, founded in 1947. This site has become more complex as buildings have been added. Oriented along the banks of the James River, this colony shows the effects of adaptation and agglomeration. There are 10 original houses, along with modern row houses, duplexes, and trailers. The site is carefully laid out, if rather dense. Google Earth, 2015.

(fig. 43). Originally, several existing buildings were adapted for colony use, and others were acquired and transported to the site. About ten of these houses are still in use, but most of the population resides in modern row housing laid out around and between the older structures. More recently, eight trailers were added to cope with the burgeoning population.

In other cases the addition of residential buildings confused the clean lines of the original colony plans and made the layouts more complex. Typical would be the irregular patterns of Barrickman and Riverdale Colonies in Manitoba and Tschetter, Glendale, and Platte Colonies in South Dakota. However, it is important to note that there is a contrast between these neat but somewhat overde-

Fig. 44. Some examples of innovative colony plans among the Schmiedeleut. *Top left*: Bloomfield Colony, Manitoba, Schmiedeleut Two, founded in 1957. The residential area is tucked into a meander of the Whitemud River. *Top right*: Starlite Colony, Manitoba, Schmiedeleut One, founded in 1991. Starlite was the first colony to adopt a circular plan. *Bottom left*: Norquay Colony, Manitoba, Schmiedeleut Two, founded in 1993. This is another circular plan, which will take a few more years to complete. *Bottom right*: Lismore Colony, Minnesota, Schmiedeleut Two, founded in 2004. The 10 duplex units are arranged in a herringbone fashion. Google Earth, 2019 and 2017.

veloped colonies and the nongeometric and more chaotic plans seen among the Dariusleut colonies.

A number of Schmiedeleut colonies, especially in Manitoba, are laid out in a boldly innovative fashion (fig. 44). Perhaps the most striking of these is Starlite Colony. This colony's plan was conceived as a circular site in which the residences would encircle the kitchen and the church. One justification for the design was that all the residences would be the same distance from the dining room, thus enhancing the principle of equality. Sibylle Becker, a student of architecture, was carrying out research at James Valley Colony when the plan for this radical design was being implemented. She was critical of the plan because of its monumental scale and the exposure of the site. Initially, the daughter colony had only sixty-five people, and the circle of residences was far from complete. Three decades later, all the homes are completed, and trees and shrubs have done much to enhance the site.[25] Additionally, James Valley Colony itself has now moved from its original design of building on three sides of a rectangle to a more obvious horseshoe format, and its daughter colony of Monarch has followed this plan as well.[26] Four other colonies, Green Acres, Norquay, Prairie Blossom, and Blue Clay, have followed Starlite's lead. In addition, it seems probable that Northern Breeze and Oak River will evolve from half-circles to complete circles when they are fully developed. Thus nearly a quarter of the Schmiedeleut colonies established in Manitoba since 1990 have chosen circular plans. Interestingly, this innovation has not been adopted outside of Manitoba.

Other experimental plans include Windy Bay, which chose to lay out its residences in a herringbone arrangement. This option has also been adopted by Bigstone Colony and its daughter colony, Lismore, in Minnesota and by Willow Bank in North Dakota. Newdale has been even more radical with its unique star shape—long, row residences pointing toward the kitchen in the center. A final anomaly is found at Sunnyside Colony, which totally rebuilt its colony on the basis of a number of residential courts each enclosing its own patch of lawn. This plan resulted from collaboration between Becker and the colony leaders.[27] Figure 45 shows several unusual colony plans.

The most unexpected finding of an overview of Schmiedeleut colony sites was the importance of single-family dwellings: photograph after photograph showed trailers or self-contained bungalows. In Manitoba, there are more colonies with such units than without (53 to 39). In the United States, the ratio is even more biased in favor of single dwellings. This is not an entirely new development. Ryan

Fig. 45. Some unusual colony plans. *Top left*: King Ranch Colony, Montana, Dariusleut, founded in 1935, with a less structured, nongeometric site plan. *Top right*: Sunnyside Colony, Manitoba, Schmiedeleut Two, founded in 1942. This colony rebuilt its housing around five courts, a radical departure. *Bottom left*: Prairie Elk Colony, Montana, Dariusleut, founded in 2006. *Bottom right*: Single-family dwellings at Ridge Valley Colony, Alberta, Dariusleut, founded in 1977. Google Earth, 2016 and 2009; Ridge Valley photograph by Simon M. Evans, 2013.

commented that "some of the newer colonies have a number of single-family dwellings which can easily be moved when the colony subdivides."[28] Clearly, there are advantages to using mobile homes or prefabricated houses for Hutterite work crews as they build the infrastructure for a daughter colony. Such accommodations can also provide overflow housing as a colony grows toward its upper population limits. In addition, many colonies will adapt the original farmhouse that came with the land to their needs and even haul in other nearby structures. These buildings may be demolished as the colony matures, and mobile homes can be moved to daughter colonies. Fairview Colony in North Dakota has incorporated eight older houses and four trailers into its plan. However, the mobile home sites on some colonies have an undeniable sense of permanence, while custom-built bungalows make up a quarter of all the housing units available on others. The pristine layout of Deerfield Colony, for instance, includes six bungalows and seven three-unit row houses. The growth of single-family housing has escaped notice until now, and it is a significant trend.

Explaining the Differences and Innovations

Increasing diversity is a central theme running through Janzen and Stanton's analysis of all aspects of Hutterite life.[29] The review of the colonies' plans and the images presented in this chapter provide evidence of yet another way Hutterite society is becoming more complex and variegated. The new landscape element—the Hutterite colony—is by no means a monolithic homogeneous entity. Differences exist both among clan groups and within each Leut.

Most colonies were laid out carefully according to a preconceived plan. In the case of the Lehrerleut, their colonies are almost exactly the same, and plans for new colonies have to be approved by a committee to ensure uniformity. The majority of Dariusleut and Schmiedeleut colonies also conform to simple geometric grid patterns, although there is more variety in detail. The kitchen complex is the functional center of the colony, and efforts are made to ensure that all residential units have much the same access to this facility. During the past few decades freestanding churches have been built on many Dariusleut and Schmiedeleut colonies, while the Lehrerleut have added a simple church room to their kitchen complex.

Innovative configurations for the dwellings in the headquarters sites of both Dariusleut and Schmiedeleut colonies are becoming more common. In Manitoba, a significant proportion of daughter colonies have adopted circular sites. In Alberta, many new colony sites are diamond or arc shaped. What does this flurry of innovation and experimentation mean? Leaders of these colonies with nontraditional designs are quick to point out that they make the kitchen complex more equidistant from each residential unit and thus enhance the basic principle of equality for all inhabitants. However, these new plans clearly signal a rejection of the old and familiar and an unwillingness to be bound by the status quo. Some observers, both Hutterites and outsiders, suggest that these departures are motivated by hubris and the desire to show off both wealth and ingenuity. There may be an element of truth in these criticisms. Becker, commenting on the radical circular design adopted by James Valley Colony for its daughter colony Starlite, says, "It seems the mother colony made a special effort to be different, to set an example for alternative designs."[30] Certainly, James Valley has proved to be outward looking in other spheres. It has a bookstore and an ongoing commitment to making Hutterite history known.

It seems probable that the Schmiedeleut's association with the Bruderhof has played a role in their adoption of alternate forms of settlement. Anthropologist Gertrude Huntington contrasts the attitudes of several Anabaptist groups toward nature in general and agricultural production in particular. She suggests that Hutterites retained a pragmatic medieval view of the natural world as being something to be subdued and made productive. On the other hand, Eberhard Arnold and his Bruderhof followers—in reaction to the industrialization and urbanization of Europe—regarded nature as pure and precious in its own right.[31] For fifty years Schmiedeleut Hutterites interacted with the Bruderhof and moved back and forth to their settlements in the east. They must have been influenced by the aesthetics they witnessed: flower gardens, tree bowers, and the careful placement of dwellings. This influence was pervasive: table 12 shows that Schmiedeleut colonies have more than double the number of innovative layouts compared with the other clan groups.

There are other explanations for the growing number of innovative designs. Hutterites have shown a sophisticated ability to monitor trends in agriculture and agricultural technology in the host society. The Brethren pride themselves, with considerable justification, on being early adopters of innovations. They have demonstrated an ability to borrow ideas and machinery, and then to adapt them to fit their particular needs. Perhaps some of this imaginative and creative energy is spilling over from the way Hutterites make a living into the more intimate sphere of how they live and organize their lives. The emergence of these dramatic new plans should not be taken out of context. It is but the latest in a series of important changes on the colonies: the move from large multistory frame buildings to single-story homes with interior plumbing during the 1960s and 1970s, the adoption of duplexes by the Schmiedeleut, and most recently, the widespread choice of both the Lehrerleut and the Dariusleut of long, low motel-style housing in the 1990s. These quite radical steps have transformed the way Hutterite families live but have apparently not breached the integrity of the culture. New layouts will be quietly absorbed in the same way.

The uniformity of geometric plans on the majority of colonies throws departures from the norm into stark relief. It is tempting to equate clean lines, careful planning, and immaculate landscaping with orthodoxy, efficiency, and adherence to tradition. What do we make of colonies where the residences, in a variety of styles, are laid out with no obvious plan? On closer examination, it becomes clear that these nongeometric colonies have a variety of different origins. Several older colonies could be labeled colonies of accumulation. Their sites have become increasingly complex, as buildings have been added piecemeal over the decades. Standoff and Pincher Creek, in Alberta, and Barrickman and Tschetter among the Schmiedeleut are examples. Several more recently established colonies, which display no regular pattern, are in transition. Lack of resources has forced them to rely on housing scavenged from the neighborhood and on mobile homes. Typical would be Cleardale, a Dariusleut colony in the Peace River Country of Alberta established in 2001. As of 2015, most families were housed in assorted buildings relocated to the site, as well as five neatly aligned mobile homes. A new kitchen complex and one multifamily row house had been completed. As funds become available and this colony is transformed, a more regular plan will emerge.[32]

Finally, a relatively small number of colonies have spurned the normative desire for order. Their buildings are disposed in a random fashion and consist of a variety of housing types. In the Lewistown area of Montana, King Ranch (1935) and its daughter colonies, Ayers

Ranch (1945), Surprise Creek (1963), and Flat Willow (1980), all exhibit these characteristics. It is probably significant that the founding colony of this group, King Ranch, came to Montana from Beadle, South Dakota, in 1935 during the worst of the Great Depression. Perhaps these circumstances embedded a hardscrabble ethic, which has been repeated through succeeding generations. These Montana colonies may not have a geometric design or specific orientation, but they are by no means dysfunctional. They have lasted many years and have established new daughter colonies at regular intervals. Their leaders might defend their unconventional layouts by pointing out that they are less worldly and adhere more closely to the ascetic ideals of the Hutterites than do their more polished and conforming neighbors.[33] However, several of these colonies are very small—Fords Creek has a population of 18; Kilby Butte, 23; and Prairie Elk, 35—and this size is not necessarily due to recent colony division. It could indicate higher-than-usual defection rates or premature hiving by a family faction. These colonies deserve more detailed study.

What is the significance of the prevalence and ubiquity of single-family dwellings on colonies, particularly among the Schmiedeleut? That so many families live separated to some extent from the community seems at first sight to be both a radical and negative development for the health of the sect. Living in a secluded trailer on the periphery of the residential area would surely provide a family with more privacy and less oversight, although these differences are likely to be relative rather than absolute; doors will always be open, and constant "dropping in" will be expected. Further reflection suggests that such an evaluation may be premature. What if most of these units are occupied by newlywed or retired couples? At two different Dariusleut colonies, the ministers showed off new single-unit bungalows with some pride and explained that they were assigned to newlywed couples.[34] The expectation was that they would move into a multifamily building when they start a family. Presently, we do not know whether such units are sought after by families or whether they are occupied with a sense of resignation until there is room elsewhere. Too many questions remain unanswered; a balanced evaluation of this trend requires more research.

10

Making a Living

Diversified Agriculture

The aim of this chapter is to tease out a single theme from the complex web of beliefs and activities that constitute Hutterite life.[1] My objective here is to describe the contribution that this growing ethnic group makes to agricultural production in Alberta and to illustrate some of the links between their cultural attributes and their success as farmers.[2] Some fifty years ago John Bennett remarked that the Hutterites were "pre-adapted to succeed" in the difficult environment of their new home.[3] His words have proved to be prescient. The scale and diversity of their farming, enabled by a large labor force and underpinned by capital accumulation made possible by a self-sufficient and ascetic way of life, have given them advantages over neighboring family farms that are often struggling to survive.[4]

In a recent article in *New York* magazine, Sarah Taber exposes some of the failings of family farms. She argues that these enterprises, "central to our nation's identity," are totally dependent on government support. She continues, "I don't think a practice that needs that much life support can truly be considered 'sustainable.'" In contrast, she explains, "despite the harsh prairies where they live, and farming about half as many acres per capita as neighboring family farmers, Hutterites are thriving and expanding when neighboring family farms are throwing in the towel." Taber stresses that Hutterite community-sized farms have "larger, more flexible labor pools," which allows them to diversify their operations. Moreover, economies of scale enable them to have their own crop-processing facilities, "so they can work directly with retailers and customers on their own terms instead of going through middlemen."[5]

This chapter weighs the contribution of colonies to agriculture in Alberta and describes the agricultural operations on sample colonies. It discusses the importance of the labor force and outlines some of the sophisticated market connections forged by the Hutterites. Finally, it examines some successful strategies for adding value to agricultural products.

Few publications have focused on Hutterite agriculture. The two detailed studies that do exist date from the 1960s and 1970s. Anthropologist John Bennett spent two field seasons living on Hutterite colonies in southeastern Saskatchewan. He was able to compare their agricultural activities, objectives, and strategies with those of other groups living in the region—indigenous peoples, farmers, and ranchers—and his conclusions were based on a detailed analysis of the purchases and sales of each group.[6] Geographer John Ryan established a relationship of trust with the leader of the Schmiedeleut in Manitoba. He obtained tax returns from all the colonies and used this unique data source to measure the contribution of the Hutterites to the agricultural output of the province.[7] Unfortunately, times have changed, and I have not been able to obtain this kind of data on a state- or province-wide scale.[8]

The Hutterites' Significance in Alberta Agriculture

A young Hutterite man, the son of the manager of a very successful and progressive colony, boasted to me that Hutterites own 10 percent of the productive capacity and produce 19 percent of the agricultural products in the province. This claim was hyperbolic, but it contained two important truths: the Hutterites do make a significant contribution to agricultural production in Alberta, and because of their involvement in varied livestock production, they do "punch above their weight." In 1996, for example, the Hutterites owned 2.9 percent of Alberta's farmland and produced 4.35 percent of farm receipts.[9] Census data on Hutterite crop production and livestock returns are not available on a regular basis for privacy reasons, but sources suggest that the colonies produce 80 percent of the province's eggs, 33 percent of the hogs, and more than 10 percent of the milk.[10]

The columns of small-town newspapers are consistently full of reports about applications for planning permission from colonies seeking to expand existing farm infrastructure. Granum Colony received approval to build a soybean-processing barn. Later it gained permission to run the facility 24 hours a day, seven days a week.[11] White Lake Colony received permission to increase the size of its chicken barn from 23,000 to 45,000 birds, while Wanham Colony received approval for a 5,200-head beef feedlot. Finally, the Peace River Regional District issued a permit for two wind farms to be constructed on land owned by South Peace Colony.[12]

In 2016 there were 175 Hutterite colonies in Alberta.[13] They owned an estimated 2.1 million acres of Alberta's 50.3 million acres of farmland, or about 4.2 percent.[14] This represented a fourfold increase since 1971, when a commission of the Alberta government reported 82 colonies with 721,559 acres, which amounted to 1 percent of the province's agricultural land.[15] A decade from now, it is likely that the numbers will increase to about 193 colonies with an average size of 13,000–14,000 acres, meaning that the Brethren will own 2.6 million acres. At the same time, it seems probable that the acreage in farms in the province will continue to decrease to around 49 million acres. As a result, the Hutterites will own about 5.3 percent of the total. A colony of 12,000 acres supports twenty families, for an average of 600 acres per family. Few family farms could survive on such a limited amount of land. Furthermore, the 175 colonies represent but 0.43 percent of all the farms in Alberta. See table 14 for a breakdown of Hutterite landownership as compared with the total amount of Alberta farmland.

The Hutterite population has continued to grow during the same time period and numbered 16,935 in 2016. But the host population has expanded at much the same rate, fueled by strong in-migration. The Hutterites represented 0.41 percent of Albertans in 1971, and that was relatively unchanged at 0.42 percent in 2016. However, the steady decline in the number of farmers means that the Brethren now make up about 14.2 percent of the Alberta farm population. The age structure of the farm population suggests that this trend will continue.[16]

Table 14. Hutterite landownership in Alberta

DATE	NUMBER OF COLONIES	HUTTERITE LAND (ACRES)	ALBERTA FARMLAND (MILLIONS OF ACRES)	HUTTERITE %
1947	33	176,000	42.9	0.41
1971	82	721,559	49.5	0.68
1996	136	1,500,000	52.0	2.90
2006	161	*1,771,000*	52.9	3.39
2011	170	2,040,000	50.5	4.04
2027	242	*3,267,000*	49.0	6.67

Sources: 1947: Zieglschmid, *Das Klein-Geschichtsbuch*; 1971: Government of Alberta, *Report on Communal Property*, 17; 1996: *Vancouver Sun*, April 8, 2000; 2006 and 2011: Statistics Canada, 2006 and 2011 Censuses; 2027: estimates based on current trends. Figures in italics are estimates based on the number of colonies and their average size.

Patterns of Agriculture Today

To proceed from a general overview to the particular characteristics of Hutterite farms, I have selected five representative colonies. Two of these were established in 1918 in the original core areas of settlement, one is from the Peace River Country, one from Vulcan County between Calgary and Lethbridge, and one from the southeastern corner of the province.[17]

The first sample colony is one of several nestled in a coulee along the tiny Rosebud River (fig. 46). It is a Dariusleut colony established in 1918, and its land base has not expanded much since that time. The colony owns 6,400 acres and leases a further 1,000 acres. It established a daughter colony in 2007 and presently has a rather small population of about fifty. The colony members grow canola, barley, wheat, and peas and have a section of irrigated hay. About half their crops are used on the colony for livestock feed. They have a milking herd of 60 Holstein cows, a major hog-raising operation, and a mixed herd of beef cattle that range on the permanent grass along the floodplain. On a smaller scale, they grow turkeys for seasonal markets and produce honey. This is a rather small and tradi-

Fig. 46. Springvale Colony in the Rosebud River Valley. Photograph by
Simon M. Evans, 2015.

tional colony, but it has two characteristics of note. First, more and
more of the bottomlands along the stream have been plowed up for
crops. During the 1970s all the floodplain was in permanent grass;
today more than half of it is cropped. This has been made possible
with improved machinery and is motivated by good grain prices.
Second, this small colony relies to a marked degree on the output
of its garden. The colony maintains a stall at the Crossroads Market
in Calgary year-round. The staples are seasonal vegetables, corn,
carrots, onions, potatoes, and beets, but the colony also sells honey,
eggs, chickens, bread, and some fruit from British Columbia (fig. 47).

The second sample colony, selected from those in the Peace River
Country, occupies a scenic site not far from Grande Prairie and is also
a Dariusleut colony. Established in 1977, it was one of the first colonies to locate in the Peace, drawn by lower land prices and a desire to
escape overcrowding of colonies in southern Alberta.[18] It has gradually doubled its land holdings and now owns 12,000 acres of rolling
cropland. There is no rangeland in permanent pasture, and for this

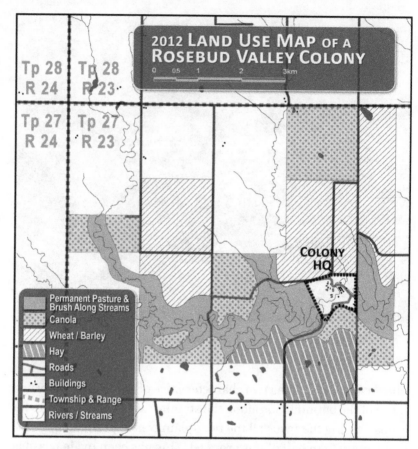

Fig. 47. Rosebud River Colony, showing cropping patterns, 2012. Drawn from air photographs and field mapping.

reason, the colony does not have a dairy or a beef herd. It concentrates on crop production and has invested in grain drying and storage equipment, but it also produces hogs, eggs, and fryer chickens.

The third colony chosen was one of the original colonies established in the southern core in 1918 and is a Lehrerleut colony (fig. 48). The colony split in 1992 to establish Miltow Colony, but the population has rebounded to 120 today. It is a relatively small colony, owning 5,500 acres. In addition to canola, wheat, and barley, the acreage sown to peas has grown considerably. The peas are used for feed, reducing the need to purchase soybean supplements. The colony also has a section of irrigated land on which it grows alfalfa

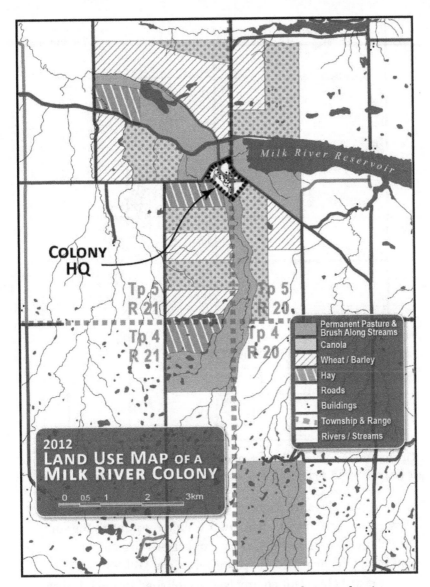

Fig. 48. A colony in the southern core of Hutterite settlement, showing crops grown in 2012. The southern portion of the colony's 5,500 acres includes sections of pasture on the Milk River Ridge. Drawn from air photographs and field mapping.

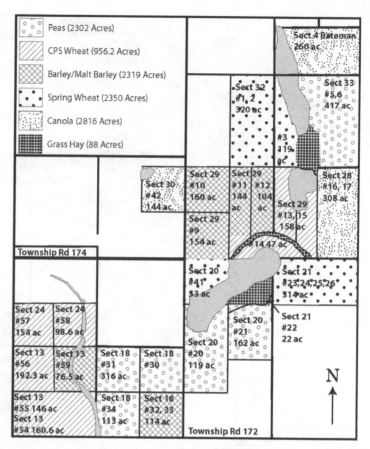

Legend:
- Peas (2302 Acres)
- CPS Wheat (956.2 Acres)
- Barley/Malt Barley (2319 Acres)
- Spring Wheat (2350 Acres)
- Canola (2816 Acres)
- Grass Hay (88 Acres)

Sect 4 Bateman 260 ac

Sect 32 #1, 2 320 ac

Sect 33 #5,6 417 ac

#3 119 ac

Sect 30 #42 144 ac

Sect 29 #10 160 ac

Sect 29 #11 144 ac

#12 104 ac

Sect 28 #16, 17 308 ac

Sect 29 #13, 15 158 ac

Sect 29 #9 154 ac

#14 47 ac

Township Rd 174

Sect 20 #41 53 ac

Sect 21 #23, 24, 25, 26 314 ac

Sect 24 #57 154 ac

Sect 24 #58 98.6 ac

Sect 20 #43 162 ac

Sect 21 #22 22 ac

Sect 13 #56 192.3 ac

Sect 13 #59 76.5 ac

Sect 18 #31 316 ac

Sect 18 #30

Sect 20 #20 119 ac

Sect 13 #55 146 ac

Sect 13 #54 160.6 ac

Sect 18 #34 113 ac

Sect 18 #32, 33 114 ac

Township Rd 172

N

Fig. 49. Part of a Vulcan County colony's cropping plan for 2016. This colony has 12,000 acres. Reformatted from map provided by the colony manager.

and corn for silage. This colony has extended its cropped acreage by plowing up former rangeland on the higher ground to the south of the colony. As well as hogs, dairy, and eggs, the colony has a large beef herd (400 head) that is pastured on the Milk River Ridge.

The next Lehrerleut colony was established in 1968. It was one of a handful of colonies that defied the Communal Property Act.[19] Individual Hutterites bought property a few years before the discriminatory act was repealed. This big, thriving colony epitomizes the innovative and progressive image of Hutterite agriculture. The pig barns and grain silos loom like an industrial plant above a shallow slough and are framed by the distant Rocky Mountains. This colony crops 11,000 acres, and not a square meter is wasted (fig. 49). Plowing is pushed aggressively to field boundaries and the margins of seasonal ponds. There is no permanent grassland and only a tiny pocket of hay land. While the primary objective is to provide feed for its livestock, this colony grows a number of special crops for contracts. The colony has three big hog barns that house 350 sows and their progeny and 100 head of Holstein dairy cows, but it is the new egg barn that demands particular attention.

This huge facility houses both 13,000 laying hens and a similar number of pullets—the next generation of egg producers. It has no constraining cages, although there are hutches where hens may retire to lay their eggs. This barn was the brainchild of the colony manager, who was acutely aware of growing concern among the urban public about the conditions under which poultry are raised. He determined to go far beyond what the law demanded and banish cages altogether. Closed-circuit cameras were installed to better monitor the well-being of the flock and provide potential customers with a picture of where their eggs are coming from. This barn is energy neutral; solar panels, heat exchangers, and extremely efficient insulation mean that enough power is generated by the building to meet its needs. The Alberta Government and Egg Farmers of Alberta have supported this endeavor.[20]

Visiting a colony in the southeastern corner of the province after more than two decades was quite an eye-opener. This is dry country, close to the heart of Palliser's Triangle. Twenty years ago it was mostly rangeland, and the limited cropland was strip-farmed using dry-farming techniques. Grudging yields of 15–20 bushels per acre were forthcoming in good years. Today field crops stretch away in all directions, and rangeland is confined to the sides of coulees. Crops of 40–50 bushels per acre are routine. This transformation has been achieved by careful rotation of crops, incorporating canola and peas; the use of drought-resistant seed varieties, bolstered by fertilizers and pesticides; and the extension of a water pipeline from Raymond Reservoir, 130 kilometers to the west, which provides water for people and stock. This line now supplies sixteen colonies and about one hundred farm families. The colony takes advantage of its dry and sunny location to produce hard durum wheat. It also grows barley, canola, peas, and lentils. It has a contract with a nutritionist who helps the colony decide what proportion of canola and peas can be incorporated into their livestock feed. The value of crop sales is balanced against the costs of buying soybeans and other supplements. This colony also has a big garden and markets some of its products across Canada. It also owns 3,000 acres of rangeland on the shores of Pacowki Lake, where it runs a herd of beef cattle.

Although each of these five colonies has its own character, leadership style, and mix of agricultural activities, they share much in common. They employ much the same rotation of crops, and all raise livestock of one kind or another. These observations of individual colonies fit comfortably into a broad survey of Hutterite colonies conducted across the prairies. Details of the revenue Alberta Hutterite colonies derive from various sources are shown in table 15. Crops, hogs, dairy, and poultry are the major dollar earners. The main difference between the Dariusleut and the Lehrerleut is that the Dariusleut colonies produce more beef. This reflects both the location of Dariusleut colonies in the more broken country along the foothills in the west and north of the province and a cultural preference for permanent pasture and cattle.

Table 15. Revenue Alberta colonies derive from various sources (percentage of total income)

	DARIUSLEUT	LEHRERLEUT
Crops	44	49
Hogs	13	17
Beef	13	3
Poultry	8	13
Dairy	14	16
Other livestock	1	0
Nonfarm	6	1
Other	2	1

Source: Blacksheep Strategy, "Understanding Business on the Colony."

Enough has been said to establish that Hutterites, by combining extensive grain farming with intensive livestock enterprises, exhibit a degree of diversity in their agricultural activities unmatched by non-Hutterites. This would be impossible without a relatively large and flexible labor force.

The Labor Force

A large workforce is a prerequisite for the diversified agriculture that the Hutterites practice. A colony of one hundred souls might have twenty retired seniors, thirty children in school, and fifty men and women to do the work. Contrast this with a family farm blessed with three sons or daughters that has a total labor force of only five. The older and more experienced men on the colony manage various departments, serving as a field boss, pig man, dairy man, and chicken man. Every morning the manager has a meeting with his department heads to determine what needs doing according to the weather and the season. Others are responsible for the vital services that help the colony run smoothly, including a carpenter, electrician, plumber, mechanic, and expert in metal fabrication.

This leaves a pool of young men from fifteen to twenty-five years of age who provide the more generalized "muscle." A sixteen-year-old may be assigned a million-dollar piece of equipment as his primary responsibility, but he will be available for other tasks when his combine or truck is not required. If you ask a young Hutterite what his job is, he is likely to reply with a laugh, "I'm a jack of all trades and a master of none." However, these young people serve an unofficial apprenticeship in a variety of fields and pick up skills that will stand them in good stead. On one colony I visited, young Chris Gross, age nineteen, was up at 4:00 a.m. milking, a task he shared on a week-on, week-off basis with a colleague. He came home for a bacon-and-egg sandwich and was off to drive a batch of chickens to be processed. Rebecca's son at Birch Lake came in from his work in the pig barn, picked up a Thermos, and hurried out to the combine.

The primary role of Hutterite women is to keep the colony clean and the people well fed. This is no mean task. They have to provide

Fig 50. Hutterite women putting up corn from their garden. Photograph by Lenita Waldner, Hutterian Brethren, http://www.hutterites.org/galleries/work-and-agriculture.

solid meals for a community of one hundred or more three times a day, while keeping their families provided with clean clothes and the whole colony spotless. Kitchen duties are rotated on a weekly basis, and this enables the women to perform a significant secondary role in agricultural production (fig. 50). They are responsible for the colony garden and for preserving the products that help make the colony relatively self-sufficient.

Another colony I visited during the summer of 2016 had had its huge garden completely wiped out by hail. The women were devastated, not primarily because of financial losses or possible shortages, but rather because they enjoyed the camaraderie of working outside together in the garden. They were also very conscious that their efforts usually make a substantial contribution to the colony. The previous year, the garden had earned close to $250,000, and this put them in a strong bargaining position when the colony discussed upgrades to the kitchen or the laundry. During my visit, the women were busy processing the produce that other colonies had gifted to make good their losses. Women contribute informally to the decisions about what to grow in the garden and how much to sow of each crop, because they do so much of the work.

Hutterite women are most certainly not shrinking violets, and they are prepared to help out wherever they are needed. The only absolute constraint on their activities is safety. Their flowing dresses can be a hazard around exposed machinery, and there can be no compromise with dress codes. Unlike the Amish women, who run thousands of small businesses, Hutterite communal culture means that the women's energy, enthusiasm, and imagination are directed toward the well-being of the colony.[21]

Gender roles are well established on the colonies and frame the daily lives of men and women. However, they are not completely rigid; the provision of childcare and the practice of rotating kitchen duties mean that women are free to do all manner of tasks around the colony. On one colony, a group of women were painting a residence, while at another they were laying floor tiles in the kitchen. In one case, the wife of the dairyman, who has a grown family, was recognized as his stand-in and helper, a role usually filled by a man. Women also work alongside male family members in the carpenter's shop, sanding and finishing furniture and kitchen cabinets. When emergencies occur, young women will turn their hands to almost any task that needs doing.[22]

During the late 1970s and 1980s there was much discussion among Hutterite leaders and researchers about surplus labor and underemployment.[23] Mechanization on the land and automation in the hog and chicken barns had reduced the need for manual labor. Ministers were concerned that "the devil would find work for idle hands." Sam Hofer describes one such situation vividly: "From the mid 1970s to the early 1980s we had more men on the field than were needed. For a few years far too many of our summer days were spent on the fields, picking rocks. We sat around a lot playing cards and listening to the radio. Incentives or feelings of accomplishment among our young people were dangerously low. . . . In a period of about nine years, Baildon Colony lost 15 young men to the outside world."[24]

This situation has been mitigated by the gradual decline in Hutterite birth rates. During the past thirty years, family size has decreased from eight to ten children to three to five. Moreover, the colonies have proved remarkably adaptable in finding new ways to make a living. Many colonies have developed light industries, especially among the Schmiedeleut. In Alberta, various enterprises have been introduced, from hauling gravel to building prefabricated sheds and from plastics to custom furniture and ironwork. Managers have found ways to use their massive shops and carpentry facilities during the winter months. These initiatives provide employment and produce valuable monetary returns. For example, Birch Hills Colony was using wood affected by the pine beetle to produce attractive beds and outdoor furniture.

Some colonies are experiencing labor shortages. One manager said he could use five or six more men immediately, and he even asked me about the temporary foreign worker program. This shortage of willing hands is a product of thirty years of declining birth rates coupled with defections among the fifteen-to-twenty-five age group. After a colony has split, the new colony might have a population of fifty or sixty, with fewer than ten male laborers. If three or four of these men leave the colony, a serious shortage could occur. Until the downturn in oil prices, the availability of high-paying jobs on the rigs was a powerful lure to young Hutterites. Four of the sample colonies have a healthy enrollment in their schools of twenty-five to thirty children, but the fifth colony, which recently split, had only seven children in school. This low figure was not uncommon among colonies I visited in the last few years. In the long term, some colonies may have to curtail the variety of their enterprises because of labor shortages. MacMillan Colony closed its dairy and disposed of its sheep flock for this reason.

While most adult colony members may have assigned roles to ensure the farm works smoothly and efficiently, the labor force is very flexible and can be redeployed to meet short-term demands. At harvest time retired men and older children will lend a hand. One of the sample colonies has recently purchased a site for a daughter colony. A school bus leaves the parent colony every morning with some 20–30 craftsmen and laborers, along with a group of women to fix lunch and snacks during the day. They return every evening and have an early breakfast before leaving again to build up the new place. Hutterite manpower enables them to respond to local emergencies, whether it is filling sand bags along the Souris River, feeding flood victims in High River, or helping contain a grassfire.

Markets

One thing that this research has revealed is the degree to which Hutterite colonies are integrated into agribusiness. The diversity and complexity of the supply chains to which they contribute are remarkable. Hutterite colonies have a number of characteristics that make them attractive to both wholesalers and processors. They produce relatively large amounts of uniform products on a regular and sustained basis. Moreover, they are responsive to the unique demands of their clients. For example, they will refine their methods to produce hogs of a certain size and fat content. The colonies have also earned a reputation for reliability. The Hutterites are involved in agricultural production for the long term to support their culture and lifestyle, and they value relationships with individuals and organizations and embrace ongoing contracts. This reduces uncertainty and risk for buyers.

One of the sample colonies illustrates this web of market connections very well. First, it is involved with three products that are regulated by the provisions of supply management: milk from the colony's 100-head herd is collected by the Alberta milk marketing board every two days; eggs, 13,000 a day, are picked up by Sparks Eggs under the auspices of the Alberta Egg Marketing Board; and its quota of turkeys are sold to Lilydale and marketed through Costco. For twelve years the colony has sold all its hogs to Maple Leaf in Lethbridge. The pork is exported to Japan, and the Hutterite manager boasted that his hogs were on the shelf in a Tokyo grocery within thirty-two days. While canola, spring wheat, and peas, which are not needed for feed, are sold on the open market, other crops are sold on contract. Since the demise of the Canadian Wheat Board, the colony has been able to sell malting barley direct to Alberta

Brewers; last year it cropped 1,500 acres. The colony is blessed with conditions of temperature and rainfall that favor soft wheat production. This product is sold to Rogers in British Columbia for baking purposes. Another of the sample colonies has an unexpected market for its hogs. They are picked up by a truck each week and delivered to Masami Food in Klamath Falls, Oregon, about 1,000 kilometers away. The specialized pork products are all sold in Japan.

Nowhere are market linkages more important than in the Peace River District. Colonies located here are several hours' drive from major urban centers and the hubs of processing and wholesaling. They face up to this challenge with characteristic ingenuity. They mitigate the problem of distance from conventional markets by ensuring that they sell as much product as possible locally. "We have our own markets," the manager of Ridge Valley Colony told me. "We have a lock on Peace River." He meant that they could sell most of their broiler chickens and eggs there, as they have a contract with IGA supermarkets and arrangements with some restaurants. Similarly, Grandview sells broilers and eggs in nearby Grand Prairie.

However, local markets cannot absorb all the hogs, beef, and lambs that are produced. Colonies have adopted a variety of strategies to connect with markets. Peace View Colony ships hogs to Vancouver using its own vehicle. The Hutterite driver makes the weekly trip and brings back fruit from British Columbia. Birch Meadows hauls its hogs to Red Deer and broiler chickens to Edmonton, while Grandview ships hogs to a plant in Dawson Creek that supplies stores throughout northern British Columbia. South Peace Colony has faced the problem of distant markets for livestock head-on and has constructed a multimillion-dollar slaughtering and packing facility on the colony. It handles beef, hogs, sheep, and buffalo for the locality. The minister at the Lehrerleut Twilight Colony explained that they had made the conscious choice to have their products picked up by the purchasers. This reduced monetary returns, but meant that "the boys are not on the road all the time." He explained, "You must not run ahead of the Lord." One further example illustrates the far-reaching nature of Hutterite market connections. When I visited Clearview Colony, north of the Peace River and arguably one of the most isolated colonies, it was expecting a visit from buyers from Japan. The purity of its honey had so impressed the colony's Vancouver agent that its Japanese clients wanted to visit this colony where bees had no contact with GMOs.

Adding Value to Agricultural Production

Most Hutterite colonies continue to devote most of their efforts to agriculture. Therefore, in response to lower returns and shrinking margins, they have looked for ways to add value to their products and reduce their dependence on middlemen by establishing cooperative marketing strategies.

Feed mills are ubiquitous on Hutterite colonies. Most colonies dry and mill some of their grain to feed their livestock. This has a long history. The group brought their skill and expertise as millers with them from Ukraine. An early visitor to the colonies along the James River described them as "distinguished by their stone buildings, by their herds of geese and flocks of pigeons and by their ice houses and tall flour mills."[25] In the frontier environment of the Dakota Territory during the 1890s and the early twentieth century, grain mills on Hutterite colonies provided an important service for the wider community. When the Hutterites were forced to relocate to Alberta, they built a flour mill on Rosebud Colony, which served the three colonies along the Rosebud River and attracted customers from miles around.[26]

One colony in southern Alberta has a particularly long and successful history in producing food products for people rather than feed for livestock. Soon after its arrival in its new location south of Magrath, Alberta, Rockport Colony started using a traditional recipe to produce a pancake mix. Ninety years later Coyote Pancake Mix is still flourishing. Don Bodnarchuk, president of NuStart Marketing, which handles the promotion and marketing of the product, explains, "The colony continues to grow their own wheat and it is something that really adds to the longevity of the product. They find it important to manufacture this mix at their colony for their large following that has grown wider and stronger over the years." Bodnarchuk says that the regionally based product is now sold across

Canada and that the traditional processes are still used, although they have incorporated technological advances and contemporary food safety standards.[27]

In contrast to the venerable processing facility at Rockport is a new soybean crushing plant under construction at Granum Colony.[28] Soybean meal is the most popular protein supplement for livestock, especially for poultry and hogs. While soybean acreages in Manitoba and southeastern Saskatchewan have been growing rapidly, cooler night temperatures and a shorter growing season inhibit similar growth in Alberta.[29] Almost all the soybean meal used by provincial farmers is imported from mills in Minnesota, to the tune of $55 million to $60 million a year. Granum Colony imports soybeans from Manitoba and plans to distribute processed meal to other colonies and farmers in southwestern Alberta. They are early adopters in this field, and their long-term investment may become increasingly profitable as shorter-season varieties are developed.[30]

A major project that illustrates both the power of cooperation among colonies and the potential benefits of investment in processing facilities is Dakota Turkey Growers of Huron, South Dakota. It is worth recounting the story of how this successful venture started. During the early 2000s Hutterite turkey growers in South Dakota were becoming frustrated over the prices they were being offered by processors. It seemed that all their efforts and investments to streamline their production were still not yielding a living for their families.[31] The colonies had already worked together with their legal advisors to organize cooperative purchase of soybean feed, and this initiative had proved highly successful. Now the Hutterite leaders wanted to explore the possibility of building their own processing facility. Neither they nor their advisors underestimated the difficulties facing them. No major turkey-processing plant had been built in the United States since the 1980s. The prospect of raising some $40 million seemed daunting.

In fact, the vague concept was translated into a finite project remarkably fast. Within a few days after the initial meeting, the state governor had been informed, and he embraced the idea of helping family farms and creating jobs. He went so far as to purchase an abandoned factory and offered it as a possible site for a processing facility. With political support and more than forty colonies committed, Dakota Turkey Growers was established in 2003. Initially the colonies provided $12 million, while the state came up with $9.2 million and some loan guarantees. Over the next three years, under the guidance of an experienced CEO, an ultramodern processing facility was built. The initial labor force of three hundred has now grown to one thousand, split into two shifts. The plant handles 40,000 birds a day and processes 200 million pounds of product a year. The company sells a variety of packaged meat products throughout the United States, and its chefs and dietitians are constantly monitoring the marketplace and looking for new niches to fill. It has recently expanded into the "ready to eat" market.[32]

Initially, it was difficult to recruit and retain a labor force from the region. With cooperation from the town of Huron, South Dakota, the company worked to attract new immigrants. After one Karen family from Myanmar moved to Huron, other families soon followed. Today there are six hundred Karen immigrants in the town. People from South America have also been drawn by the prospect of jobs and currently make up about 16 percent of the labor force. The town has helped the new arrivals with housing arrangements, and the schools have hired ESL instructors to teach the children of immigrants, who now make up nearly half the student body. The cooperation between the company and the town to provide for the needs of newcomers has yielded positive results. The turnover of workers has declined to 15–20 percent, much lower than elsewhere in the meatpacking industry. Overall, this has been a very positive investment on the part of participating colonies. They not only have a say in the prices paid them for their turkeys but also share in the profits of Dakota Provisions.[33]

Many colonies are investing in slaughtering facilities and are preparing livestock products for niche markets. When I visited South Peace Colony, British Columbia, in 2011, I visited the recently completed meat-processing facility. It had been designed and built by the colony and represented a large capital outlay. As I considered the relative isolation of the colony, I could not help but wonder if the facility would attract enough customers to ensure viability. I need not have worried; it now has more work than it can handle. A recent visitor reported that the facility is operating five days a week and employs three or four men full-time. In addition to beef and pork, they process buffalo and are especially busy during the hunting season. A German neighbor has taught them much about making sausages and salami.[34]

Viking Colony has invested in deboning equipment to maintain and expand its sales of chicken to Chinese restaurants in Edmonton.[35] Lisa Guenther asks, "Why ship poultry to Lilydale when they can process the birds on farm?" Paul Wipf, the colony's manager, explains, "What makes Hutterite chicken better than the usual grocery-store birds? It's the freshness." He says, "People seem to trust Hutterites and the way that they do a good job of raising their food."[36] The same trend is apparent at Iron Creek Colony, which slaughters its own pigs and cuts and wraps pork for specialized markets.[37]

A cooperative venture among Hutterite colonies around Great Falls, Montana, is transforming egg production there. Thirty colonies came together in 2006 to form a company called Montana Eggs. Working with the well-established distribution company Wilcox Family Farms, this new cooperative planned and built an egg-sorting plant. The $6.6 million facility employs twenty people and ships 280 million eggs annually. It has a full-time USDA inspector. The company has obtained a contract to supply eggs to Costco stores in Montana and eastern Washington. With this assured market and streamlined processing facilities, colonies have been investing heavily in new free-range chicken barns and expanding their flocks significantly.[38]

Future Developments

It is evident that Hutterite agriculture is flourishing. The next decade or two will surely see a continuation of these trends. There will be more colonies, and they will be larger. On the colonies, there will be an ongoing process of experimentation and fine-tuning of technology to meet their needs. Every effort will be made to reduce energy inputs, first in the barns and later in the residences. The use of solar energy and methane gas will become widespread. The provincial government will partner with innovative colonies to encourage them to be early adopters of new developments. The sophisticated web of distribution contracts will be extended.

These trends over the next generation will exacerbate the differences between the large, aggressively run colonies and the smaller, more traditional and conservative colonies. Here the preoccupation will be with maintenance and compliance with the law rather than monitoring market trends. This increasing diversity among colonies in the economic sphere matches developments in the social and cultural life of the Brethren, which form such an important theme of Janzen and Stanton's book.[39]

One area where we can expect to see marked expansion in Hutterite agriculture is in horticulture. Over the past decades, a shift has occurred in the way colonies manage the surplus of their prolific gardens. At first they gave away produce as an act of neighborliness. They say of the good old days, "We fed the district." Gradually, locals came to the colonies to buy eggs and chicken and seasonal vegetables. With the rise of farmers' markets, a majority of colonies became involved, and trucks left the colonies for destinations in both small towns and major cities. As the public has become more and more interested in eating locally, using organic products, and forging links with producers, the Hutterites have been able to capitalize on their image as Old World, earthy, "peasant" producers. They have a great reputation and brand name, although they are actually using all the science and advanced technology available to them. Some colonies have gone a step further and established contracts to supply wholesalers.[40]

Because no single colony can supply a full range of vegetables over a season, groups of colonies are coming together to avoid competition and to specialize in particular items so that they can supply produce over longer periods.[41] Thus the garden, originally cultivated to ensure that the colony had plenty of vegetables year-round, has become a valued source of financial returns. Expansion in this area would be a good fit for smaller colonies where territorial expansion

Fig. 51. Hutterite women serving at a small suburban farmers' market in Calgary, Alberta. Photograph by Simon M. Evans, 2015.

is not feasible. Some are already experimenting with greenhouses, not only to germinate seeds in the spring but also for producing tomatoes, cucumbers, and even melons.[42]

Success in this area has not been without its problems. The stalls at farmers' markets have to be staffed, and young women often perform these tasks (fig. 51). Some ministers regard this as a dangerous new exposure to "the world."[43] Competition among colonies for the busiest markets has become another problem, while the investment in time and resources must be weighed against returns. Some colonies drive more than 150 kilometers to their chosen locations.

The rosy outlook outlined here could be disrupted, however. The larger, more aggressive colonies of today are exposed as never before to environmental and economic vagaries. The Brethren have moved a long way from the image of the Hutterite ark serenely sailing over the worldly sea. How will they weather the next prolonged drought or growing consumer fads that might reduce demand for meat and milk? Their very successes, and the fact that they have longer to prepare to establish a daughter colony, have made it harder for leaders to impose an ascetic way of life in order to save for the next generation. Although defections have by no means reached epidemic proportions, the loss of a handful of key young people could have profound effects. Most worrying of all are the staggering costs of starting a new colony. In addition to buying land and putting up buildings, the parent colony has to pay millions of dollars to buy quotas for eggs, milk, and broiler chickens. The total cost of these quotas could easily exceed $50 million. One man I spoke with said that it was going to take twenty-six years to pay off their debts incurred when founding a daughter colony.

Hutterite agriculture makes a considerable and growing contribution to agricultural production in Alberta. The Hutterites have proved remarkably adaptable and are innovators in some branches of agricultural technology. Their success has been based on their large labor pool, which allows them to pursue diversified mixed farming, and on their ability to accumulate capital for expansion by pursuing a culture of austerity. In turn, these attributes rest on the foundation of their faith and their communal lifestyle. The "Hutterite way" demands surrender of the self to the building of Christ's kingdom here on earth. This vision has sustained them for four hundred years, yet it is also because the Hutterites have been able to adapt to changing circumstances that they have survived and prospered in both good times and bad.

11

Beating the Squeeze

Adaptive Strategies

The success of the Hutterites in maintaining their cultural identity, their remarkable growth in numbers, and their territorial diffusion has been sustained by their ability to make a good living from agriculture.[1] Working the land has allowed them to locate their colonies discreetly in the countryside and to maintain their distance from the host society. The Hutterites see themselves as an ark afloat and tossed about on the sea of the sinful world. They seek to control and limit their contacts with non-Hutterites to a minimum. The scale and diversity of their agricultural operations have protected them from the worst vagaries of environmental and economic cycles. Philosophically, too, agriculture has demanded the wholehearted commitment of the community, while it provides meaningful jobs for men, women, and older children. Victor Peters, who knew the Brethren well, went so far as to say, "The Hutterian dedication to farm life is motivated by a conviction that for them this way of life is most pleasing in the eyes of God."[2]

During the last twenty years, the dominant all-pervasive role of agriculture has been challenged by mechanization and globalization. Clearly, mechanization of field operations has a long history on the colonies, but the scale and sophistication of new equipment are unprecedented and have further decreased the need for field hands. At the same time, machines have replaced workers in the livestock barns, whether for egg sorting and packing, milking, or slaughtering and meatpacking. Globalization has increased competition, lengthened the supply chain, and reduced returns to primary producers. Farmers everywhere have been squeezed by declining profit margins as production costs have risen and returns have stagnated.

The Hutterites have responded to this evolving economic environment in a number of ways. Some colonies have fine-tuned their cropping patterns to exploit new cash crops. Others, as discussed in the previous chapter, have explored ways of adding value to their products by cutting out the middlemen or processing products on the colony. An alternative strategy has been to slash energy costs by adopting innovative systems based on renewable resources. Finally, the past few decades have seen a significant growth in the number of nonfarm enterprises on the colonies. Led by the Schmiedeleut in Manitoba and South Dakota, more and more colonies have started to use their metal-working facilities and carpenters' shops to provide goods and services for regional markets. This is by no means a new departure. Many colonies have worked on neighbors' farm machinery during the winter or undertaken some custom carpentry on an ad hoc basis. However, it is entirely new to find a colony like Baker, Manitoba, which has rented most of its land and concentrates on producing ventilation systems and heat exchangers for a North American market.

The aim of this chapter is to examine and describe these responses to twentieth-century economic realities and to evaluate the prevalence of nonfarm activities on the colonies. This will help answer the broader question, What are the implications of these developments for the "Hutterite way"? Do they represent the first perilous step on a slippery slope toward assimilation and integration of the sect into the host society? Or are they merely a logical extension of a long-standing practice, another example of what Joseph Eaton called "controlled acculturation" all those years ago?[3]

The chapter examines the pressures for change, weighs the motives for adopting new strategies, and establishes the links to Hutterite history. It describes various experiments adopted to slash the costs of heating and power, then looks at examples of the kinds of manufacturing currently employed on the colonies. Finally, it introduces some objections to adopting new ways and summarizes the findings in order to reach some tentative conclusions concerning change and the future of the Hutterites.

The Nature of the "Squeeze"

For over a century the Hutterites' success as farmers has enabled them to accumulate capital to establish new colonies when they become necessary. As Paul Wipf, manager of Viking Colony, explains, "The whole plan of a colony is to take care of the next generations. It is no different from your parents helping you through university. . . . But we do it to a greater extent."[4] Saving for a daughter colony is a constant and pressing obligation; indeed, if Hutterite culture is to survive, provision must be made for the next generation. However, it is becoming more and more difficult to generate monetary surpluses from agriculture. A paradigm shift is occurring among colony leaders from reliance on agriculture to an economic plan that is more diversified and includes a variety of light manufacturing ventures. Already almost half of the Schmiedeleut colonies have adopted some nonfarm enterprises. Dariusleut colonies are not far behind, and the momentum of change is quickening.

This profound shift in orientation is being driven by three factors that are affecting colonies from South Dakota, through the Peace River Country of Alberta, to Washington and Oregon. The first is the inexorable rise in the costs of establishing a new colony. The second is the declining profit margins in agriculture. Hutterites, like most Canadian farmers, are being squeezed between rising costs of production and stable or declining returns. The third factor occupying the minds of Hutterite leaders is how to find meaningful year-round jobs for their young people.

The Costs of Establishing a Daughter Colony

The role of colony division in maintaining the culture by limiting the size of communities has been discussed in earlier chapters, as has the manner in which splitting multiplies the number of managerial jobs. The fact that fission or branching provides an opportunity to release social tensions and to dissipate bad feelings among subgroups has been noted elsewhere.[5] However, little detail has been forthcoming about the costs involved in this vital undertaking. As Theron Schlabach has noted about their fellow Anabaptists,

"Surprisingly few authors writing on North American Mennonite history have investigated the influence of market forces on individual and group behaviors."[6]

The work of John Bennett is an exception. Based on his fieldwork during the 1950s and 1960s, he estimated that the total cost of establishing a daughter colony was about $315,000. His case study was in an area of marginal land in southwestern Saskatchewan. The land purchase—11,000 acres at $17 an acre—accounted for almost two-thirds of the total.[7] A brief but penetrating economic description of the Hutterites in Montana by Hans Radtke states that land purchases for new colonies averaged around $400,000 in the early 1960s but had doubled to $800,000 per colony by 1969. Radtke estimates the value of a typical colony at $1 million.[8] In Alberta, a special committee of the assembly had access to the tax returns of almost all the existing colonies for their report on communal property. However, the authors had little to say about the costs of establishing a new colony; they merely quoted a researcher who estimated that a colony would have to save some $59,000 per annum if it were to be ready to establish a new colony after 17.3 years.[9] John Ryan, to whom we owe a debt for his detailed analysis of the costs and returns of Manitoba colonies, has nothing to say about the establishment of new colonies.[10]

Recent books on Hutterites continue to emphasize the important role of colony division in Hutterite culture, but they do not go beyond generalities. Janzen and Stanton state that "colonies start saving money for expansion, that is, the establishment of daughter colonies, as soon as their debts are paid off or the population exceeds one hundred. Hutterites are always saving money and looking for available land."[11] In a similar vein, Katz and Lehr stress that a colony "must accumulate large capital resources to establish a daughter colony. To achieve this they must maximize income from work and minimize living expenses."[12] Neither book mentions figures for land acquisition and construction costs of infrastructure. My research suggests that the race to generate capital savings to fund a new daughter colony may be more and more difficult to win. The incentive to explore new revenue streams is growing.

In the absence of precise data, this study has been forced to rely on partial and anecdotal information about the costs involved in establishing a new colony. These scraps of information—inadequate as they are—hint at the way such costs have increased to reach startling new heights. In Canada, the need to acquire quotas for the production of milk, eggs, and poultry add significantly to these costs. A dairy herd has been the sheet anchor of the economy of many colonies because it provides cash returns throughout the year. But the quota to establish a new dairy herd of 100 cows would cost about $4 million for the quota alone. The quota for laying hens costs around $400 per bird, so a modest barn with 13,000 layers would mean an outlay of $5.2 million. These are daunting figures, indeed, especially when added to the rising costs of land and buildings. It is little wonder that Hutterite leaders are exploring new ways of making a living, which they hope will offer better and more regular returns on investment.[13]

Sascha Hausmann spent several months living on a colony in southern Alberta during 2017. He had ample opportunity to hear discussions about hiving and stories about various colonies that had recently split. He reports that Hutterites generally felt it would require at least $50 million to establish a daughter colony.[14] This figure corresponds to my own findings. I visited a colony in southeastern Alberta in 2016 that was well into the process of colony division. The parent colony had purchased a huge ranch of 15,000 acres at $3,000 an acre. The land had cost $45 million, and the necessary quotas and construction costs would push the total figure well above $60 million.[15] This big, prosperous colony faced the prospect of being deeply in debt for more than twenty years, making it vulnerable to increasing interest rates. On the basis of the fragmentary evidence, one must agree with Gordon Tait, who has spent over thirty years working with the Hutterites, when he remarked, "Today they [Hutterite leaders] are making million dollar decisions that ten years ago were only $100,000 decisions."[16]

Declining Profit Margins in Agriculture

In Canada, farm income was forecast to decline modestly in 2016 and 2017, mostly because of lower livestock prices resulting from increased meat production in the United States. Total operating expenses were expected to increase somewhat in 2017.[17] South of the border, analysts were less sanguine. In an article titled "The Great Margin Squeeze," the authors note the "unprecedented" expected level of losses for 2015 and go on to explain that the prevalence of fixed costs in agriculture, land, equipment, and labor make the industry slow to adjust to changing output conditions.[18]

In light of these general trends, Hutterite farm managers view the future with some apprehension. They feel that over the next few years, their focus will be on increasing efficiency rather than acreage, and they predict a decline in the importance of livestock.[19] The concentration of large hog operations in parts of Manitoba raised concerns about the disposal of effluent and its possible effects on surface water and groundwater. In 2008 further expansion in the Red River Valley and Interlake regions was forbidden.[20] Later this measure was extended to cover the whole province. This effectively stopped any plans for expansion and cast a chill over the hog industry in Manitoba. In March 2017 the new Conservative government removed the restrictions, but attempts to streamline planning applications have been only partially successful.[21]

Profit margins on hogs are slim, and the costs of expanding infrastructure to meet ever more stringent regulations have risen sharply. As one Hutterite farm manager remarked, "Most of our income used to come from hogs, but that's a thing of the past. Not much is going to be invested in that anymore." One of his peers explained, "We actually went out of beef because it just didn't turn out. In my opinion . . . with all the legislation that's out there on food safety and this stuff, I can't see us expanding. I think eventually they are going to kill us. . . . With pigs, we've been in pigs all our lives since we've been here, but I can't see us surviving with pigs."[22] These pessimistic forecasts suggest that demand for hogs and prices have been steadily declining. In fact, such is not the case. Although the price index shows considerable volatility from year to year, the trend has been stable or slightly upward. The point is that margins have been eroded by increased input costs. Some colonies have been able to sidestep these strictures by establishing long-term relationships with agribusiness. Brant Colony, for example, produces custom hogs for the Japanese market through its contract with Maple Leaf Foods in Lethbridge. Across the border in Montana, colonies have links to veterinarians in Minnesota and slaughterhouses in California, as well as to markets in Japan and China.[23] But not all colonies have been as successful.

Providing Work for All Colony Members

On a Hutterite colony, working in the fields or stock barns is much more than a mere job. Work is worship for these communal people, and wholehearted commitment to labor for the community is as important to their spiritual welfare as attendance at the evening service.[24] As Victor Peters observes, "To the Hutterite, work itself is a purposeful ingredient of life, and idleness is almost sinful."[25] Thus a primary responsibility for colony leaders is to ensure that there is regular meaningful work for all of their flock. As larger and more efficient machines have replaced laborers in the fields and the hog and egg barns, this duty has become more and more difficult to fulfill. In particular, the declining emphasis on livestock will reduce the need for a team of dairymen to carry out milking twice a day and for others to feed hogs and clean their barns. The number of these full-time and responsible jobs may be reduced. Perhaps work in manufacturing will provide an alternative.

Given the circumstances, the creation of year-round jobs in non-farm occupations must seem like an appealing prospect, both to managers and to young Hutterites. The task of colony leaders to keep their community meaningfully occupied is complicated by the seasonal nature of the demand for labor. As one farm manager explained, "I would have to say it's a problem to keep everybody employed on the farm. . . . There's a couple of times of year when you need everybody and then when it rains or something, all of a sudden you've got a bunch of people unemployed. And it's a big problem and I am always out there looking for opportunities where we can maybe do something seasonally during the winter."[26]

However, not all colonies will have a pool of under-employed labor looking for meaningful and exciting jobs. A newly established daughter colony of sixty souls might have fifteen to twenty adult males. Of these, the senior men would be responsible for various agricultural endeavors; one would be the field boss, others departmental heads and tradespeople. This would leave fewer than ten young men to provide the muscle—to drive tractors, clean the barns, and respond to myriad daily requests for help from the managers. Some colonies are even experiencing labor shortages. One minister said that he could use five or six men immediately and, surprisingly, asked me about the Temporary Foreign Worker Program.[27] Jake Hofer, manager of Airport Colony, Manitoba, remarked, "We are just as shorthanded as the other guys—now we have three outside guys working on the colony. Help is hard to find for everyone."[28] Thirty-five years of declining birth rates coupled with defections among the fifteen-to-twenty-five age cohort mean that some colonies have had to close one or more enterprises because of labor shortages. Serious underemployment occurs only during the later stages of a colony's population cycle, when the community has reached 120 people or more.

The cycle of the gradual growth of a colony over decades and then its split and the establishment of a daughter colony has another, less obvious impact on the availability of skilled labor for starting a nonfarm enterprise. For several years prior to colony division, the skilled craftsmen on the colony are fully occupied building the new colony. After the daughter colony has finally become a separate functioning entity, the tradesmen at the parent colony are faced with an equally herculean task: the older buildings now require a makeover so that they conform to the elevated standards of the daughter colony. This refurbishment of the parent colony may take several years.[29] Thus it would be a serious oversimplification to view the adoption of nonfarm businesses as a means of finding jobs for underemployed Hutterites. Some colonies are labor deficient, while on others key personnel are fully occupied. New enterprises will likely involve the reassignment of colony members from one job to another. Already on some colonies during the winter months, men spend the mornings in the barns and the afternoons in the various workshops.[30]

Hutterite leaders often make the point that the adoption of nonfarm activities on the colonies is far from being an innovative departure; it is, in fact, a return to Hutterite tradition and cultural roots. They point out that during the "golden age" in southern Moravia in the late sixteenth and early seventeenth centuries, the economic success of the Bruderhof was based on their craft skills.[31] Those men were also leaders in education and medicine.

Two hundred years later, during their sojourn in Ukraine, Hutterite communities concentrated on agricultural production and learned progressive techniques from their Mennonite neighbors. But their craft skills continued to thrive. In the 1860s they were producing pottery, clocks, cabinets, and fine linen. As some of these industries flourished, some Hutterite leaders expressed concern that the participants might become too worldly.[32]

Not surprisingly, the Hutterites brought these skills with them when they established their first colonies along the James River in Dakota Territory in 1874. Their construction skills are attested by the survival of many original buildings, especially at Bon Homme Colony, South Dakota. The new arrivals soon established mills to grind their own and their neighbors' corn. By 1897 there were five water-powered flour mills, and the colonists were engaged in spinning, weaving, carpentry, shoemaking, tanning, blacksmithing, and bookbinding.[33] A visitor in 1912 remarked on the modernity of their operations. Gasoline engines powered cream separators and butter churns, water flowed to houses and barns from artesian wells, and a large tractor was used for plowing, although horse teams were in evidence everywhere. One colony already had a dynamo for electric lights, and other colonies were following suit.[34]

No account of the emergence of nonfarm activities on the colonies during the twentieth century would be complete without a discussion of the role of Jake Kleinsasser of Crystal Springs Colony. A charismatic and visionary leader, Kleinsasser became *Altester* (bishop) in 1978 and has had an indelible impact on the Schmiedeleut for the past four decades.[35] Kleinsasser immersed himself in the writings of the Hutterite leaders of the sixteenth century and in the history of the sect in Europe. He became concerned lest contemporary Hutterites might grow complacent without the stimulus of outside hostility. In his view, worship had become moribund, and change was needed to reinvigorate spiritual life and to regain some of the passion and intensity of their ancestors. To this end, he encouraged Hutterite youth to embrace education, envisioning a day when all Schmiedeleut children would complete high school and many would attend college. He was committed to outreach and the mission field, and he renewed the connection between the Hutterites and the Bruderhof. This group was founded by Eberhard Arnold in the 1920s and had enjoyed a close relationship with the Hutterites during the 1930s and 1940s. Kleinsasser visited the headquarters of the Bruderhof at Woodcrest Colony in Rifton, New York. Impressed with the joy and spontaneous enthusiasm of their worship, he introduced musical instruments and praise songs to some Schmiedeleut colonies.[36]

The Bruderhof drew its recruits from urban centers and from all walks of life. They sustained their communities with light industries and craft production. An astute observer of the Hutterites wrote in the 1990s, "The Bishop [Kleinsasser] saw the difficulties in acquiring sufficient land, dairying and egg quotas and so on. Thinking ahead he was looking to the eastern communities as models for non-agricultural communal life that the Hutterites might someday need to adopt."[37] Thus Kleinsasser was prescient and foresaw pressures on the status quo that would become difficult to ignore twenty years later. During a visit to Crystal Springs Colony in the early 1980s, I saw a huge machine for drying and making pellets from alfalfa, a machine shop devoted to turning out equipment for pig barns, and a classroom full of computers.

Unfortunately, Kleinsasser's activism and his determination to push a revisionist agenda led to a widespread perception that he was an authoritarian leader. He used the threat of excommunication to daunt opposition and took Hutterites that refused to be cowed to civil court, an action that was contrary to Hutterite culture and almost unprecedented in their long history.[38] Thus Kleinsasser was largely responsible for the division of the Schmiedeleut into two groups: Schmiedeleut One, his followers and the more reform minded, and Schmiedeleut Two, the majority of the more traditional communities.[39] His replacement, Bishop Arnold Hofer of Acadia Colony, would have a difficult task ahead of him. However, it is clear that some of the trends foreseen by "Jake Vetter" ("Uncle Jake," the way Hutterites refer to a senior member of their community) have come to pass in the new millennium.

All farmers are by necessity wonderfully skilled at fixing things and making temperamental machinery work. The Hutterites have an advantage in that because of their relatively large labor force, they can specialize. Young men with particular skills and attributes become full-time carpenters, welders, mechanics, electricians, and plumbers. They employ their talents in maintaining the complex systems at their home colony and in building a daughter colony from ground up. Youth who leave school at age fifteen or sixteen are apprenticed to the established tradesmen. Thus the colony has a pool of skilled laborers, brought up in a rural and agricultural milieu but available to develop nonagricultural enterprises.

Slashing Costs by Exploring New Technologies

One of the largest expenses the colonies incur is the cost of heating and cooling residences and barns. Poultry and hogs require carefully monitored constant temperatures to flourish. Humans are somewhat more tolerant of summer heat and winter cold, but residential heating costs are by no means inconsequential. Individual colonies have been exploring ways to reduce energy costs for decades. In this quest, they have two major advantages: they can experiment and invest for the long term without having to answer to impatient shareholders, and each colony enjoys some economies of scale in comparison with a family farm. Energy is required to sustain a community of one hundred or more, along with the extensive livestock infrastructure.[40]

Political, economic, and technological developments have combined to create a very favorable environment for the expansion of renewable energy resources in western Canada. Hutterites have been quick to "jump on the green band wagon," as Jeff Collins puts it.[41] The Alberta government's 2016 Climate Leadership Plan aimed at reducing greenhouse gas emissions by phasing out coal-fired energy generation and promoting renewable energy.[42] Currently, renewable sources account for about 16 percent of Canada's primary energy production. According to the 2017 *Southeast Alberta Energy Diversification Report*, "Solar photovoltaic and wind energy are the fastest growing sources of electricity in Canada. In June of 2016, CBC reported that over the next decade up to $50 billion dollars will be invested into renewable energy in Alberta and Saskatchewan."[43]

Technological developments coupled with the momentum generated by increasingly rapid uptake have meant a 64 percent decrease in utility-scale solar photovoltaic costs from 2008 to 2014. Likewise, the costs of land-based wind energy projects have decreased by 41 percent. There is a sense of excitement in the field as research and experimentation continue on methods of storing electrical power and transmitting it more economically. Those involved in the field believe that the development of renewable energy in western Canada has reached a critical mass and that the momentum generated will withstand political changes. At the end of 2016 Alberta Electric System Operator listed eighty-five proposed and operating projects over 1 megawatt; of these, thirty-three were solar and fifty-two were wind based.[44]

Hutterite colonies play a significant role in promoting the growth of renewable energy on farms and in rural areas. In addition to direct investment, some colonies have provided land for wind farms or extensive arrays of solar panels, others have developed revolutionary new boilers that halve heating costs, and still others have plumbed the earth's surface to exploit geothermal energy.

Wind Power

Pincher Creek Colony was among the first to host a wind farm in the eminently suitable area near the Crow's Nest Pass. The first turbines started turning in 2000, and today there are sixty on the 8,500-acre colony. They provide both electricity and cash flow to the colony year-round. According to the colony's former manager,

Mike Gross, "At the time of the year when there's no crop—in winter time—these windmills, they pay very, very good."[45] Across the border in Montana, Springwater Colony is in a somewhat similar windy location in the Judith Gap between the Little Belt and the Big Snowy Mountains. Opened in 2006, the wind farm of ninety turbines has been a boon to the county and a second source of income to the colony, which collects a substantial rent while still using the land around the turbines. As one commentator describes it, "The landscape tells the picture with wind turbines sprouting out of wheat fields and sheep grazing right up to the doorstep."[46] Not far away, at Martinsdale Colony, the relationship between the renewable energy company Two Dot Wind and the colony was even closer—a perfect marriage of Hutterite mechanical expertise and the company's far-reaching contacts—before the wind farm was sold in 2017 to North-Western Energy for $18.5 million.[47] Colony blacksmiths, welders, and electricians refurbish used turbines, and this reduces the costs of installation by two-thirds. The nearby shop at Forty Mile Colony shares the work. The power generated is sold to Montana Power.

In British Columbia, on the margins of the boreal forest close to Dawson Creek, two wind farms, each containing seven turbines, have been established on South Peace Colony. The company involved, Renewable Energy Systems Canada, was prompted to invest by BC Power's Standing Offer Program, which enables small power projects to feed into the grid.[48] Farther south, Sunshine Colony received approval to construct four 600-kilowatt turbines, generating 2.4 megagrams, in March 2014. The colony bought its turbines from Tacke Windtechnik, and they provide enough power for all the colony's needs. Surplus power flows through the Fortis distribution network. Similarly, O.K. Colony purchased two used turbines from a Danish company, Bonus Energy, which generate 300 kilowatts. Pine Meadows is expecting to benefit from the growth of Next Era Energy Canada, which has fifty-one turbines already operating as part of its Ghost Pine Wind Energy Center in Kneehill County.[49] These examples hint at the excitement and momentum developing in this field, but the pace of development means that many other projects have not been mentioned.

Solar Energy

The seventy-six hundred solar modules at Green Acres Colony, near Bassano, Alberta, generate 2 megawatts of electricity and make it one of western Canada's largest solar farms.[50] The colony leaders embarked on the $4.6 million project with the objective of providing a long-term solution to the soaring costs of power. They stress that harvesting the power of the sun is consistent with their philosophy of self-sufficiency. Their "solar harvest" is just another crop, albeit one that continues to amaze Jake Hofer, the colony electrician responsible for much of the installation work: "It still blows me away to this day. Yes, you look at the system, day after day, and there's nothing moving, no moving parts, and yet it creates all this energy."[51] Indeed, one of the reasons they decided to pursue a solar project rather than a wind power installation was the lower maintenance costs. Hofer boasts that after four years of operation, his main maintenance headache is weed control. Colony labor inputs during the installation reduced costs from $2.80 per watt to $2.40. One megawatt of power is used in the colony's plastics recycling plant, while the other serves the residences and barns. The original business plan based on 2015 electricity prices projected a fifteen-year payback on their investment, but decreasing prices have extended this period.[52]

The solar installation at Brant Colony is much smaller, but it may play a significant role as a model of what can be achieved using the power of the sun.[53] The colony's net-zero chicken barn generates as much power as it uses. The project is a partnership among the colony, Egg Farmers of Alberta, and Alberta Agriculture. It was supported by a $250,000 grant from the Albert government's Growing Forward 2 plan.[54] Tom Mandel, the colony manager, explained that the colony was going to build a new chicken barn anyway to replace its cage system with a free-range barn. The colony leaders were persuaded by Egg Farmers of Alberta researchers to look carefully at a solar-heating option. The potential savings made sense, and it was clear that a Brant net-zero barn, through the colony's partners, might be a model for other chicken farmers and livestock producers.

At the opening, an expert on sustainability praised the barn: "This project really is the first of its kind in Canada [and] is trialing new technologies that could potentially define the new normal for energy efficiency and reducing climate impacts for animal husbandry."[55]

A hidden cost to the colony was a certain loss of autonomy. While the barn was under construction by colony tradesmen, every input and output was measured and documented by outsiders. The one hundred solar panels on the barn roof produce 25.5 kilowatts of electricity, while heat exchange pumps, LED lighting, and extreme insulation techniques all contribute to efficiency. The careful instrumentation of every step in the process has produced data that will be invaluable to those who follow after. Closed-circuit television cameras help monitor the well-being of the birds and provide opportunities for the public to view the barn. Much of the electronic equipment installed came from the Netherlands, and Darrel Mandel, the colony chicken boss, said he was in frequent contact with the Dutch firm. The boilers came from Germany.[56] At the barn opening, the Alberta minister of agriculture, Oneil Carlier, said, "The colony here has taken a leap of faith."[57] It is hoped that other producers may follow their lead.

Turin Colony was a real pioneer in 2006 when it built a solar-thermal system. Philip Waldner looks after the system, which has met the colony's needs for heat for more than a decade with very little maintenance. He emphasizes what a good fit "harvesting the sun" is for the Hutterites. It is just another crop, he says, and plays a role in reducing greenhouse gases.[58]

Granum Colony is playing a more passive role in another solar energy project. It is providing land northeast of Claresholm, Alberta, for a $210 million farm with 880 solar modules.[59] The project manager in Alberta is Daniel Andres of Perimeter Solar, but a key partner is Obton A/S, a Danish firm, one of the largest solar farm operators in Europe. According to Andres, "We got interested because the cost of solar has come down so quickly in the last eight years. It has come down about ten fold, making solar costs competitive with other sources of power generation."[60] The site selected is in a saline basin and is marginal agricultural land. This reduces speciesat-risk issues that would occur if native prairie land were involved. It is also adjacent to a transmission line.[61] From the colony's point of view, the project is a win-win situation. It gets paid rent for the land—which exceeds the returns from agricultural use—while at the same time continuing to graze sheep under the solar panels. The project has been under review by the Alberta Utilities Commission and, after several delays, is currently under construction and should be operational by the fall of 2021.

Improved Boilers

For several decades Decker Colony was well known throughout western Canada as the maker and distributor of Decker Brand Boilers.[62] The colony's integrated system produced savings of more than 70 percent in heating costs for greenhouses, manufacturing plants, livestock facilities, and machine shops. Although designed for multifuels—coal, biomass, biofuels, wood pellets, natural gas, and fuel oil—most of their boilers in fact used coal. However, the Decker boiler is among the cleanest-burning boilers in the industry, and mandatory emission testing ensured that government standards were exceeded. Quality materials and careful engineering mean that the heating system required little maintenance and provided years of trouble-free service.

How did a rather isolated Hutterite colony on the parkland margins of Manitoba become the production center for a much sought-after boiler with distribution across western Canada, into the United States, and even to Europe? As is so often the case, the story of the boilers began with the needs of the colony.[63] Soon after the colony formally separated from its parent colony, Britestone, in 1981, the costs of heating the barns and shops with propane "went through the roof." The colony found an alternative-heating source: the All Canadian Boiler. It worked so well that it reduced heating costs substantially. The colony bought a second boiler and became a dealer for the system.

Through the early 1990s Hutterite engineers worked to integrate and streamline each step in the process, from fuel hopper to ash auger and multiclone dust collector. The biggest innovation was to move from an open to a closed system. This increased efficiency and allowed the use of rust inhibitors, which greatly extended the life of the boiler. The downside of this major step was that it meant government regulation and a flood of red tape. However, sales continued to grow, as did the reputation of the Decker boiler. Both employment in the metalworking shop and income from the enterprise provided a good balance to the ongoing agricultural activities at the colony.[64] Pincher Creek Colony, faced with natural gas bills of $8,000 a month for its new pig barn, bought a Decker boiler in 1999 and slashed costs to $1,200 a month.[65]

However, sales have fallen off in the past decade, and when I visited during the spring of 2018, the demonstration boiler system was gathering dust at the back of the shop. Colony leaders were weighing whether it was worth the costs and the time spent to keep their certifications current. Two external changes undermined the competitive edge that the colony product had enjoyed. First, fracking opened new natural gas fields and reduced the price of gas to a point where it could compete with the economies achieved by coal-fired boilers. Second, governments introduced carbon taxes and moved to ban the use of coal. While the boilers can use a variety of biomass fuels as alternatives, they are in short supply and therefore expensive.

Iron Creek is a small colony in Alberta that has grown slowly since it was established in 1979. Today it is home to eighty Hutterites. However, it has proved to be a dynamic center of innovation. Faced with high heating and water costs, as well as nagging problems with effluent disposal from its pig barns, the colony worked with BioGem Power Systems to install a furnace that used methane gas from hog manure to generate electricity.[66] The Alberta Environmentally Sustainable Agriculture Council reported in 2006 that the colony was saving $145,000 in electricity and $203,000 in heating costs.[67] The plant was generating enough power to sell a surplus back to the grid. Perhaps the greatest achievements of the scheme were to reduce odor and water use and to eliminate the costs of injecting manure.[68] Unfortunately, this imaginative and potentially lucrative solution to a major problem plaguing many colonies—

effluent disposal—hit some snags, and the furnace was mothballed after three years of operation. The furnace was installed when the price of natural gas was rising and the cost of electricity was soaring. Since that time, the price of electricity has decreased and has been deregulated. The colony also had to truck water to the site to maintain the anaerobic digestion process.

The hub of innovation using biomass furnaces has moved to Manitoba, where more suitable material is available, from wood chips to cattails. Two years ago Vermillion Hutterite Colony near Sanford, Manitoba, faced a decision. The coal-fired furnace that the colony used to heat its chicken barn was being phased out by the government. A new natural gas system could be installed for $450,000, but thereafter the annual energy cost would top $100,000. Alternatively, a biomass furnace would cost $600,000 to install, but the annual energy cost would be much lower. The colony chose the innovative alternative, and the costs for the first two years of operation have been between $15,000 and $20,000 a year. "It's already paid for itself," said colony manager Shawn Gross. The colony buys wood chips from South-East Pallet and Wood Products of Blumenort, Manitoba. A side benefit is that the wood is not left to rot and produce methane gas. Sturgeon Creek Welding, a Hutterite manufacturing business on Sturgeon Creek Colony outside Headingley, makes the biomass generators. Triple Green Energy, which promotes and sells the system, reports that twenty of the generators have been sold in Manitoba, mostly to other colonies. As of 2018, six more colonies had furnaces on order.[69]

Geothermal Heating

Millbrook Colony, South Dakota, could lay claim to be the "poster child" of colonies that have embraced nonfarm enterprises. The fact that a relatively isolated agricultural ethnic community could develop a highly sophisticated geothermal heating system with sales across North America has attracted considerable attention.[70] Not long after their split from parent colony Rosedale in 1983, Millbrook leaders started to look for activities that would provide year-round jobs for their people and additional income to supplement returns from their mixed farming operations. They concluded that a geothermal system would provide big savings in heating costs while at the same time having a benign ecological footprint.[71]

A geothermal heating and cooling system exploits the difference in temperature between the constant temperatures found at some depth beneath the earth's surface and the variable temperatures at the surface.[72] The key component in such a system is a pump that circulates liquids deep underground and maximizes the heat differential on the surface. Hutterite engineers developed and patented the Hydron Module ground source heat pump. It worked so well that demand for the pump increased rapidly. In 1995 Energy Dynamics was founded to act as the exclusive distributor of the pump, which was manufactured in expanded facilities close to the colony. Continuing success and growth meant that more and more non-Hutterites were hired, putting the primary function of the colony as a faith community in jeopardy. In 2007 the business was sold to Enertech Manufacturing, which again remodeled and expanded the plant at Mitchell, South Dakota.

The advantageous sale of the geothermal enterprise underwrote the establishment of two daughter colonies: Spruce Grove, at Blanchard, South Dakota, and Meadow View at Bridgewater, South Dakota.[73] The parent colony has been reduced in number to only fifty souls. The story of Millbrook Colony over the past few decades is one of extraordinary innovation and entrepreneurship. One could argue that the success of the heat pump exposed the colony to "worldly influences." If this were indeed the case, it is clear that the present much-reduced colony is firmly reestablishing its Hutterite roots, and its invention has provided a unique heating option for many other colonies.

When White Lake built its daughter colony, Jumbo Lake, the colony's leaders decided to install geothermal heating and cooling systems to all the residences.[74] They felt that "harvesting heat from the ground" was in line with their philosophy and their tradition of innovation. It was an expensive undertaking, although Hutterite electricians did most of the work. It will take a generation to pay off the installation costs and reap the benefits of negligible running costs. When I visited Eli Hofer in his spacious new home on a hot day in August, the house was deliciously cool. Eli said that he did not ever have to adjust the temperature.[75] The parent colony, White Lake, has used the principle of geothermal heating to develop and patent an innovative stock watering system. It consists of a thick rubber tube of insulation that can be sunk eight 8 feet into the ground. This protects the water pipes, allowing the slightly warmer groundwater to prevent the surface water from freezing. Its major advantages are that it does not require an external energy source and it is easily maintained. The colony has agents in Montana, Manitoba, Pennsylvania, and Arizona, and a trailer load of units had just been shipped the morning I visited.[76]

Light Manufacturing Enterprises

The most overt response by Hutterites to changes in the economic milieu has been their willingness to use existing infrastructure and the skills of their people to develop a variety of light industrial enterprises.

Metalworking

Holden Colony, Alberta, is the original home of VersaFrame, a metal fabrication company with fifteen participating sites across western Canada, several of them on Hutterite colonies.[77] They make metal siding and roofing. Here again, the colony's venture into manufacturing grew out of its own needs. It was buying a lot of construction materials from an Edmonton producer that had cramped facilities and had trouble meeting the colony's needs.[78] The colony had space and skilled labor available. The brothers who owned the business and the colony leaders reached a deal. A large barn on the colony, which had been used for seed potatoes, now houses three rolling mills and associated presses. Rolls of steel in thirty-four colors are imported from South Korea via Vancouver. The mill employs five men full-time. Most of the output moves to a warehouse and sales center in Nisku, just south of Edmonton, but when I visited, two contractors were loading finished products at the factory door.

Most of the sales and contacts with customers are handled by non-Hutterites, allowing the colony to concentrate on production.

Just across the road on the colony looms another large building with its own reception center and sales room, Holden Colony Manufacturing. This facility uses the building materials produced on the colony to turn out a variety of portable buildings, including storage sheds, garages, and summer cottages. These buildings can be tailored to customers' requirements, and delivery and setup are included in the price. Attractive show homes are displayed at the colony, and its website is comprehensive and easy to use.

Valley View Colony, Alberta, planned to make manufacturing a central part of its daughter colony from the inception. The colony started turning out sidewalls, roof cladding, and structures for the oil industry, at the site of the new May City Colony in 2006, long before formal colony division. The new plant was recognized by VersaFrame, the parent company, for having the most aggressive first quarter sales in 2007, and output grew by 10 percent in 2012.[79] Across the border in central Montana, Golden Valley Colony has launched a million-dollar facility, Valley Steel, to produce custom steel trim, siding, and roofing for both commercial and residential customers.[80] Goldridge Industries, owned and run by Turin Colony, has a successful history reaching back to 1994. The colony produces a wide range of products for the cattle feedlot industry and for the oil and gas industry. "We manufacture anything that has to do with moving water in the oil patch, from pumps to road crossings and more—pretty much anything you need for pumping water," explained the manager.[81]

Baker Colony has been successful in creating a manufacturing industry that has expanded to fill a niche in North American agricultural support infrastructure. Under the company name Better Air, the colony manufactures and sells complete ventilation systems for animal barns and for facilities that store vegetables and fruits like potatoes and apples. Hogs, dairy cattle, and poultry produce humid air contaminated with carbon dioxide, methane, and solid dust particles from food. A negative ventilation system extracts the foul air and draws in clean air, which can be controlled for temperature and humidity according to daily and seasonal changes in the external environment. A key component in the Better Air system is a heat exchanger, which uses the hot stale air to partially warm clean incoming air. This item and several robotic machines used in production were invented and built on the colony. As well as complete ventilation systems, the facility produces a variety of plastic and PVC products, including chimneys, fan hoods, feed carts, and auger hoppers.

The factory provides year-round work for the majority of adult males on the colony. In addition, five non-Hutterites are employed to handle sales and promotion, while some other young men from the neighborhood work on the production line. Retired seniors from the colony help with packing small items, and women provide additional hands when there is a deadline to meet. The factory's sales area reaches westward deep into Saskatchewan and Alberta and, to a more limited extent, eastward into Ontario. Better Air has penetrated the U.S. market and has had customers in Texas. The manager remarked that the size of the U.S. market made it a rather daunting prospect, as they would have to start producing thousands of items instead of hundreds. The colony plans to control growth and continue to emphasize quality.

Most of Baker Colony's land is rented to Mennonite neighbors. The colony manager explained that the rental returns usually exceeded those they could expect from agriculture. Nevertheless, although the hog barns are empty, the colony had just invested $250,000 to seed several hundred acres of corn and was planting a big garden. A small barn houses goats, chickens, hogs, horses, and rabbits so that colony children do not lose their farm heritage, and they play a major role in looking after the livestock.[82]

Whiteshell Colony was established from Iberville in 1962. For over thirty years it prospered and grew, supported by diversified agriculture, which saw the majority of the colony's crops of soybeans, canola, and wheat fed to hogs, chickens, and dairy cows. In the late 1990s the colony sold its dairy herd and expanded its hog operation. A decade later it was experiencing "irregular cash flow and surplus labor." Or as the manager put it more forcefully, "Hog prices tanked and we had some bad years. Moreover, environmental regulations prevented us draining some of our heavy land." A communal decision was made to establish Whiteshell Chairs, a manufacturing business that would provide chairs and tables for the hospitality industry. The company started production in the old dairy building. Today it has a modern production facility complete with a showroom. Sales have gone well, with contracts to supply Days Inn hotels and sales in the Northwest Territories and Mexico. Building on its initial successes, the company has widened its product line to include picnic tables, firepits, and bike racks. All products are powder coated at the plant for quality and durability. In 2013 the company purchased Homestyle Roofing to further diversify the output of its metalworking shop. Seven or eight Hutterite men are employed full-time in the plant, while four or five women handle the upholstering work. Today the problem is finding extra hands to do the work rather than having an underemployed labor force. In the manager's view, this is a much healthier state of affairs.

In spite of this successful diversification, farming and livestock remain the main source of income for the colony, which has 5,000 acres sown to soybeans, canola, and wheat, along with 1,200 sows and 10,000 laying hens. The manager's task is to manage his labor force to keep both factory and farm running smoothly and, perhaps more importantly, to keep his brothers and sisters supplied with varied and meaningful work.[83]

Metalworking, using a colony's existing shop and the skills of Hutterite workers, is widespread among the colonies. Among others, Millerdale, South Dakota, and White Lake, Alberta, produce all kinds of doors and windows; Starland Colony, Minnesota, makes steel tools, metal parts, and accessories for manufacturing companies in the Twin Cities; and Riverside Colony, South Dakota, produces stainless steel equipment.[84]

Woodworking

The development of woodworking at Springfield Colony, Manitoba, was rather typical. During the 1990s the colony started using its carpentry shop to make custom bedroom furniture for neighbors and other colonies. One customer then asked for kitchen cabinets, and thus began the gradual shift from hobby shop to sleek, highly automated production facility. Today the 70,000-square-foot factory produces 100–150 cabinets a day and is among the leading suppliers in Manitoba. It boasts $50 million of woodworking, finishing, and painting equipment from Germany and the United States. Twenty Hutterite men are employed, and the labor force is augmented with an equal number of non-Hutterites. This is a colony in which more girls have been born than boys, and women play a key role in the office and are also involved in the final sanding and polishing of the products.[85]

The dramatic growth of this enterprise owes much to the drive and vision of the CEO, Pauly Kleinsasser. He explained, "As a young punk of 16, I traveled to New York State to the Bruderhof. There I worked in the carpenters' shop and loved it. I promised that I would have my own shop one day."[86] He has traveled frequently and widely to evaluate and purchase state-of-the-art machinery and materials. His enthusiastic promotion of Springfield Woodworking is matched by his overt expression of his commitment to his faith and the Hutterite way of life.[87] The colony has a showroom in Winnipeg for its products, and its sales area reaches eastward to the cottage country around Lake of the Woods.

The woodworking business balances the colony's farming activities, which include 6,000 acres of soybeans, canola, barley, and wheat, as well as hogs and chickens. Young colony members are rotated among different jobs so that they gain experience in the fields and garden, with the livestock, and in the factory.

Two colonies in the Peace River Country use local timber to produce wood products. Birch Hills Colony, Alberta, makes attractive, if rather massive, beds and furniture using wood ravaged by the pine beetle.[88] Cleardale Colony, Alberta, turns out a variety of sizes of sheds and storage facilities on an assembly line. This enterprise is a major contributor to the income of this young and rather isolated colony. When I visited, the German teacher was preparing to travel to the U.S. Midwest to look at automated precision saw equipment with a view to further investment.[89]

Construction

Many of the Hutterite-run enterprises already mentioned sell products to contractors and the building trades. Some colonies have gone further and offer one-stop supplies to their customers. Hutterite-owned companies have staked out a growing foothold in the supply of construction materials to Manitoba builders. This area of manufacturing is a natural fit for colonies because they build their own homes and agricultural infrastructure. Their shops already have some of the metal- and woodworking equipment they need, and colony members have skills and experience. It is not surprising that their market share has been growing during the past three decades.[90] In Manitoba, two big companies lead the way: Domtek Building Products, owned by Newdale Colony, and Can-American Corrugating Company, run by its neighbors, CanAm Colony. Other colonies produce siding or roofing materials as part of their product lines but sell more locally.

Newdale Colony is totally committed to manufacturing. Almost all its land is rented to neighbors, and the colony relies on its company, Domtek, for its livelihood. The company has grown steadily over the past twenty-five years. Ten colony members work in the plant full-time, while five or six non-Hutterites look after the state-of-the-art office on the colony and the salesroom in Winnipeg. Domtek products include steel panels for the walls or roofs of agricultural, residential, and commercial buildings. Selling points include features developed on the colony, like special panel overlap and hidden fasteners, as well as a five-step painting system that allows Domtek to offer a forty-year warranty with confidence. For interiors, it produces PVC interlocking liner panels, which compete well with more traditional systems like painted drywall. The colony's sales area is centered in Winnipeg but reaches into Saskatchewan and Alberta.[91]

Near neighbor CanAm Colony, in Margaret, Manitoba, is another important producer of building materials. Founded in 1999, Can-American Corrugating Company has grown into one of the largest dealers for metal roofing, laminated poles, and rebar in western Canada. Its use of the latest in manufacturing equipment and high-quality materials have earned the company a solid reputation. It emphasizes customer service and ongoing technical support. The huge facility employs twenty-five colony members and seven non-Hutterites. The colony has retained 2,600 acres of land and grows dairy-grade alfalfa as a cash crop.[92]

Brentwood Colony, in Faulkton, South Dakota, has developed an extremely successful business that fits well into colony life: it builds custom homes. When its leaders were looking for an enterprise to balance the colony's agricultural output and contribute to its bottom line, the shortage of housing in North Dakota, caused by the shale oil boom, was constantly in the news. This sparked the idea of building homes, though ironically, none of the completed products have been sold in the oil-rich region.[93]

ProComm Builders was established in 2010, and five show homes were constructed. However, sales proved elusive.[94] In 2012 the colony developed the idea that the prospective buyer should call all the shots, from the size and plan of the home to the kitchen cabinets, the colors, and the carpets. Since then, it has sold seventy homes, each one unique, and there is a comfortable waiting list of orders. One of the selling points is that this takes much of the mystery and intimidation out of building a new home. The customer can make all the choices, with the help of an experienced designer, before construction starts. But it is the quality of the materials and the workmanship that command the admiration of buyers.[95]

The construction takes place in a 33,000-square-foot production center, where three homes can be built at a time. When I visited, two men were completing the base of a new house, while a second home was framed and roofed, and work was being done on interior drywall. One could appreciate the advantages of working in a controlled environment rather than on a wet and windy building site. The homes are extremely energy-efficient. ProComm offers houses of 1,300 to 2,600 square feet, with a maximum footprint of 35 by 85 feet. The huge production facility includes cutting-edge design extractor fans for dust, as well as changing rooms, lockers, and showers for the work crew. It takes about fourteen weeks to complete a home, and customers are encouraged to visit while building is in progress. Outside, there were two more houses, one completed and awaiting delivery, the other nearing completion. The carpets were laid, the painting was completed, and two Hutterite tradesmen were installing kitchen equipment. Seven men are employed full-time, while four or five more help out when their other responsibilities allow. A team of women clean and polish a completed home before delivery. As many as nine local suppliers are involved. They provide floor materials, bathroom accessories, cabinetry, kitchenware, countertops, electrical fittings, and carpets.

Typical customers include retiring farmers who are moving to small towns, first-time homebuyers, and those looking for a lakeside cottage as a second home. Most deliveries are made within a radius of 80 kilometers, but deliveries can be completed up to 160 kilometers. In the past, the colony had sales centers in Faulkton and Aberdeen, but now the sales staff prefers to draw potential customers to the site. Word of mouth and an excellent website entice new customers.

Plastics

A number of colonies have established successful businesses based on plastics. A pioneer in this field was Green Acres Colony, Alberta. Its company, Crowfoot Plastics, performs an invaluable service by providing a place for farmers to recycle their plastic waste. Giant silage and grain bags, resembling huge white sausages, are a common site on Alberta farms. They are used to protect fodder crops from the weather. The disposal of large quantities of this plastic material posed a problem. Some chose to burn it, others to bury it; neither is a good option. Now the farmers simply have to roll their bags and take them to the Crowfoot Plastics plant, where they receive some compensation that at least pays for their gas. The Hofer brothers run the company, and they report: "Our company is five years old and we recycle approximately 5 million pounds of plastic a year, high density polyethylene plastic and gas pipe and low density polyethylene grain bags."[96]

In the plant, which runs on solar power, materials are shredded, washed, dried, ground up, melted at 200°c, and extruded as plastic beads. This output makes up a vital part of the raw materials used at Crawling Valley Plastics, on nearby Clearview Colony, Alberta. The company produces plastic bags both for garbage and for the food and service industries. The availability of relatively low-cost recycled plastic makes the business viable. Five full-time operators run the extrusion machines and the presses, which are housed in the old dairy barn.[97] The computers in the modern office run spreadsheets that track the progress of every order. When the colony started the company, it employed an outside agent to handle sales and distribution. Today the company has a well-established base of three hundred customers and handles all sales from the colony. Its location close to the Trans-Canada Highway provides easy access for tractor-trailers that can move the products to Calgary and Edmonton.[98] Here, as is so often the case, Hutterite engineers have fine-tuned the machines they bought to reduce waste, while manager John Hofer uses his years of experience working to optimize the diet of his hogs, tinker with raw material inputs, and ensure the right weight and strength of the bags his plant produces.

Clearview's daughter colony, Ridgeland Colony, Alberta, operates Seiu Lake Plastics, which has a more diverse product line. It produces bubble wrap packaging and plastic foam products. In Manitoba, Maple Grove Colony runs Maple Grove Plastics, which produces air and radiator filters, patented under the name Screen-O-Matic, and hot-water heating pads for farrowing crates. It also uses plastic tubing in its custom-built boat docks.[99]

After the setback with its biomass boiler, Iron Creek soon found another interesting manufacturing venture to explore: producing Fox Blocks for the Airlite Plastics Company of Omaha, Nebraska. These are large LEGO-like plastic blocks that clip together to form walls. The hollow core of each block is stiffened with rebar and filled with concrete, providing a tough wall with about 5 inches of insulation. Both interior and exterior surfaces are ready to cover with stucco or paint. The raw material consists of bags of plastic granules that look like salt, imported from South Korea. Heated and extruded through a number of machines, the plastic is formed into blocks in which steel spreaders are fitted.

The plant provides jobs for four or five Hutterites, sometimes more when they run the machines for twenty-four hours to catch up with back orders. When I visited, the huge barn was stacked to the rooftop with relatively light and easily shipped bundles of prefabricated walls. At present, much of the output moves to Vancouver and southern British Columbia. The parent company, Airlite Plastics, has three other Canadian production centers: at Starbuck, Manitoba; Cap Pele, New Brunswick; and Montreal. The company handles management and sales, and the colony's responsibilities are confined to manufacturing.

I had a chance to see Fox Blocks being used to construct new residences on the colony. All the forty-year-old houses were being replaced. Stucco was being applied to the Fox Block walls on the outside of one house, while the interior was completely finished and occupied. Windows with triple glazing and doors had been imported from Germany.[100]

Oak Bluff Colony, like other Manitoba colonies, was forced to look for a new enterprise when its hog business collapsed about a decade ago. The leaders cast around for a green business opportunity. As manager Jack Maendel explained, "There are too many colonies in woodworking and metalworking already. We don't want to be copycats. We wanted something unique, and it is hard to find anything unique anymore." They came up with EcoPoxy, which uses bioingredients to make an odorless epoxy glue. Its advantages are that it uses renewable materials, rather than being oil based, and it can be more easily and safely used by do-it-yourself customers and professionals alike. At present, the product is made with linseed and cashew oil, but the company is experimenting with soybeans, which will cut costs significantly. The company has landed a government grant for $167,000 to enable it to develop its own laboratory facilities. There are fifteen employees, including five non-Hutterite chemists, salespeople, and accountants.[101]

Sand and Gravel

Many colonies in Alberta and Saskatchewan have opened quarries, making use of the outwash sands and gravels deposited by the glaciers to provide materials for use in constructing their colonies and maintaining their roads. In some cases, they have invested in crushing and washing infrastructure. These colonies sell sand and gravel to neighbors, contractors, and municipalities. Examples are Cayley Colony, Riverbend Colony, and White Lake Colony, all in Alberta. Peace View Colony, British Columbia, is a special case. When it opened a small quarry on its newly acquired property, the colony found a valuable deposit of pea-size gravel, which hardly needed any treatment. It has exploited this resource over the past decade and has ongoing contracts with the British Columbia Roads Department. Farther to the east, but still in the Peace River Country, Birch Meadows Colony, Alberta, has a cement truck and carries out custom work for both private and municipal customers.

A trio of colonies in central Alberta and Saskatchewan have exploited deposits of clay and sand to make precast concrete walls. Spring Ridge Colony, near Wainwright, Alberta, began manufacturing walls for use in construction projects on the colony in 2000. In 2006 it incorporated the enterprise as Twin Valley Precast and began to sell to customers. In 2015 the plant was upgraded and expanded. It now has two bays each with a 20-ton crane and can handle large projects such as wall panels and oil pump bases. The Workers' Compensation Board of Alberta has determined that the colony should insure those Hutterites working in the plant.[102]

Miscellaneous Enterprises

Colonies have a multitude of other initiatives that fall outside the generalized categories. A few examples hint at the breadth of these eclectic enterprises. Millerdale Colony, South Dakota, has a flourishing business producing promotional items for companies. When I visited, three young Hutterite women were minding a bank of eight automated sewing machines, which were turning out baseball caps with embroidered company logos. Teams of women rotate from kitchen and garden duties to work in the shop. It takes hours to digitize each new pattern for the machines to copy. An older Hutterite, who was confined to a wheelchair, manages a laser engraving machine that turns out knives and pens with company names.

The colony even customizes three sizes of clocks for retirement gifts.[103] At Lajord Colony, Saskatchewan, the manager, Darius Hofer, was having trouble finding a suitable weigh scale for the colony's trucks. The colony decided to build its own, but before the scale was installed, a neighboring colony bought it. Since that time, the colony has kept building and selling the scales, and it keeps a stock on hand to meet the demand. Recent sales were to Hynes Lake Colony in the Peace River Country and to a colony in Montana.[104]

Greenwald Colony, Manitoba, exploits its proximity to the Trans-Canada Highway to run a salvage business. It recovers wrecked semi-trailers and sells their contents, whether they be women's clothing or chocolate bars. Then the colony either fixes the rig or breaks it up for scrap and parts. Birch Hills Colony, at Wanham, Alberta, does the same kind of work, although it also handles damaged grain bins and obsolete agricultural machinery.[105] Miami Colony, Manitoba, runs a redolent but profitable tanning business. It processes bison, moose, and deer hides, as well as cattle hides, and makes gloves, bridles and leather goods.[106] Finally, Ayers Ranch, Montana, runs a popular meat shop that processes wild game during hunting season, while Clear Lake Colony, Alberta, promotes its "Traditional Hutterite" meats online, boasting that it has been processing meats since 1547.[107]

Some Objections to Change

Some colonies' leaders remain dubious about the wisdom of adopting light industrial enterprises. They fear that this change from the seasonal rhythms of agriculture, and the varied tasks it involves, may be detrimental to the "Hutterite way."[108] They envision their people harnessed to machines, their days arbitrarily divided into eight-hour shifts, and their ability to interact with their brothers and sisters inhibited by their specialized tasks and the safety equipment that they are forced to wear. They suggest that there could be resentment between those working in the shop's warm, dry conditions and those facing the elements on the farm. They worry, too, that businesses dealing with customers and suppliers will increase the interaction between colony members and the outside world, and they point to the fact that several colonies have hired outside workers, thus bringing the outside world right into the colony. Professor Joanita Kant described this problem graphically, suggesting that one envision a young Hutterite working alongside a young man from the local town, who was boasting about the truck he was saving for with his wages or the stock-car races he was going to attend.[109]

I raised these questions with the leaders of colonies that had adopted light manufacturing enterprises. They reported that their family men welcomed the regular hours in the shop, which allowed them more time at home, and that working in the plant and taking coffee breaks in the rest area actually brought the workers closer together.[110] They said that shop managers are not "time management experts"; some of the leisurely tempo of work in the fields is carried over to work on the production line. The work must get done, but they are relaxed about timing; what does not get done today will get done tomorrow. Finally, they pointed out that not all young people were suited to farm life. One young Hutterite told us in no uncertain terms that he hated animals. One hopes that he was fascinated by machines and computers. I asked Pauly Kleinsasser at Springfield Colony, Manitoba, which employs twenty non-Hutterites, whether employing outsiders posed a threat to young Hutterites and their beliefs. He replied that it all depended on how you brought up your young people. If they were firmly rooted and grounded in their faith, there was little danger of worldly influences.[111]

In my admittedly limited observations, I found that the colonies regarded light manufacturing activities as just another set of possible jobs, adding diversity and interest to those offered on the farm. There was a lot of flexibility, with men and women spending mornings in the garden or the livestock barns and afternoons in the shop. One manager explained that they were running behind on a contract for doors and windows, but they would soon catch up when seeding was finished and extra hands became available. Only a handful of colonies rely entirely on manufacturing.

The growing number of colonies engaged in various nonfarm activities may result in competition with non-Hutterite companies. This is particularly true in the building supply industry. Construction companies in Manitoba asked the government to step in and end what they believed was the unfair advantage given to Hutterite competitors. Gino Koko, general sales manager of Vicwest, a company that manufactured metal building supplies, said, "Every year they gain a bit more market share and they gain a bigger customer base. When the playing field is different and there's advantages that are outside something we could do, that's when we don't like the competition." But Jonathan Wollman of Newdale Colony, the home of Domtek Building Products, ridiculed the idea that Hutterites do not have to pay wages: "We have to pay the workers, not in the form of money, we pay them with a well-furnished house and three, four or five meals a day. They should take their employees, build them a house, furnish it, feed them and totally look after them. They'd be surprised."[112] Similar objections were voiced when Hutterville Colony, South Dakota, sought a zoning change for its daughter colony Sunrise, also in South Dakota, so it could develop a blacksmith's shop and garage for truck repairs.[113] Millbrook Colony, South Dakota, likewise provoked a hostile response when it proposed a manufacturing plant for its daughter colony Spruce Lane, North Dakota.[114]

There are dangers inherent in the adoption of nonfarm activities, an important one being that manufacturing enterprises enjoy shorter product runs than is customary in farming. The businesses face a constant need to reinvent themselves, to innovate and to pursue new market niches, and to react to regulatory changes with respect to the environment and to health and safety standards. But Hutterite businesses have established an enviable reputation for the quality of their workmanship and the reliability of their products. They display integrity and a commitment to excellence. Outside firms can establish contracts with the colonies knowing that they are not going anywhere. They can build trust, which gives them the stability they desire.

Change and the Future of the Hutterites

To what extent have Hutterite colonies adopted new enterprises to improve their bottom line and to accumulate capital? The concepts and language of diffusion theory are helpful in framing an answer to this question.[115] There are wide differences among the clan groups. The Schmiedeleut were "early adopters" and have pursued nonfarm activities most vigorously. They started manufacturing enterprises during the 1980s, and with each success, more colonies have come on board. With 67 percent of Schmiedeleut colonies reporting nonfarm enterprises, they are classified as being in the "late majority" stage of diffusion. Their early adoption of new strategies owes much to the dynamic leadership of Jake Kleinsasser, who acted as a change agent, and to the Leut's intense interaction over several decades with the Bruderhof in New York State, a group whose primary source of income was from light manufacturing. More recently, escalating land prices have encouraged Schmiedeleut colonies to look for alternatives to farming; when planning a daughter colony, they will purchase only enough land to ensure privacy and invest in manufacturing enterprises. These businesses will benefit from the expertise, skills, and contacts already fostered at the parent colony.

Almost one-third of Dariusleut colonies have taken up some nonfarm activities, placing them in the "early majority" category. There are pockets of innovation in central Alberta, like the colonies around Holden, Iron Creek, and Viking, and also in the Peace River Country. As far as I could see, few Dariusleut colonies in the core area south of Lethbridge were transitioning to new manufacturing endeavors, and it is here that further change may be anticipated.

The Lehrerleut are still in the early adopter stage of diffusion, with less than 10 percent of colonies having nonfarm activities. This Leut is the most conservative of the clan groups and has the strongest intercolony organization, which may inhibit individual colonies from innovating. Moreover, the Lehrerleut tend to have large, well-established farms where the emphasis is on grain production rather than livestock. So far, the colonies in this group have reinvested in agriculture rather than manufacturing. It seems likely that some may follow the lead of Brant Colony and look to slash energy costs by adopting new technology, while other Lehrerleut colonies may look for ways to add value to their farm products.

The differences among clan groups are mirrored by those within each Leut. The colonies blessed with vigorous entrepreneurial leadership and a willingness to take risks demonstrate innovation in not one, but several fields. For the sake of organizational clarity, various categories of nonfarm enterprises have been discussed separately, but in fact, some colonies are pursuing a range of strategies. They may be investing in innovative energy solutions while adding value to their agricultural products by processing and paying careful attention to marketing, as well as pursuing one or more manufacturing activities. When I spent a morning with one colony manager, I was impressed with the number of active files on his desk. These included a progress report on a new automated dairy barn, a soybean crushing plant, a solar energy project, and a plan to extend the gravel pit. At another colony, I was shown the shop and manufacturing enterprise that had brought me to the colony, and then the manager took me on a tour. I saw the new drive-through sheep barn, which had greatly increased returns by cutting down on losses during lambing. Then the manager explained that the colony had doubled its acreage of potatoes because it had secured one of the first contracts with a new processing plant in Lethbridge. Success in one area spills over into others. "For to everyone who has, more will be given, and he will have abundance."[116]

In complete contrast, there are colonies in each of the clan groups where leadership does not have the drive or vision to pursue new paths.[117] They are risk-averse and insist that what has been done in the past will continue to sustain them in the future. These are old colonies, and it has been at least forty years since they split. Their population is aging, they are losing young people to the outside world, and the young men who remain find it hard to attract wives. Their housing stock is old, and even their agricultural infrastructure is obsolescent. If the continuing health of Hutterite culture depends on finding the means to establish daughter colonies when division becomes necessary, then the dangers of not employing new strategies to generate capital far outweigh the risks inherent in innovation.

At the start of this project, I expected to be investigating a shift in emphasis from agriculture to light manufacturing industry that was revolutionary in nature, involving precipitate change and resulting in tumult. How wrong I was. There has indeed been a steady expansion of nonfarm enterprises on the colonies, but it started decades ago and has proceeded at a measured pace. Innovation has been accommodated within the fabric of existing colonies. Buildings once used for agriculture are now used for light engineering. Skills honed in colony shops and used to build daughter colonies and refurbish older headquarters are now deployed in enterprises that help the colony pay its way and accumulate capital. Only a handful of colonies rely solely on manufacturing. In most cases, new ventures employ four or five Hutterite workers and earn some 10 percent of the colony turnover. Agriculture remains an economic sheet anchor and a source of seed capital for new endeavors. What I observed was incremental change in response to a changing economic environment. It is a situation very close to what Joseph Eaton referred to as "controlled acculturation" and a process that will strengthen rather than threaten the continuity of the "Hutterite way."[118]

12

Coda

Musings on the Future

The foregoing chapters have worked through the three principal themes set out in the introduction: exploring the diffusion and present distribution of Hutterite colonies, describing their contributions to the changing cultural landscape, and charting the ways in which they make a living and interact with the land they occupy. Those chapters have looked at the growth and expansion of Hutterite colonies and outlined some of the obstacles they have faced. In the third volume of his encyclopedic assessment of communal groups in the United States, Timothy Miller writes, "The Hutterites present the greatest independent communal success story in history—larger and longer-lived than any other communal movement not anchored in some larger religious tradition, such as a branch of Buddhism or Christianity."[1]

The narrative of the diffusion of Hutterite colonies in the first six chapters of this book provides a background to, and evidence for, Miller's assertion. Three colonies of refugees, tenuously planted in the Dakota Territory, have multiplied to five hundred spread widely over the Canadian prairies and the northern Great Plains. This vigorous diffusion has occurred in the face of hostility and suspicion that at times has found expression in overt political action. The Brethren have been forced to flee, had borders closed against them, and had their right to purchase land curtailed.

I argue that regular colony division has channeled the Hutterites' exceptional demographic energy in a positive way. Maximum colony sizes of 120–150 became established as norms during their early decades in North America, and they worked out the means of achieving colony division without rancor. For half a century high birth rates meant that daughter colonies had to be established every fifteen years. Today smaller families mean longer periods between splits. Nevertheless, given the Hutterites' demographic momentum, several new colonies are still established every year.

The steady multiplication of colonies has added a new element to the cultural landscape of the plains. Most colonies share common characteristics, but there are differences among the clan groups, and a range of innovative layouts and housing types have been adopted by some colonies.

Agriculture remains the most important way in which Hutterites make a living. This book has described some typical farms and the diversity of their operations. On my colony visits, I found sensitivity to changing market demands and imaginative attempts to fine-tune crop choices and to modify animal products to meet emerging trends. I was surprised and impressed by the sophisticated and intricate links many colonies have established with agribusiness.

Profit margins are critically low in agriculture, and this has encouraged more and more colonies to develop light manufacturing enterprises. What often started as sidelines to keep tradesmen busy during the winter have morphed into full-time businesses providing year-round employment and contributing a substantial return to the colony economy. Some colonies have rented out most of their land to neighbors and rely entirely on their manufacturing enterprises that often flow into markets across North America. Most integrate their new light industrial activities into the colony and regard them as another semi-independent department, much like the hog operation or the egg barn.

As attention turns to the future, I should start by saying how impressed I have been by the resiliency and adaptability of the Hutterites. In the face of a tsunami of change in the host society, they have already achieved remarkable transformations within their closed society without losing their cultural integrity. Over a period of four or five decades they have gone through a critical demographic transition as average family size has plunged from ten or more children to only three or four. Evidence suggests that they have reached an acceptable new level of stability.

The Hutterites no longer face overt hostility from governments. Indeed, often their leaders are invited to join marketing boards, while some colonies are drawn into partnerships with government or industry to develop innovations such as solar egg barns. This change has mainly been achieved by a softening of attitudes on the part of the host society. But the Hutterites have also played a role. Their leaders have become increasingly confident and willing to serve in responsible posts, while the Hutterites' growing contribution to the agricultural economy have made such appointments appropriate.

But in the countryside, attitudes toward the Brethren are more conflicted. While there is still a deep undercurrent of resentment and hostility, it is definitely more muted than in the past. Farmers often see the local colony as ideal neighbors, while remaining suspicious of Hutterite expansion more generally.

Nowhere is change more evident than on the colonies themselves. The first colonies I visited during the early 1970s had big, high wood-frame houses, each providing drafty apartments for six or eight families. They had outside toilets. What a contrast to the duplex on a new colony in which I was entertained in the summer of 2018! It had a high cathedral ceiling, big windows, and a geothermal heating system laid under the hardwood floor. Colonies both new and old have reached new levels of comfort, modernity, and in some cases aesthetic appeal. They boast airy and functional school buildings, many with gymnasiums.

A transition is also taking place on the economic front. Most colony leaders would agree that the model of diversified agriculture that has stood them in good stead for a century now needs modification. While some colonies have responded by fine-tuning production and paying more attention to marketing strategies, others have come together to form cooperatives that reduce input costs and increase their heft in the marketplace. A more radical alternative has been to develop nonfarm enterprises, an option adopted by more and more colonies. Information passes freely among colonies, and a successful venture will soon be emulated elsewhere. The challenge will be to find new industrial niches to exploit. But the presence of a willing and disciplined workforce will surely prove a lure for small local firms looking to expand, and links with multinational producers have already been established.[2]

The Brethren still face several problems. As the number of colonies has increased, so too has their diversity, both within and among the clan groups. This is inevitable and may even be a sign of vigor. However, the increasing gap between rich and poor colonies is a cause for concern in an egalitarian society. There is no denying the sharp contrast between a big, prosperous, forward-looking colony with modern infrastructure and a small, traditional colony with a more limited range of outputs, making do with older machinery and facilities. Mechanisms exist within the Hutterite organization for providing both advisory management and ongoing financial support. Nevertheless, the widening gap between the haves and the have nots remains an obstinate reality.

A closely related problem is due to affluence. Although these are plain people who have traditionally adopted what John Bennett refers to as a "culture of austerity—a way of living with less, and doing so with dignity and purpose," some colonies display obvious signs of conspicuous consumption.[3] One cannot help thinking that an element of competition has developed among colonies. Affluence can also result in an increasing demand for consumer goods, as well as a slide away from the self-sufficient and inward-looking community set apart from the world and toward a more individualistic and materialistic consumer culture.

For a generation, colony leaders have wrestled with how to cope with the threats posed to their way of life by the internet and cell phones. Some have recognized the futility of attempting to maintain strict boundaries with the outside world and give cell phones to every school graduate, while others continue to fight a losing battle to limit the use of new technology. For computers *do* play a vital and legitimate role in the economic life of a colony. They are used to monitor milk yields, manage the efficient use of fertilizers in the fields, or keep an inventory of supplies and customers in a new light industry. Cell phones provide a means of instant communication between workers and managers across the sprawling fields and provide links to veterinarians, mechanics, accountants, and suppliers. But although these technologies have become indispensable, they also represent an invasion of the outside world into the confines of the colony. As one leader remarked, the outcome depends on how well young people have been nurtured to make good choices and on the spiritual vitality of the community itself.

How the Hutterites deal with these problems depends on their continued success in imbuing each new generation with their all-pervasive faith. It is this faith, based on communal Anabaptism, that is the reason for their longevity. Faith is what makes living in community possible. At the same time, communal living is the ultimate expression of their faith. Their God is present with the women as they shell the peas for the communal supper and with the men as they do the milking or combining. From the mature grandmothers working in the kindergarten, trying to instill the importance of the group over the insistent demands of the individual child, to the teenager caring for an infirm aunt, every action is an expression of service. Thus the daily church service and Sunday observances are but one aspect of the Hutterites' faith journey. Though they are treasured as opportunities to pause and reflect, they are not the only way that God is served or the only time the divine is present.

Nevertheless, there is widespread concern among leaders of all the clan groups that the rigid traditional structure of the *Gebet* (daily worship service) has become atrophied. Ministers are exploring ways of making the precious *Lehren* (or sermons) of the seventeenth century more accessible to church members by linking their truths to contemporary events or introducing new musical forms into their services. At the same time, the leaders are reviewing the ways Hutterite history is taught. How can the rich and textured culture of the Hutterites be made more meaningful to young people? The aim must be to move from teaching Hutterite history by rote learning, focusing on the memorization of key figures, places, and dates, to a more imaginative evocation of what has been accomplished in the past and a mapping out of exciting new pathways to a communal future together. Can ministers and German teachers achieve the same kind of slow evolutionary transformation in matters of faith and education as has been achieved in material matters? I am both hopeful and confident that they can. After all, the Hutterite way of life has long provided an unconventional, even radical solution to many of the problems facing the contemporary world, such as the emptiness of materialism and rampant consumerism, anomie and the longing for greater meaning, unemployment and poverty, the difficulties of finding affordable quality childcare, and the loneliness and sense of rejection faced by many isolated elderly.

Notes

Introduction

1. Acts 2:44 (KJV); Peters, *All Things Common*. For a thorough introduction to all aspects of Hutterite life, see Janzen and Stanton, *Hutterites in North America*.
2. Kraybill and Bowman, *On the Backroad to Heaven*.
3. Janzen and Stanton, *Hutterites in North America*, chap. 4, "Four Hutterite Branches."
4. Janzen, *Prairie People*. The majority of the Hutterites living in Ukraine were not living communally. It was only the Schmiedeleut in Scheromet and the Dariusleut in Hutterdorf who had embraced *Gemeinschaft*. Hostetler, *Hutterite Society*, 110.
5. See chap. 2 for details.
6. For a sympathetic account of this bitter split, see Janzen and Stanton, *Hutterites in North America*, 62–73.
7. For the legal case, which the Hutterites eventually lost, see *Calgary Herald*, July 25–26, 2009. The significance of the dispute was evaluated by Ogilvie, "Failure of Proportionality Tests." For the advertisement, see Andy, Kurt, and Shawn Wipf of Viking Colony on the back of the July–August 2009 issue of *Alberta Views*.
8. The landmark general history of the Hutterites is Hostetler, *Hutterite Society*. For European origins, see Gross, *Golden Years*.
9. Referred to as the *Lehren*, this collection of 400 sermons, written while the Hutterites were living in Slovakia, are the only sacred texts allowed in the church service, as they represent the orthodox Hutterite interpretation of the Holy Books and thus help preserve the Hutterite past.
10. Horsch, *Hutterian Brethren*.
11. For an overview see Hofer, *History of the Hutterites*.
12. Huntington, "Living in the Ark."
13. See, for example, Ingoldsby, "Hutterite Family in Transition"; The Nine, *Hutterites*.

14. For example, Cook, "North American Hutterites"; Pluzhnikov et al., "Correlation of Intergenerational Family Size"; Loeb et al., "Effects of Influenza Vaccination."

15. Earlier work was summarized in Peter, *Dynamics of Hutterite Society.* More recently, Ingoldsby and Smith have examined various aspects of the Hutterite family in a series of articles. See, for instance, Ingoldsby and Smith, "Role of Discipline."

16. Kraybill and Bowman, *On the Backroad to Heaven.*

17. Janzen and Stanton, *Hutterites in North America,* xiv.

18. Janzen and Stanton, *Hutterites in North America.*

19. Katz and Lehr, *Inside the Ark.*

20. Hostetler, *Hutterite Society*; Ryan, *Agricultural Economy*; Bennett, *Hutterian Brethren*; Eaton and Mayer, *Man's Capacity to Reproduce*; Peter, *Dynamics of Hutterite Society.*

21. In particular, Winkelbauer, *Österreichische Geschichte* and "Die Vertreibung der Hutterer"; von Schlachta, *Die Hutterer zwischen Tirol* and *Täufergemeinschaften.*

1. Forging a Home on the Frontier

1. An exception is Zieglschmid, *Das Klein-Geschichtsbuch der Hutterischen Bruder,* translated from the German as the two-volume *Chronicle of the Hutterian Brethren* by the Hutterian Brethren of Crystal Springs Colony, Ste. Agathe, 1987 and 1998.

2. To put together this account, I have drawn on brief references from several sources. Rather than adding a citation for each sentence, I would like to acknowledge my debt to the following: Peters, *All Things Common,* 41–43; Hostetler, *Hutterite Society,* 120–25; Janzen and Stanton, *Hutterites in North America,* 38–45.

3. Young, "Mennonites in South Dakota," 487.

4. *Dakota Herald,* August 4, 1874.

5. Canadian prices are given in Canadian dollars throughout the book, while U.S. prices are in U.S. dollars.

6. The Homestead Act in the United States was established to provide free 160-acre farms to individuals who "proved up" by staying on the property and making improvements. No provision was made for group settlement. The same was true in Canada, but some exceptions were made for block grants to Mennonites and others.

7. This group had been extremely successful and amassed considerable wealth, but its members were aging, and their adherence to celibacy meant that there was no younger generation to take up the mantle.

8. Conkin, *Two Paths to Utopia,* 50.

9. To maintain fidelity with historical sources, U.S. units of measure are used for U.S. locations and for those in Canada up until the 1970s, at which time Canada switched to the metric system.

10. Samuel Hofer, *Hutterites*, 95.

11. See figure 27 in chap. 7.

12. Peters, *All Things Common*, 116–18; Peters, "Process of Colony Division," 57–64; Janzen and Stanton, *Hutterites in North America*, 235–40.

13. Hostetler, *Hutterite Society*, 123.

14. Willms, "Brethren Known as Hutterians," 392.

15. Anderson, "Hutterite Colonies."

16. Willms, "Brethren Known as Hutterians," 391.

17. Conkin, *Two Paths to Utopia*, 54.

2. The Exodus

1. Parts of this chapter were published in Evans and Peller, "Hutterites Come to Alberta," and are adapted here with the kind permission of the editor of *Alberta History*.

2. Willms, "Brethren Known as Hutterians," 391.

3. Stoltzfus, *Pacifists in Chains*, 52–53. This wonderful book focuses on the tragic story of the Hutterite martyrs, but it also describes the rise of hysterical patriotism that repudiated the very principles for which the war was being fought.

4. Teichroew, "Military Surveillance of Mennonites," 96. The German-speaking Hutterites, although they had spent a century in Russia and had no ties at all with Germany, were tarred with the same brush.

5. Stoltzfus, *Pacifists in Chains*, viii.

6. Teichroew, "Military Surveillance of Mennonites," 95.

7. Quoted in Unruh, "Hutterites during World War I," 135. This incident is widely reported in the literature: see Peters, *All Things Common*, 44; Hostetler, *Hutterite Society*, 130; Conkin, *Two Paths to Utopia*, 59.

8. Photograph reproduced in Janzen and Stanton, *Hutterites in North America*, 49. Janzen describes the incident and provides a thorough account of the treatment and behavior of noncommunal Hutterites. See Janzen, *Prairie People*, 137–43.

9. Accounts of torture and harassment are included in all the major sources: Janzen and Stanton, *Hutterites in North America*, 46–48; Stoltzfus, *Patriots in Chains*, 37 for a particular example and the whole text for persecution and injustice; Hostetler, *Hutterite Society*, 127–30; Conkin, *Two Paths to Utopia*, 56–59; Unruh, "Hutterites during World War I," 130–36.

10. See Stoltzfus, *Pacifists in Chains*, for the whole story.

11. Peters, *All Things Common*, 45.

12. Peters, *All Things Common*, 45. Interview given by the secretary of the State Council of Defense to the *Mitchell (SD) Republican*, September 26, 1919. This issue was finally settled by the State Supreme Court in October 1922. It ruled that the Hutterites could continue to function as a religious association. Conkin, *Two Paths to Utopia*, 63.

13. *Sioux Falls (SD) Argus-Leader*, September 11, 1918. Some authorities state that the levy was 5 percent; see Hostetler, *Hutterite Society*, 131.

14. We have found figures for only four colonies: Spink Colony paid $4,150 for Liberty Bonds and $825 for the Red Cross; Lake Byron Colony paid $3,750 for Liberty Bonds and $750 for the Red Cross; Richards Colony paid $2,000 for Liberty Bonds and $400 for the Red Cross; and Bon Homme paid $3,650 for Liberty Bonds and $731 for the Red Cross. The average tax paid was $4,000. If all fouteen colonies paid up, the total was $56,000. *Sioux Falls (SD) Argus-Leader*, September 11, 1918.

15. Conkin, *Two Paths to Utopia*, 60.

16. They proved to be forgiving: several Schmiedeleut colonies established daughter colonies in South Dakota during the 1930s.

17. Willms, "Brethren Known as Hutterians," 392.

18. Epp, *Mennonite Exodus*, 94.

19. Epp, *Mennonite Exodus*, 101.

20. Much of the detail in this section comes from Hiebert, "Story of a Pure Church." Hiebert's interviews with aging Hutterites, who remembered details of the move from South Dakota or possessed documentary evidence, have provided us with a valuable resource. I use his work here with thanks.

21. Rockyford and District History Book Society, *Where We Crossed*, 67.

22. Hiebert, "Story of a Pure Church," 82. Hiebert reports that the newly arrived Brethren lost at least twenty members to the epidemic.

23. Beiseker Historical Society, *Beiseker's Golden Heritage*, 117.

24. Hiebert, "Story of a Pure Church," 84.

25. Anderson, "Prudent Plain People."

26. Peter Peller has analyzed the 1921 Nominal Census of Canada to provide a demographic profile of the Hutterites two years after their arrival in Canada.

27. Rockyford and District History Book Society, *Where We Crossed*, 67–68.

28. See, for example, *Lethbridge (AB) Herald*, October 16, 1918; Magrath and District History Association, *Irrigation Builders*, 297–301.

29. *Lethbridge (AB) Herald*, September 6, 1918.

30. *Lethbridge (AB) Herald*, October 24, 1918.

31. Holzach, *Forgotten People*, 57–58. The farm animals in the barns and feedlots fared better than the residences in this regard.

32. Hiebert, "Story of a Pure Church," 78–81.

33. Esau, *Courts and the Colonies*.

34. There were three families of Hofers, consisting of six adults and seventeen children. Nominal Census of Canada, 1921, District 7, Subdistrict 14.

35. Nominal Census of Canada, 1921.

36. For an overview of postwar conditions, see Bright, "1919," 413–41.

37. *Calgary Herald*, quoted in Bright, "1919," 426.

38. Bright, "1919," 421.

39. "Macleod Citizens in Huge Demonstration against Mennonites," *Lethbridge (AB) Daily Herald*, September 21, 1918.

40. Epp, *Mennonites in Canada*, 395.

41. *Calgary Eye Opener*, October 5, 1918.

42. Canada, *Debates of the House of Commons*, Session 1919, vol. 2, 1913.

43. Epp, *Mennonites in Canada*, 408.

44. Bright, "1919," 423.

45. *Lethbridge (AB) Herald*, October 16, 1918.

46. Armishaw, "Hutterites' Story," 236.

47. Willms, "Brethren Known as Hutterians," 393.

48. Armishaw, "Hutterites' Story," 235. Calder discussed the case of the "Russian" Hutterites with his cabinet colleagues, and they agreed to ignore the order in council in this particular case.

49. Armishaw, "Hutterites' Story," 237.

50. "It is surprising that so astute a politician as Mr. Calder, who was, moreover, well versed in western affairs, should have found himself so far off base in this matter." Willms "Brethren Known as Hutterians," 393.

51. Armishaw, "Hutterites' Story," 236.

52. Barnhart, "Calder, James Alexander."

53. See, for example, *Toronto Globe and Mail*, March 31, 1921.

54. Statistics Canada, Table 17-10-0063-01.

55. Epp, *Mennonite Exodus*, 94.

56. Jones, *Empire of Dust*, 254, table 1.

57. Hopkins, *Canadian Annual Review of Public Affairs*, 427.

58. See Robert Everett-Green, "Canada's Other Western Front," *Toronto Globe and Mail*, June 28, 2014. Green points out that although the cultivated acreage rose by 21 percent in 1918, grain production actually fell by 19 percent, due in part to bad weather but also to the shortage of labor.

59. Canada, Debates of the House of Commons, Session 1917, 1748.

60. Armishaw, "Hutterites' Story," 228.

61. "Hutterites Defended," *Winnipeg Free Press*, August 12, 1919.

62. Armishaw, "Hutterites' Story," 239.

63. Statistics Canada, Table 17-10-0063-01.

64. Epp, *Mennonite Exodus*, 105.

65. It had been their unwillingness to take up arms and to follow the dictates of emerging nationalism that had caused them to flee Moravia in the early seventeenth century and Russia in the late nineteenth century. Hostetler, *Hutterite Society*, 67–112.

66. Stoltzfus, *Pacifists in Chains*, 213–17; Mark 12:17 (KJV).

67. Clark, "Hutterian Communities," 357–74.

68. Willms, "Brethren Known as Hutterians," 394.

69. Conkin, *Two Paths to Utopia*, 62.

70. Troth, "Migration of Milltown Colony."

71. Armishaw, "Hutterites' Story," 240

72. Conkin, *Two Paths to Utopia*, 61–62

73. This tendency to name a new colony after an old one can be a source of confusion.

74. Willms, "Brethren Known as Hutterians," 393.

75. Canada, Debates of the House of Commons, May 19, 1919, 2570.

76. These were Bon Homme, Milltown, Wolf Creek, Lake Byron, Old Elmspring, and Rockport.

3. Consolidation and Acceptance

1. Berton, *Great Depression*, 9.

2. Francis and Ganzevoort, *Dirty Thirties in Prairie Canada*, 5.

3. Friesen, *Canadian Prairies*, 396; Broadfoot, *Ten Lost Years*.

4. Beaudoin, "What They Saw"; Sauchyn and Beaudoin, "Recent Environmental Change."

5. Joern and Keeler, *Changing Prairie*.

6. Chakravarti, "Precipitation Deficiency Patterns."

7. Samuel Hofer, *Hutterites*, 103.

8. Kells, "Hutterite Commune."

9. Thomas, "Survey of Hutterite Groups," 12.

10. Hofer, *Treasures of Time*, 699.

11. Brief by L. S. Turcotte on behalf of the Hutterites to the Committee of the Legislative Assembly of the Province of Alberta, February 10, 1947.

12. Joseph Y. Card to the Rt. Hon. R. B. Bennett, March 2, 1934.

13. Kells, "Hutterite Commune," 53.

14. Swan, "400-Year-Old Commune," 95.

15. Gross, *Hutterite Way*, 114.

4. "Enemy Aliens"

1. Only an estimated 276 young men from both the United States and Canada went to alternative service camps. See Zieglschmid, "Must the Hutterites?," 1270.
2. Conkin, *Two Paths to Utopia*, 72.
3. Peters, *All Things Common*, 61.
4. Eaton, "Canada's Scapegoats," 253–54.
5. Peters, *All Things Common*, 56–65.
6. Janzen, *Limits on Liberty*, 64.
7. "Voluntary Hutterite Curb," *Winnipeg Tribune*, April 29, 1957.
8. Ryan, *Agricultural Economy*, 40–43.
9. Conkin, *Two Paths to Utopia*, 72.
10. Riley and Johnson, *South Dakota's Hutterite Colonies*; Riley, *The Hutterites and Their Agriculture*.
11. Initially the act was challenged by the federal government because "enemy aliens" were within federal jurisdiction. The Alberta law was reworded to apply to Hutterites and Doukhobors, and the prohibition on sales of land was extended to include leases. See Land Sales Prohibition Act, 1942, c. 16; Act to Prohibit the Sale of Lands to Any Hutterites for the Duration of the War, 1944, c. 15; and Communal Property Act, 1947, c. 16.
12. Janzen, *Limits on Liberty*; Palmer, "Hutterite Land Expansion Controversy."
13. Rideman, *Confession of Faith*, 102.
14. Radtke, *Hutterites in Montana*, 45.
15. Howard, "Hutterites," 40.
16. Petersen, "Hilldale," 3–5.
17. Interview, minister of Elm Spring Colony, Alberta, July 1972.
18. Bennett, *Hutterian Brethren*, 53.
19. Lobb and Agnew, *Hutterites and Saskatchewan*.
20. Serl, "Final Report."
21. Government of Alberta, *Report of the Hutterite Investigation Committee*.
22. Communal Property Act, 1960, c. 16.
23. Sanders, "Hutterites," 230; Sanders, "Communal Property Decision."
24. *Calgary Herald*, May 4, 1961; *Albertan*, June 2, 11, 1960.
25. Communal Property Act, 1962, c. 8.
26. Palmer, "Hutterite Land Expansion Controversy," 30–38.
27. Becker, "Hutterites Survive 400 Years."
28. Graham, "Hutterites Elect Unique Body."
29. Government of Alberta, *Report on Communal Property*.

30. This section is based on Evans, "Spatial Bias," 1–16.

31. Zwarun, "Model Citizens."

32. Pratt, "Anabaptist Explosion," 18–23.

33. Meinig, "Cultural Geography," 100.

34. For a discussion of "neighboring" strategy, see Bennett, *Hutterian Brethren*, 80.

35. Evans, "Dispersal of Hutterite Colonies," 145.

36. *Albertan*, June 2, 1960.

37. *Albertan*, June 11, 1960.

38. O.K. Colony did finally purchase the Henninger property without publicity in 1974. Rev. Jacob Waldner, personal communication, February 1974.

39. *Albertan*, December 15, 1960.

40. *Calgary Herald*, April 8, 1974.

41. *Calgary Herald*, December 30, 1971.

42. *Calgary Herald*, December 3, 1971.

43. Conkin, *Two Paths to Utopia*, 73.

44. Peters, *All Things Common*, 57.

5. Some Freedom of Locational Choice

1. Kobayashi, "Multiculturalism," 205–6.

2. In one case a colony paid $75 an acre when the prevailing rate "at home" was ten times as much. *Gemein* is the church; *gemeinshaft* includes the idea of owning and sharing material goods in common, a practice that binds the community together.

3. For a discussion of underemployment, see Boldt and Roberts, "Decline of Hutterite Population Growth."

4. See Bennett, "Change and Transition"; Peter and Whitaker, "Acquisition of Personal Property."

5. Ryan, "Hutterite Settlements," 92.

6. Government of Alberta, *Report on Communal Property*, Appendix J.

7. Ryan, "Hutterite Settlements," 109.

8. Boldt, "Structural Tightness," Boldt, "Plain People"; Peter and Whitaker, "Changing Role of Hutterite Women."

6. Unfettered Diffusion

1. This chapter is based on Evans and Peller, "Mapping an Ethnic Isolate," an article I coauthored with Peter Peller. His preliminary work digitizing data on all five hundred colonies enabled us to measure with some precision the time between colony splits and the distances moved at fission. We could also produce maps of Hutterite settlement

patterns at different time periods. The article is adapted here with the kind permission of the editors of *Great Plains Quarterly*.

2. Peters, *All Things Common*, 116–18 and "Process of Colony Division"; Janzen and Stanton, *Hutterites in North America*, 235–40.

3. Ryan, "Hutterite Settlements"; Riley, *Hutterites and Their Agriculture*.

4. Evans and Peller, "Hutterite Demography."

5. Doe River Farm is the daughter colony of Craigmyle Colony, which is located in Starland County between Delia and Hanna. The distance between the two colonies is about 700 kilometers.

6. For details, see Evans, "Some Developments" and "Hutterites in Alberta."

7. The five longer-distance Schmiedeleut moves all involved daughter colonies established in Minnesota, such as Pembroke, South Dakota, to Starland, Minnesota, 346 kilometers; and Fordham, South Dakota, to Altona, Minnesota, 295 kilometers.

8. Examples would be Craigmyle to Bear Canyon, Alberta, 726 kilometers; Cluny to Silver Valley, Alberta, 740 kilometers; and Ewelme, Alberta, to Raymore, Saskatchewan, 690 kilometers.

9. The number of Schmiedeleut colonies establishing daughter colonies during the 1990s may reflect the period of turmoil experienced when the clan group split into two groups. A colony division may have occurred to resolve irreconcilable differences within colonies. See Janzen and Stanton, *Hutterites in North America*, 62–67.

10. *Calgary Herald*, September 30, 2016.

11. Colony visit, July 13, 2016.

12. Springdale Colony was established from Milford, Alberta, in 1959, but this was an individual decision, and the new colony was located close to White Sulphur Springs, far removed from any previous settlement.

13. Thomas, "Survey of Hutterite Groups," 65.

14. These colonies all have randomly organized sites, unlike most colonies. See chap. 9 for details.

15. Originally referred to as Espanola Colony, it is now named Spokane. See Gross, *Hutterite Way*.

16. *Spokane (WA) Spokesman Review*, April 23, 2017.

17. *Spokane (WA) Spokesman Review*, April 23, 2017.

18. Lobb and Agnew, *Hutterites and Saskatchewan*; Serl, "Final Report."

19. Spring Creek, Alberta, to Crystal Lake, Saskatchewan, Dariusleut farm; Mixburn, Alberta, to Winding River, Saskatchewan, Dariusleut farm; Rocklake, Alberta, to Loreburn, Saskatchewan, Lehrerleut farm; and Jenna, Alberta, to Garden Plane, Saskatchewan, Lehrerleut farm.

20. See Barker, "Understanding Business." An extensive survey of colony managers found that about one-third of the colonies had nonfarm businesses, but this figure included the Lehrerleut, who have very few. Overall income from nonfarm sources was only 6 percent, but it would be much higher among the Schmiedeleut. These developments are discussed more fully in chap. 11.

21. McCurry, "Study of Recent Hutterite Outmigration"; Kant, *Hutterites of South Dakota*; Janzen and Stanton, *Hutterites in North America*, 215–17.

22. Typical quota costs: 13,000 laying birds at $400 per bird, $5.2 million; 100 milk cows at $40,000 per cow, $4 million; possible addition of 20,000 broiler chickens at $200 per bird, $4 million.

23. Interview, MacMillan Colony, June 2015. Peace View Colony has postponed investing in a new dairy because the future of supply management is uncertain, interview, July 2013.

24. Janzen and Stanton, *Hutterites in North America*.

25. The Nine, *Hutterites*; Alleway, "How to Get to Heaven"; Kelly Hofer, *Hutterites*.

7. The Driving Force behind Diffusion

1. This chapter is based on Evans and Peller, "Brief History of Hutterite Demography," an article I coauthored with Peter Peller. I acknowledge with gratitude his major contribution, particularly the method he developed for unpacking the U.S. 2010 Census to provide information on Hutterite numbers. The article is adapted here with the kind permission of the editors of *Great Plains Quarterly*. Until fairly recently, Hutterites have successfully kept all but a handful of their number on the colonies. Permanent defection has been less than 5 percent. Change in this area is discussed later in this chapter.

2. Eaton and Weil, *Culture and Mental Disorders*.

3. Eaton and Mayer, *Man's Capacity to Reproduce*.

4. Sheps, "Analysis of the Reproductive Patterns"; Cook, "North American Hutterites"; Mange, "Growth and Inbreeding."

5. Friedmann, "Hutterite Census for 1969"; Hofer, *History of the Hutterites*.

6. The names and addresses of colonies are much easier to find than population data. Hutterites in both Alberta and Manitoba have published a series of directories, such as *The Holden Hutterite Directory, 2008* and *Hutterite Directory, 2011*.

7. One exception is Nonaka, Miura, and Peter, "Recent Fertility Decline."

8. Details of these and other sources are included in the bibliography.

9. Peter, *Dynamics of Hutterite Society*, 154–55.

10. Evans, "Alberta Hutterite Colonies."

11. Janzen and Stanton, *Hutterites in North America*, xiii; Katz and Lehr, *Inside the Ark*, 202. It should be noted that in the second edition of their book (2014), Katz and Lehr provide the number 48,500, which is much more in line with our own calculations, though they do not discuss in any detail how they arrived at this figure.

12. I acknowledge with gratitude the work done by Michael McCurry at South Dakota State University and his generosity in sharing his methods with me.

13. Statistics Canada, "Selected Collective Dwelling"; U.S. Census Bureau, "2010 Census Block Boundary Files" and "Table P12: Sex by Age."

14. Statistics Canada, "Type of Collective Dwelling"; Birch Hills Colony, *Hutterite Telephone & Address Directory*.

15. Pratt, "Anabaptist Explosion"; Cook, "Pockets of High Fertility."

16. See the graph in Katz and Lehr, *Inside the Ark*, appendix 3, 229.

17. Eaton and Mayer, *Man's Capacity to Reproduce*, 39.

18. Eaton and Mayer, *Man's Capacity to Reproduce*, 47.

19. Laing, "Declining Fertility."

20. The parameters used in the formulas were derived from 50 nations with reliable statistics for the period 1955–60. The accuracy of the equations when applied to data for later time periods might be questioned.

21. McCurry, "Study of Recent Hutterite Outmigration."

22. Janzen, "Hutterites and the Bruderhof."

23. Katz and Lehr, *Inside the Ark*, 27.

24. Eaton and Mayer, *Man's Capacity to Reproduce*, 32.

25. Morgan, "Mortality Changes."

26. I have found no statistics on this topic but have noticed several newspaper reports. See, for example, "Tragic Shooting on Colony," *Edmonton Journal*, April 12, 2008; "John Waldner Killed in an Accident," *Ottawa Citizen*, September 19, 2004; "Community Mourns Teen Accident," *Calgary Herald*, November 25, 1996.

27. Eaton and Mayer, *Man's Capacity to Reproduce*, 22.

28. Peter, *Dynamics of Hutterite Society*, 169.

29. Eaton and Mayer, *Man's Capacity to Reproduce*, 47.

30. Peter, *Dynamics of Hutterite Society*, 170.

31. Nonaka, Miura, and Peter, "Recent Fertility Decline."

32. It also suggests that demographic trends on the colonies can be affected by the behavior of the host society, as I argue later in this chapter.

33. For the methodology used to calculate these values, see Hauer, Baker and Brown, "Indirect Estimates."
34. Eaton and Mayer, *Man's Capacity to Reproduce*, 11.
35. Laing, "Declining Fertility," 298.
36. Morgan and Holmes, "Population Structure."
37. Boldt, "Recent Development."
38. McCurry, "Study of Recent Hutterite Outmigration."
39. Janzen and Stanton, *Hutterites in North America*, 66.
40. The Canadian Census amalgamates the figures for the three younger age cohorts, which cannot therefore be presented as a pyramid.
41. Hostetler, *Hutterite Society*, 143.
42. Ingoldsby and Stanton, "Hutterites and Fertility Control."
43. White, "Declining Fertility."
44. For a thorough analysis of defection, see Janzen and Stanton, *Hutterites in North America*, 240–52; see also McCurry, "Study of Recent Hutterite Outmigration"; Rich, "Hutterite Defectors."
45. Hartse, "Social and Religious Change."
46. The Nine, *Hutterites*.
47. Janzen and Stanton, *Hutterites in North America*, xii.
48. Laing, "Declining Fertility," 305.
49. White, "Declining Fertility," 60.
50. Peter, *Dynamics of Hutterite Society*, 161.
51. Samuel Hofer, *Hutterites*, 173.
52. Evans, "Alberta Hutterite Colonies," 51.
53. Boldt, "Plain People"; Boldt and Roberts, "Decline of Hutterite Population Growth."
54. Ingoldsby, "Hutterite Family in Transition," 391.
55. Here I am using the term "controlled acculturation" loosely. Eaton measured change in the written regulations of the Schmiedeleut. But the gradual adoption of birth control does conform to his definition: "It is the process by which one culture accepts a practice from another culture, but integrates the new practice into its own existing value system." Eaton, "Controlled Acculturation," 338.
56. White, "Declining Fertility," 68. This development has also been reported in Amish and Mennonite societies. See Ericksen et al., "Fertility Patterns and Trends"; Stevenson, Everson, and Crawford, "Changes in Completed Family Size."
57. Ingoldsby and Stanton, "Hutterites and Fertility Control," 141.
58. Quoted in Katz and Lehr, *Inside the Ark*, 90. A young mother with four children told us almost exactly the same thing during a colony visit in 2013.

59. Hostetler, Hutterite Society, 210; Ingoldsby, "Hutterite Family in Transition," 380.
60. In 1965 A. J. Hooke, minister of municipal affairs, predicted the disappearance of Hutterite culture: "I am convinced that there will be no Hutterite problem in 20 years as the younger people take over there will be a trend away from colonies; the problem will solve itself." *Red Deer (AB) Advocate*, April 8, 1965. See also Frideres, "Death of Hutterite Culture"; Peter, "Death of Hutterite Culture"; Boldt, "Death of Hutterite Culture."

8. Bones of Contention

1. A version of this chapter was published as Evans, "Some Factors Shaping the Expansion." It is adapted here with the kind permission of the editors of *Canadian Ethnic Studies*
2. Land Sales Prohibition Act, 1942, c. 16.
3. *Calgary Herald*, February 12, 14, 1947. For context, see Breen, "1947."
4. Communal Property Act, 1947, c. 16. The full text of the act is included as an appendix in Government of Alberta, *Report on Communal Property*.
5. Flint, *Hutterites*. Peters, *All Things Common*, has a chapter titled "Hutterian Expansion, a Cause of Controversy"; see also Palmer, "Hutterite Land Expansion Controversy"; Sanders, "Hutterites"; Evans, "Spatial Bias"; Janzen, *Limits on Liberty*.
6. "Hutterite Freedom," *Calgary Herald*, November 7, 1972.
7. "Tory MLA Wants Limits on Farm Size," *Edmonton Journal*, January 18, 2000.
8. "Hutterites Offended by MLA's Farm-Size Bill," *Edmonton Journal*, January 23, 2000.
9. Interestingly, the same fears seem to have motivated ex-legislator Bob Sivertsen in his attempts to organize a boycott of Hutterite goods in Havre, Montana. *Missoula Current*, June 25, 2019.
10. Since 1973 there have been five cases of Alberta colonies establishing daughter colonies in Saskatchewan: Jenner to Garden Plane, Sandhills to Eagle Creek, Holt to Belle Plaine, Ewelma to Raymore, and Valley View to Spring Water.
11. Government of Alberta, *Report on Communal Property*, 80.
12. Statistics Canada, "Type of Collective Dwelling."
13. Although the focus of the chapter is on Alberta and the particular shifts and changes of perception that have taken place there, the story of hostility toward Hutterite expansion and the issues raised by protagonists are remarkably similar elsewhere. See, for instance, Huntley,

"Discrimination against the Hutterites"; Gillis, "A Built-In Advantage"; "Hutterite Advantage," letter to the editor, *Maclean's* 124 (January 17, 2011): 7.

14. Marsh, "Alberta's Quiet Revolution."
15. Government of Alberta, *Report on Communal Property.*
16. Hoeppner, *Ordinary Genius,* 236.
17. "Request to Hutterites for Silence Explained," *Calgary Herald,* January 13, 1973.
18. "Hutterites Told Don't Stir Public," *Calgary Herald,* January 12, 1973.
19. "Premier Stands Firm on Repeal," *Calgary Herald,* February 19, & February 24, 1973.
20. "Vulcan Remains Firm: Hutterites Aren't Welcome," *Lethbridge* (AB) *Herald,* March 23, 1973.
21. Hoeppner, *Ordinary Genius,* 241–42.
22. Hoeppner, *Ordinary Genius,* 242.
23. "Fear of Hutterites Easing, but Still There," *Toronto Globe and Mail,* November 29, 1973.
24. For example, Fairview to Grandview, New Elm to Ponderosa, and Springpoint to Ridge Valley.
25. Government of Alberta, *Interim Report to the Minister of Municipal Affairs;* Government of Alberta, *Reports to the Minister,* October 1974 and 1975.
26. "Hutterite Land Purchases Regulated by Board," *Medicine Hat* (AB) *News,* September 8, 1980.
27. "Smiles Making the Hutterites Feel at Home—at Last," *Edmonton Journal,* November 21, 1979.
28. "Anti-expansion Group Still Pushes;" *Lethbridge* (AB) *Herald,* January 24, 1983; "Beware the Hutterites," *Alberta Report,* December 20, 1983.
29. "Hutterites Battle Odds to Establish New Colony," *Medicine Hat* (AB) *News,* May 12, 1983.
30. "Hutterite Expansion Sparks Debate," *Edmonton Journal,* May 10, 1989.
31. Erskine Colony bought a block of land for its daughter colony Alix later the same month. "Hutterite Plan Tearing Community Apart," *Edmonton Journal,* May 28, 1989.
32. Ken Hoeppner, personal communication, March 2012.
33. "Province Controlling Growth of Hutterite Colonies," *Edmonton Journal,* May 11, 1989.
34. "Province Controlling Growth of Hutterite Colonies," *Edmonton Journal,* May 11, 1989.
35. Government of Alberta, *Interim Report to the Minister of Municipal Affairs,* 5.

36. Government of Alberta, *Interim Report to the Minister of Municipal Affairs*, 17.

37. "Hutterite Guidelines Are Discriminatory," *Edmonton Journal*, May 13, 1989.

38. "The Hutterites Again," *Edmonton Journal*, May 12, 1989.

39. This was mentioned as a possibility by Don Getty during the Stettler by-election and later by Ray Speaker, the new minister of municipal affairs. See also "Hutterites Urged to Choose Sparse Regions," *Edmonton Journal*, January 10, 1990.

40. For decades our image of the Hutterites was shaped by Hostetler and Huntington, *Hutterites in North America*, and Hostetler, *Hutterite Society*.

41. For a comprehensive new treatment of the Hutterites, see Janzen and Stanton, *Hutterites in North America*.

42. Janzen and Stanton, *Hutterites in North America*, 62–73; Kraybill and Bowman, *On the Backroad to Heaven*, 283n3; Janzen, "Hutterites and the Bruderhof."

43. Samuel Hofer, *Hutterites*, 15; Scheer, "Hutterian German Dialect."

44. There are hundreds of accounts of this dispute spread over a three-year period. For a summary, see Ogilvie, "Failure of Proportionality Tests." See also *Calgary Herald*, November 30, 2007, through to *Edmonton Journal*, March 3, 2010; Andy, Kurt, and Shawn Wipf of Viking Colony, full-page advertisement, *Alberta Views* (July–August 2009).

45. Janzen and Stanton, *Hutterites in North America*, 170.

46. Barker, "Understanding Business."

47. Evans, "Some Developments."

48. Hostetler, *Hutterite Society*, 185–90; Peters, "Process of Colony Division"; Evans, "Some Developments," 334.

49. "Deer Field Colony under Construction: Hutterville to Split," *Lethbridge (AB) Herald*, October 3, 1990.

50. Pine Hill bought land in 1990 and split in 2000, establishing daughter colony Rainbow. *Red Deer (AB) Advocate*, February 27, 1990.

51. On figure 22 in chapter 6, for instance, see Clearview Colony, Lomond, and High River. Elsewhere, examples can be found from both Leut, but they are more common among the Dariusleut. Gadsby (Dariusleut), 8 pieces of land; Manville (Dariusleut), 9; Three Hills (Dariusleut), 10; and Cloverleaf (Lehrerleut), 9.

52. From "Court Rules Hutterites Should Get Taxes Back," *Calgary Herald*, February 1, 1975, to "Hutterite Tax Trial Concludes," *Calgary Herald*, November 25, 1978. For analysis, see Esau, *Courts and the Colonies*.

53. Janzen and Stanton, *Hutterites in North America*, 64–73; Janzen, "Hutterites and the Bruderhof."

54. See *Calgary Herald,* May 12, 2006, for the start of the case and *Calgary Herald,* August 20, 2009, for its conclusion. There were more than 50 newspaper citations for this case.

55. Esau, *Courts and the Colonies*; this quotation comes from the book cover. For discussion, see 79 and "Concluding Reflections."

56. An informal survey found six colonies at one market in Calgary and six others at other markets around the city.

57. There is a wonderful photograph of Flames star Jarome Iginla talking to two Hutterite women outside the Saddledome in *Calgary Herald,* October 27, 2009.

58. This process was initiated by Arnold Platt and his committee, which developed an information kit that was circulated to schools. The process is sustained by the number of young teachers who serve in colony schools for a period before returning to classrooms in the cities.

59. Kirkby, *I Am Hutterite*; Hofer, *Born Hutterite*, made into a film by the same name directed by Smith.

60. Allard, "Solace at Surprise Creek"; Nikiforuk, "Community Life."

61. Government of Alberta, *Report on Communal Property*, 1, 15.

62. Epp, "1996."

63. Roger Gibbons of Canada West Foundation, quoted in Rampton, "Urban West Growing."

64. Epp, "1996."

65. Kraybill and Bowman, *On the Backroad to Heaven*, 18.

66. Kraybill and Bowman comment, "We are troubled by folks who limit education, restrict occupations, curb personal freedom, and stifle personal achievement and artistic expression." Kraybill and Bowman, *On the Backroad to Heaven*, 277.

67. "Hutterite Freedom: A First-Class Report," *Calgary Herald,* November 7, 1972.

68. "A Poor Start," *Calgary Herald,* December 9, 1972.

69. "This Is Democracy?," *Lethbridge (AB) Herald,* February 4, 1975.

70. "Hutterite Control Is Racism and Envy," *Medicine Hat (AB) News,* December 4, 1982.

71. Ryan, *Agricultural Economy.*

72. "Rights of Hutterites," *Edmonton Journal,* January 15, 1990.

73. "Religious Persecution," *Calgary Herald,* January 21, 2000; "Stop This Attack on Hutterites," *Edmonton Journal,* January 22, 2000.

74. Zwarun, "Model Citizens"; "Fear of Hutterites Easing, but Still There," *Toronto Globe and Mail,* November 29, 1973. See also *Toronto Globe and Mail,* November 19, 1982; February 3, 1983; March 16, 1984.

75. "Alberta's Hutterites Threatened with Limits on Growth of Farms," *Vancouver Sun,* April 8, 2000.

76. *Toronto Globe and Mail*, November 25, 1982. The resolution did indeed result in a media firestorm and reactions from civil rights watchdogs.

77. "Tory MLA Wants Limits on Farm Size," *Edmonton Journal*, January 18, 2000.

78. *National Post*, January 19, 2000.

79. Vulcan Chamber of Commerce, "Brief to Premier Peter Lougheed."

80. "Hutterites Offended by MLA's Farm-Size Bill," *Edmonton Journal*, January 23, 2000.

81. For discussion of these trends, see Evans, "Hutterites in Alberta."

82. Janzen and Stanton, *Hutterites in North America*, 253–58; McCurry, "Study of Recent Hutterite Outmigration."

83. *Fort Macleod (AB) Gazette*, February 8, 1985.

84. *Edmonton Journal*, May 28, 1989.

85. *Fort Macleod (AB) Gazette*, February 8, 1985.

86. *Fort Macleod (AB) Gazette*, February 8, 1985.

87. Zieglschmid, *Das Klein-Geschichtsbuch*, 631.

88. Of Alberta's forty-two school districts, twenty-four have colony schools. Janzen and Stanton, *Hutterites in North America*, 181. This 2010 account of Hutterite life contains a chapter titled "Education and Cultural Continuity."

89. *Calgary Herald*, October 13, 1997.

90. Ingoldsby and Smith, "Public School Teachers Perspectives," 252.

91. Ingoldsby and Smith, "Role of Discipline," 287.

92. Government of Alberta, *Report on Communal Property*, 32.

93. The Schmiedeleut organize a much larger conference that brings together teachers from both the United States and Canada. Janzen and Stanton, *Hutterites in North America*, 183.

94. Ingoldsby and Smith, "Public School Teachers Perspectives," 253.

95. Roy McMurren, personal communication, June 25, 2009. McMurren was an instructor at Lethbridge College, in Alberta, and had taught several Hutterites about large machines.

96. Janzen and Stanton, *Hutterites in North America*, 184. The authors report that 40 percent of Schmiedeleut One colonies employ Hutterite teachers.

97. MacDonald, "Hutterite Education in Alberta," 134.

98. Quoted in MacDonald, "Hutterite Education in Alberta," 134.

99. *Calgary Herald*, August 19, 1967.

100. *Calgary Herald*, February 11, 1990.

101. *Edmonton Journal*, May 28, 1989.

102. *Edmonton Journal*, May 28, 1989.

103. *Red Deer (AB) Advocate*, November 11, 1996.

104. It could be that my focus on larger newspapers means that I missed reports in smaller local papers. However, in the past, any news of clashes was picked up swiftly by the larger organizations.

105. Huntington, "Living in the Ark."

106. *High River (AB) Times*, February 20, 1958.

107. *Edmonton Journal*, January 23, 2000.

108. *Calgary Herald*, January 14, 1961.

109. Government of Alberta, *Report on Communal Property*, 21.

110. Bennett, *Hutterian Brethren*. In 1977 John Ryan found that 80 percent of Hutterites' farm machinery was purchased within a 40-kilometer radius of a given colony. Purchases of fuel, fertilizer, farm chemicals, and lumber were also made locally. Ryan, *Agricultural Economy*.

111. *Edmonton Journal*, May 28, 1989.

112. *Red Deer (AB) Advocate*, November 11, 1996.

113. Janzen and Stanton, *Hutterites in North America*, 280; Barker, "Understanding Business."

114. See the work of Jack Stabler over the past thirty years, in particular, Stabler and Olfert, "Economic Structure."

115. *Eagleview (AB) Post*, July 2, 1990.

116. *Fort Macleod (AB) Gazette*, March 22, 1995. The board required that the colony have an engineer supervise the building of the sewage lagoon and instructed that liquid manure be injected into the ground rather than sprayed on top.

117. *Calgary Herald*, August 15, 1991.

118. *Edmonton Journal*, December 11, 1991; *Lethbridge (AB) Herald*, December 9, 1991. A few years later Beaver County residents were less successful in opposing planned expansion of hog-raising facilities at the newly established Tofield Colony, southeast of Edmonton. The appeal board gave the colony the go-ahead, stating that all suitable methods were being employed to control lagoon odors. *Edmonton Journal*, March 29, 1997.

119. McGarvey, "Alberta Village."

120. This controversy is summarized in Bonta, "Opposition to a New Hutterite Colony."

121. David Waldner, personal communication, July 1, 2020. He also told me about a recent meeting with the National Resource Conservation Board during which the chairman did nothing to prevent open mockery of the Hutterites in attendance, and he spoke with frustration about the long history of hostility in the Vulcan area.

122. *Ottawa Citizen*, September 14, 1997.

123. Colony visit, June 2009. There are 2 kilometers of pipe, a reservoir, and six electric motors, which make water available to a pivot irrigation system.

124. *Calgary Herald*, December 2, 2007.

125. *Spokane (WA) Spokesman Review*, August 2, 2000, April 23, 2002; *Calgary Herald*, August 16, 2006.

126. Brett Penosky, "Opinion: Fair, Respectable and Responsible Solution," *East Central Alberta Review*, June 28, 2018.

127. A doubling time of twenty years would have meant that the 82 colonies that existed in 1972 would have multiplied to 328 by 2012.

128. There have been contrary voices both within the cabinet and among the backbenchers, but as discussed earlier, they had limited effect.

129. Starting from a base of 181 colonies reported in 2009, a doubling time of thirty-two years would mean 362 colonies in 2041, or about 271 in 2025. Defection of individuals, and even renegade colonies, might reduce these totals by 10 to 20 percent, giving a conservative total of 230 colonies in 2025. For growth rates, see Janzen and Stanton, *Hutterites in North America*, 307; Evans, "Alberta Hutterite Colonies," 45.

9. The Legacy of Diffusion

1. This chapter is based on Evans and Peller, "Hutterite Colonies and the Cultural Landscape," an article I coauthored with Peter Peller. His ability to manage large data sets proved invaluable, and without his patient diligence, this analysis could not have been completed. The article is adapted here with the kind permission of the editor of the *Journal of Amish and Plain Anabaptist Studies*. The satellite images used as illustrations for this chapter have been updated from those in the original research so as to provide the best resolution possible.

2. Data retrieved May 2016 from GAMEO and Hutterian Brethren, *HB Directory*.

3. Over the course of forty years I have visited some 125 colonies.

4. Statistics Canada, "Type of Collective Dwelling."

5. First proposed by Popper and Popper in the late 1980s. See Popper and Popper, "Great Plains." For an overview of the debate, see Manning, *Rewilding the West*.

6. This is not a historical phenomenon, but rather an ongoing process. Thirty years ago the farm population of Alberta numbered 176,940 and made up 7 percent of the province's population. Statistics Canada Agriculture Division, "Trends and Highlights." In 2011 the corresponding numbers were 129,810 and 3.6 percent. Statistics Canada, CANSIM Table 004-0126.

7. Epp, "1996."

8. See the work of Jack Stabler over the past thirty years, in particular, Stabler, *Changing Role of Rural Communities*, and Stabler and Olfert, "Economic Structure."

9. The average time between colony splits is thirty years. This would mean 237 new colonies in the period 2010–25, for a total of 752, less some defections.

10. In 2011 in Alberta there were 165 Hutterite colonies and 95 census villages. Statistics Canada, "Geosuite: 2011 Census." The mean population of the Hutterites colonies was 95 and for the census villages was 408, and 15,600 Hutterites made up approximately 12 percent of the total farm population. See note 6. Statistics Canada, "2011 Census of Canada."

11. Hostetler, *Hutterite Society*, 156; Janzen and Stanton, *Hutterites in North America*, xiii; Melland, "Change in Hutterite House Types."

12. Main Centre Colony in Saskatchewan is another example where residential buildings have been completely replaced. Janzen cites the example of Miller Colony, Montana, where all the new houses on the daughter colony and the home place were built to the same specifications at the same time. "They were designed identically in layout and furnishings, though with differences related to family size." Janzen and Stanton, *Hutterites in North America*, 57.

13. Hostetler, *Hutterite Society*, 153.

14. Hostetler, *Hutterite Society*, 155.

15. Sixty-one colonies (14 percent) show slight deviation from north-south or east-west orientation. Examples are Huron and Milltown in Manitoba, and Camrose and Ferrybank in Alberta.

16. Katz and Lehr, *Inside the Ark*, 190. The author is referring to a "living unit" or apartment in one of the old frame houses, which were home to as many as eight families under one roof.

17. Ryan, *Agricultural Economy*, 29; Becker, "Hutterites," part 1.

18. Melland, "Changes in Hutterite House Types," 209.

19. The figures are Dariusleut, 19; Lehrerleut, 26; and Schmiedeleut, 21.

20. Hostetler, *Hutterite Society*, 156.

21. Janzen and Stanton, *Hutterites in North America*, 62.

22. Becker, "Hutterites," 137.

23. Ryan, *Agricultural Economy*, 24

24. Katz and Lehr, *Inside the Ark*, 190.

25. Becker, "Hutterites," 137–38.

26. I am grateful to an anonymous reviewer of a draft of this chapter for this additional information.

27. Becker, "Hutterites," Part 3.
28. Ryan, *Agricultural Economy*, 26.
29. Janzen and Stanton, *Hutterites in North America*.
30. Becker, "Hutterites," 137.
31. Huntington, "Ideology, History, and Agriculture."
32. Raymore (2003) in Saskatchewan and Haven (1989) and Neuhof (1994) in Minnesota are other examples of colonies with plans that are still evolving.
33. It is interesting that these colonies are the ones that have welcomed outsiders from the media. King Ranch Colony was explored in *American Colony: Meet the Hutterites*, a 10-episode documentary on the National Geographic Channel in 2012. Surprise Creek was featured in an article in *National Geographic* (Allard, "Solace at Surprise Creek"). It is perhaps unfortunate that such atypical colonies should be portrayed as the norm to the general public. In Alberta, the focus on Standoff Colony by Karl Peter and the Glenbow Museum is rather similar (see the photos in Spiteri and Dempsy, *Hutterites*).
34. Interviews, Sandhills Colony, June 2014, and Ridge Valley Colony, July 2013. On these occasions, the topic came up in general conversation. Because I had not realized how common single-family units were, I did not make them a focus of inquiry.

10. Making a Living

1. An earlier version of this chapter was published as Evans, "Hutterite Agriculture in Alberta." The article is adapted here with the kind permission of the editor of *Agricultural History*.
2. Analysis has to be limited to a single ecological and political regime. While Hutterite agriculture throughout North America is framed by the same belief system, the details are very different. For example, colonies in Canada adjust their strategies to maximize benefits from supply management arrangements for milk, poultry, and eggs. Colonies in neighboring Montana respond to federal land management initiatives.
3. Bennett, *Hutterian Brethren*, 162.
4. This has often resulted in resentment. Relations between Hutterites and their rural neighbors are reviewed in chap. 8.
5. Taber, "America Loves the Idea."
6. Bennett, *Hutterian Brethren*.
7. Ryan, *Agricultural Economy*. See also Janzen and Stanton, *Hutterites in North America*, chap. 9.
8. Statistics Canada and product marketing boards will not isolate data on Hutterite production for privacy reasons. The *Vancouver Sun*

obtained a special tabulation from Statistics Canada by in 1993, but our request for similar data was denied. This report on Hutterite agriculture in Alberta is based on my years of interest in the Brethren and an attempt to stay abreast of the scholarly and popular media reports concerning them. I have had the privilege and pleasure of visiting many colonies. In recent years I was able to visit eleven of the twelve colonies in the Peace River District. During 2016 I interviewed the leaders of the colonies chosen as case studies, and in 2018 I revisited a number of colonies in Manitoba and South Dakota. I am very grateful for the hospitality, patience, and courtesy with which I have been welcomed.

9. Hutterites owned 607,500 of 21 million hectares of farmland in the province and produced $344 million of the $7.9 billion gross farm receipts. These figures were obtained through a special inquiry initiated by the *Vancouver Sun*. *Vancouver Sun*, April 8, 2000.

10. For example, Janzen and Stanton, *Hutterites in North America*. As of 2010, Hutterites in Montana produced more than 90 percent of the state's hogs and 98 percent of its eggs. In South Dakota, 50–60 percent of the state's hogs were raised on Hutterite colonies. Janzen and Stanton, *Hutterites in North America*, 212.

11. *Fort Macleod (AB) Gazette*, October 29, 2014, February 25, 2015.

12. *Claresholm Local Press*, February 8, 2017; *Signal*, Rycroft, September 2, 2014; *Alaska Highway News*, August 18, 2016.

13. Statistics Canada, "Type of Collective Dwelling."

14. Calculations were based on the assumption that the average size of colonies in Alberta was 12,000 acres. See Barker, "Understanding Business."

15. Government of Alberta, *Report on Communal Property*, Appendix E.

16. Evans, "Alberta Hutterite Colonies," 57.

17. For the purposes of this study, I visited the colony in the Peace Country in 2013 and the other four during the summer of 2016.

18. Interestingly, the colony's minister explained in 2013 that a neighbor was asking $500,000 for 160 acres, which the Hutterites wanted to round out their land.

19. Government of Alberta, *Report on Communal Property*, 8. The Communal Property Act was repealed in March 1973 because it conflicted with the provincial bill of rights.

20. Research director of Egg Farmers of Alberta, personal communication, July 17, 2016; "How Does an Egg Farm Work?," *Calgary Herald*, October 26, 2013.

21. Kraybill, Johnson-Weiner, and Nolt, *Amish*, 293. However, there is a small-scale but widespread black market. Women knit and crochet articles that are sold to tourists.

22. Janzen's analysis of gender relationships is both penetrating and amusing. He emphasizes that although women may not have a formal presence on the colony management committee, they exert considerable indirect influence. He also points out that Hutterite women are often better read than male Hutterites and are playing a growing role in Hutterite education. Janzen and Stanton, *Hutterites in North America*, 219–26; see also Ingoldsby, "Hutterite Family in Transition."

23. Karl Peter notes that "unemployable and idle young men are a source of social problems, undermining the social order of the community." Peter, *Dynamics of Hutterite Society*, 160.

24. Samuel Hofer, *Hutterites*, 128. Only two of the men returned to the colony.

25. Conkin, *Two Paths to Utopia*, 55.

26. Rockyford and District History Book Society, *Where We Crossed*, 67; Evans and Peller, "Hutterites Come to Alberta."

27. Knight, "Magrath Area's Rockport Hutterite Colony."

28. Colony visit, Granum Colony, August 1, 2018.

29. Gietz, "Potential for Soybeans in Alberta."

30. Ron Gietz, personal communication, August 13, 2018.

31. The colonies raise about 80 percent of the 6.2 million turkeys grown in the state. Cobb, "Color Them Plain."

32. I am extremely grateful to Jeff Sveen, a lawyer with the firm of Siegel, Barnett and Schulz of Aberdeen, South Dakota, who met with me to tell me the story of Dakota Turkey Growers, with the permission of his clients, May 17, 2018. He has worked with the colonies for twenty-five years. See also the Dakota Turkey Growers website (doing business as Dakota Provisions), https://dakotaprovisions.com.

33. PBS NewsHour, "South Dakota Town Embraces New Immigrants Vital to Meat Industry," July 2, 2016, https://www.pbs.org/newshour /show/south-dakota-town-embraces-new-immigrants-vital-to-meat -industry. One colony manager reminded me that the colonies are also exposed to the risks faced by food-processing companies—however diligent they are—of an outbreak of *E. coli* or salmonella.

34. Colony visit, Granum Colony, August 1, 2018. Leonard Hofer's daughter lives at South Peace, and he had recently returned from a four-day visit there.

35. Colony visit, Viking Colony, June 28, 2018.

36. Guenther, "New Venture."

37. Colony visit, Iron Creek Colony, June 28, 2018.

38. *Great Falls Tribune*, "$6.6 million sorting plant coming to Great Falls," September 2, 2016. The adoption of cage-free nesting systems is part of the deal with Costco.

39. Janzen and Stanton, *Hutterites in North America*, 5.
40. The brand name Hutterite Gardens is available at my local co-op in Calgary.
41. Thirteen colonies in southern Saskatchewan are pursuing this experiment.
42. Colony visits, Sandhills and Grandview Colonies; Janzen and Stanton, *Hutterites in North America*, 211.
43. Urban farmers' markets are usually open on Sundays; the colonies employ non-Hutterites to open their stalls on a limited basis.

11. Beating the Squeeze

1. A version of this chapter is to be published in a forthcoming volume edited by Kenny Wollman, titled *Navigating Tradition and Innovation*. The essay is adapted here with the kind permission of the editor.
2. Peters, *All Things Common*, 107.
3. Eaton, "Controlled Acculturation," 331–40.
4. Quoted in Guenther, "A New Venture."
5. For an overview, see Janzen and Stanton, *Hutterites in North America*, 235–40; Hostetler, *Hutterite Society*, 185–90. For a case study, see Peters, "Process of Colony Division."
6. Schlabach, "Historiography of Mennonites and Amish," 61.
7. Bennett, *Hutterian Brethren*, 69, 185–87.
8. Radtke, *Hutterites in Montana*.
9. Government of Alberta, *Report on Communal Property*.
10. Ryan, *Agricultural Economy*.
11. Janzen and Stanton, *Hutterites in North America*, 236.
12. Katz and Lehr, *Inside the Ark*, 103.
13. Hutterite colonies in the United States do not have to purchase quotas; however, their returns from milk, eggs, and poultry are much lower than the price-supported ceilings mandated in Canada.
14. Hausmann, "Working at the Hutterites," 16.
15. Colony visit, July 2016.
16. "Business Lessons from the Colonies," *AgAdvance*, September 22, 2014. Tait is the director of Hutterite services with MNP, a financial consulting company that has acted as advisor to 95 percent of the Hutterites in western Canada for over fifty years.
17. Agriculture and Agri-Food Canada, "Canadian Agricultural Outlook 2017," https://m.farms.com/news/canadian-agricultural-outlook-2017-119180.aspx.
18. Gloy, Boehlje, and Widmar, "Great Margin Squeeze."
19. Blacksheep Strategy, "Farm Shift," 14.

20. Katz and Lehr, *Inside the Ark*, 104.
21. In Ontario, Alberta, and Saskatchewan, planning approval can be obtained in two to four months, while in Manitoba, it takes more than a year. *Western Producer*, December 7, 2017.
22. Blacksheep Strategy, "Farm Shift," 41.
23. See chap. 10; see also "Montana Hutterites Key to Region's Hog Industry," *Grand Forks Herald*, November 26, 2013; Kant, *Gentle People*, 7.
24. Janzen and Stanton, *Hutterites in North America*, 197.
25. Peters, *All Things Common*, 106.
26. Blacksheep Strategy, "Farm Shift," 43; Kant, *Hutterites of South Dakota*, 21.
27. Colony visit, Codesa Colony, July 13, 2013. For general context, see Evans, "Hutterite Agriculture in Alberta."
28. "Business Lessons from the Colonies," *AgAdvance*, September 22, 2014.
29. See chap. 9 in this book.
30. Hausmann, "Working at the Hutterites," 55.
31. Hostetler, *Hutterite Society*, 42. Hostetler lists more than 30 different crafts.
32. Janzen and Stanton, *Hutterites in North America*, 29.
33. Hostetler, *Hutterite Society*, 125.
34. Conkin, *Two Paths to Utopia*, 52–55.
35. Kleinsasser died in August 2017. His obituaries hint at his controversial leadership style. To some, he was "energetic, creative and visionary" and should be recognized as one of the greatest Hutterite leaders. *Winnipeg Free Press*, August 9, 2017. To others, his death "marked the end of the most internally divisive era in our 500 years of existence." Kirkby, "New Bishop." See also *Mennonite World Review*, September 5, 2017.
36. For an account of the interaction between the Hutterites and the Bruderhof, and Kleinsasser's role, see Preston, "Jacob's Ladder."
37. Samuel Hofer, *Hutterites*. John Ryan, an economic geographer at the University of Winnipeg who was a close acquaintance of Kleinsasser's, expressed a similar idea: "Jake is ahead of his time. He says 'In order to survive, we will have to change. In the past, Hutterites were craftsmen, not farmers. Just because we were farmers for the past hundred years or so doesn't mean we'll always be farmers.'" Preston, "Jacob's Ladder," 80.
38. Esau, *Courts and the Colonies*.
39. Janzen and Stanton, *Hutterites in North America*, 62–73.
40. Professor Jim Frederes, interviewed in Collins, "Hutterite Harvest."
41. Collins, "Hutterite Harvest."

42. For a summary, see Solbak, "Renewable Energy Strategies."

43. Moore, *Southeast Alberta Energy Diversification*, 5.

44. Moore, *Southeast Alberta Energy Diversification*, 7.

45. Castle River, TransAlta, https://www.transalta.com/facilities/plants -operation/castle-river/; *Alberta Venture*, October 1, 2010.

46. *Prairie Populist*, August 1, 2018.

47. *Billings Gazette*, July 9, 2005.

48. *Dawson Creek Mirror*, August 12, 2016.

49. Alberta Utilities Commission (AUC), Decision 2014-074, March 27, 2014, Sunshine Colony; AUC Decision 2010-365, December 8, 2010, O.K. Colony; AUC Decision 2011-173, April 26, 2011, Prairie Home Colony; *Virden Empire-Advance*, June 30, 2018.

50. Dodge and Thompson, "Green Acres."

51. Dodge and Thompson, "Green Acres."

52. When the project came online, the price of electricity was 14–15 cents per kilowatt-hour. Today it is only 2–3 cents. David Vonesch of SkyFire Energy, personal communication, September 14, 2017.

53. Colony visits, July 6, 2016, October 25, 2017. A video of the Brant barn was shown at the annual meeting of the Egg Farmers of Canada, Calgary, Alberta, July 13, 2018.

54. "Barn Aims to Make the Energy It Uses," *Western Producer*, August 18, 2016.

55. Professor Nathan Pelletier, "Net-Zero Egg Barn with Solar Energy Opens in Alberta," *Canadian Government News*, July 27, 2016.

56. Colony visit, October 25, 2017.

57. Egg Farmers of Alberta, "Brant Colony Net-0 Grand Opening."

58. Collins, "Hutterite Harvest."

59. Colony visit, Granum Colony, August 1, 2018.

60. "Solar Farm Proposed for East of Claresholm," *Claresholm Local Press*, August 9, 2017.

61. Daniel Andres, personal communication, August 14, 2018.

62. Colony visit, May 9, 2018.

63. The following paragraphs draw heavily on a personal e-mail from the colony manager, Jacob Waldner, June 6, 2018.

64. CBC News, January 22, 2012, mentioned that sales amounted to $2 million, more than half of the annual turnover of the colony.

65. Morgan, "Power of Change."

66. The original digestion technology came from Luxembourg. Europe is twenty years ahead of North America in this area because of high costs of energy and government subsidies.

67. AESA, "More from Manure," 2.

68. *Manure Manager*, July 10, 2008, https://www.manuremanager.com/manure-biogas-developer-ready-for-round-two-as-green-power-trend-grows-1598/.

69. "Hutterite Colonies Greening Up Their Act," *Winnipeg Free Press*, March 28, 2018. Interestingly enough, the residences at Vermillion Colony are heated with a geothermal system.

70. Janzen and Stanton, *Hutterites in North America*, 215; Cobb, "Color Them Plain"; Kant, *Hutterites of South Dakota*, 21.

71. Colony visit, Millbrook Colony, South Dakota, May 16, 2018.

72. For detailed information about geothermal systems, see the website of Enertech Global, https://enertechusa.com/.

73. "New Hutterite Colony Planned near Hillsboro," *Rapid City Journal*, December 18, 2011.

74. Collins, "Hutterite Harvest."

75. Colony visit, Jumbo Lake Colony, August 1, 2018.

76. Colony visit, White Lake Colony, August 1, 2018.

77. These include Pilbroch, Hillview, Rockport, and Box Elder in Alberta; Leask, Springwater, and Arm River in Saskatchewan; and Sommerfeld and Decker in Manitoba.

78. Colony visit, June 27, 2018.

79. "Valley View Hutterites Launch Ambitious Plans for New Colony," *Mountain View Gazette*, May 7, 2013. Several other colonies have built manufacturing facilities at daughter colony sites before building residences or agricultural facilities. Examples are Millbrook Colony, in South Dakota, and daughter Spruce Grove, in North Dakota, and Fairview Colony and daughter Wheatland, both in North Dakota.

80. Rogers, "After Centuries of Farming."

81. Hoshowsky, "Alberta-Based Manufacturing Expertise."

82. Colony visit, Baker Colony, May 11, 2018. This was a most interesting visit. Jonathan Maendel explained the unique origins of the colony and its commitment to education and outreach in Haiti and Nigeria. See also the company website at https://www.betterair.ca/; Janzen and Stanton, *Hutterites in North America*, 216.

83. Colony visit, May 12, 2018; "Whiteshell Colony Farms."

84. Cobb, "Color Them Plain"; Kant, *Hutterites of South Dakota*.

85. Colony visit, May 12, 2018.

86. During the 1980s the Schmiedeleut leader Jake Kleinsasser sought to reestablish relations with the Bruderhof, a twentieth-century religious movement. Exchanges of personnel took place in both directions. For an account of this, see Janzen and Stanton, *Hutterites in North America*, 62–73.

87. Pauly Kleinsasser regularly attends European trade fairs and has visited the historic Hutterite sites in Austria and Moravia. He has also traveled to Asia five times in search of countertop materials.

88. Colony visit, Birch Hills Colony, July 16, 2013.

89. Colony visit, Cleardale Colony, July 19, 2013. Other examples of woodworking enterprises are Fab-a-Tek, at White Rock Colony, South Dakota; Mayfield Truss at Mayfield Colony, South Dakota; and Douse Woodworking at Lakeside Colony, Manitoba.

90. "Unfair Competition," CBC News, November 10, 2010.

91. Colony visit, May 10, 2018; see also http://www.domtek.ca.

92. Colony visit, May 10, 2018; William Waldner, personal communication, June 4, 2018.

93. Colony visit, May 16, 2018.

94. *Outdoor Forum*, June 29, 2013.

95. Customer comments, ProComm Builders, https://procommbuilders .com.

96. Maendel, "Who Will Help Recycle?"

97. Colony visit, Clearview Colony, July 21, 2018. John Hofer, the manager, explained that the dairy barn was old-fashioned and due to be replaced, but to make it economic, the colony would have to increase the size of its milking herd. This was deemed impossible because of the costs of milk quotas.

98. A rather similar plastics business at O.K. Colony, south of Raymond, Alberta, failed after two or three years because of high transport costs.

99. Maple Grove Plastics, http://maplegroveplastics.com.

100. Colony visit, Iron Creek Colony, June 28, 2018. Eastend Colony in Saskatchewan handles imports of these top-of-the-line articles and distributes them to other colonies. The door had six locks rather than the customary one near the handle, which was somewhat ironic, as the Hutterites seldom lock anything up.

101. Redekop, "Hutterite Colony Carving."

102. *Western Producer*, November 14, 2017, https://www.producer.com/ daily/alberta-hutterite-colony-ordered-to-pay-wcb-dues-for-workers -in-concrete-plant/.

103. Colony visit, Millerdale Colony, May 16, 2018.

104. Colony visit, Lajord Colony, May 8, 2018.

105. Colony visit, Birch Hills Colony, July 17, 2013.

106. Miami Leather Company, https://www.miamileather.ca.

107. Clear Lake Colony's "Traditional Hutterite" meats, http://www.traditionalhutterite.ca. The year 1547 is a date toward the end of the Hutter-

ites' "golden period" in Moravia. See Janzen and Stanton, *Hutterites in North America*, 20–22.

108. Hausmann, "Working at the Hutterites," 56; Janzen and Stanton, *Hutterites in North America*, 216.

109. Interview with Professor Joanita Kant, South Dakota State University, Brookings, May 15, 2018.

110. Interview with Jonathan Maendel, Baker Colony, Mennonite Conference, Winnipeg, October 31, 2016.

111. Colony visit, Springfield Colony, May 12, 2018. Kleinsasser's thoughts were echoed by Wayne Waldner at Millbrook Colony, South Dakota, which has a number of non-Hutterites working in its feed mill. Colony visit, Millbrook Colony, May 16, 2018.

112. CBC News, November 8, 2010.

113. J. S. R. wrote, "Giving exemption is a slap in the face to other businesses who are already in commercial classification. At this new shop no labor will be hired, no wages will be paid." *Dakota Free Press*, July 8, 2015.

114. *Rapid City Journal*, December 18, 2011.

115. Rogers, *Diffusion of Innovations*. For the geography of diffusion, see Brown, *Diffusion Processes and Location*.

116. Matt. 25:29 (KJV).

117. The following remarks should not be taken as an indictment of all colonies that have not yet adopted nonfarm activities. As explained earlier, some young colonies will employ all their capital to build up their farms, and all their tradespeople will be fully occupied.

118. See chap. 7, note 55.

12. Coda

1. Miller, *Communes in America*, 3.

2. An example is Airlite Plastics Company of Omaha, Nebraska, making Fox Blocks at Iron Creek Colony, Alberta. See chap. 11.

3. Bennett, *Hutterian Brethren*, 173.

Bibliography

AESA (Alberta Environmentally Sustainable Agriculture Council). "More from Manure." *Green Matters* 27 (Spring 2006): 2.

Allard, William Albert. "Solace at Surprise Creek." *National Geographic* 209, no. 6 (June 2006): 120–47.

Alleway, Lynn, dir. *How to Get to Heaven with the Hutterites*. Aired July 3, 2013, on BBC Two.

Anderson, Lawrence C. "Hutterite Colonies: Toponymic Identification." Paper presented at the Tenth Annual Historic Communal Societies Conference, New Harmony, Indiana, 1983.

———. "Prudent Plain People on the Plains and Prairies of North America: The Hutterian Brethren." Unpublished paper, Dakota State History Conference, 1983.

Armishaw, Bradley. "The Hutterites' Story of War Time Migration from South Dakota to Manitoba and Alberta." *Journal of Mennonite Studies* 28 (2010): 225–46.

Barnhart, Gordon. "Calder, James Alexander, 1868–1956." In *Encyclopedia of Saskatchewan*. Regina SK: Canadian Plains Research Center, 2005. https://esask.uregina.ca/entry/calder_james_alexander_1868-1956.jsp.

Beaudoin, Alwynne B. "What They Saw: The Climatic and Environmental Context for Euro-Canadian Settlement in Alberta." *Prairie Forum* 24, no. 1 (Spring 1999): 1–40.

Becker, Jane. "Hutterites Survive 400 Years of Hardship." *Red Deer* (AB) *Advocate*, April 8, 1965.

Becker, Sibylle. "Hutterites: Architecture and Community." Master's thesis, University of Calgary, 1989.

Beiseker Historical Society. *Beiseker's Golden Heritage*. Beiseker AB: Beiseker Historical Society, 1977.

Bennett, John W. "Change and Transition in Hutterite Society." In *Western Canada: Past and Present*, edited by Anthony W. Rasporich, 120–32. Calgary: McClelland and Stewart West, 1975.

———. *The Hutterian Brethren: The Agricultural Economy and Social Organization of a Communal People*. Stanford CA: Stanford University Press, 1967.

Berton, Pierre. *The Great Depression, 1929–1939.* Toronto: McClellend and Stewart, 1990.

Birch Hills Colony. *Hutterite Telephone & Address Directory.* Accessed June 18, 2019. https://hutterite.directory/Hutterite.Directory.pdf.

Blacksheep Strategy. "Farm Shift: Insight from Canada's Leading Farmers." Winnipeg: Blacksheep Strategy, 2009.

———. "Understanding Business on a Colony: A Syndicated Survey of Hutterite Farm Bosses." Winnipeg: Blacksheep Strategy, 2010.

Boldt, Edward D. "The Death of Hutterite Culture: An Alternative Interpretation." *Phylon* 41, no. 4 (1980): 390–95.

———. "The Plain People: Notes on Their Continuity and Change." *Canadian Ethnic Studies* 11 (1979): 17–28.

———. "The Recent Development of a Unique Population: The Hutterites of North America." *Prairie Forum* 8, no. 2 (1983): 235–40.

———. "Structural Tightness, Autonomy and Observability: An Analysis of Hutterite Conformity and Orderliness." *Canadian Journal of Sociology* 3 (1978): 349–63.

Boldt, Edward D., and Lance W. Roberts. "The Decline of Hutterite Population Growth: Causes and Consequences—A Comment." *Canadian Ethnic Studies* 12 (1980): 111–17.

Bonta, Bruce. "Opposition to a New Hutterite Colony." Peaceful Societies Series. University of North Carolina. May 11, 2017. https://peacefulsocieties.uncg.edu/2017/05/11/opposition-new-hutterite-colony/.

Breen, David. "1947: The Making of Modern Alberta." In Payne, Wetherell, and Cavanaugh, *Alberta Formed*, 551–53.

Bright, David. "1919: A Year of Extraordinary Difficulty." In Payne, Wetherell, and Cavanaugh, *Alberta Formed*, 413–41.

Broadfoot, Barry. *Ten Lost Years, 1929–39: Memories of Canadians Who Survived the Depression.* Toronto: McClelland and Stewart, 1997.

Brown, Lawrence A. *Diffusion Processes and Location.* Philadelphia: Regional Science Research Institute, 1968.

Chakravarti, A. K. "Precipitation Deficiency Patterns in the Canadian Prairies, 1921 to 1970." *Prairie Forum* 1, no. 2 (November 1976): 95–110.

Clark, Bertha W. "The Hutterian Communities." Pts. 1 and 2. *Journal of Political Economy* 32, nos. 3 and 4 (1924): 357–74, 468–86.

Cobb, Kathy. "Color Them Plain but Successful." *Fedgazette* 18 (January 2006): 11–13.

Collins, Jeff. "Hutterite Harvest." *The Cache Project.* Season 2, October 12, 2017. Video, available at https://thecacheproject.ca/the-cache-project-season-2/.

Conkin, Paul K. *Two Paths to Utopia*. Lincoln: University of Nebraska Press, 1964.

Cook, Robert C. "The North American Hutterites: A Study in Human Multiplication." *Population Bulletin* 10 (December 1954): 97–107.

———. "Pockets of High Fertility in the United States." *Population Bulletin* 24 (1968): 25–55.

Deets, Lee Emerson. *The Hutterites: A Study in Social Cohesion*. Gettysburg PA: printed by the author, 1939.

Dodge, David, and Dylan Thompson. "Green Acres: The Largest Solar Farm in Western Canada." *Green Energy Futures*. November 16, 2015. http://www.greenenergyfutures.ca/episode/hutterite-solar-western-canada-biggest.

Eaton, Joseph W. "Canada's Scapegoats." *Nation* 169 (1949): 253–54.

———. "Controlled Acculturation: A Survival Technique of the Hutterites." *American Sociological Review* 17 (June 1952): 331–40.

Eaton, Joseph W., and Albert J. Mayer. *Man's Capacity to Reproduce: The Demography of a Unique Population*. Glencoe IL: Free Press, 1954.

Eaton, Joseph W., and Robert J. Weil. *Culture and Mental Disorders*. Glencoe IL: Free Press, 1955.

Egg Farmers of Alberta. "Brant Colony Net-0 Grand Opening." August 23, 2016. YouTube video. https://www.youtube.com/watch?v=G72xHCXYoC0.

Epp, Frank H. *Mennonite Exodus: The Rescue and Resettlement of the Russian Mennonites since the Russian Revolution*. Altona MB: D. W. Friesen, 1962.

———. *Mennonites in Canada, 1786–1920: The History of a Separate People*. Toronto: Macmillan, 1974.

Epp, Roger. "1996: Two Albertas; Rural and Urban Trajectories." In Payne, Wetherell, and Cavanaugh, *Alberta Formed*, 727–48.

Ericksen, Julia A., Eugene P. Ericksen, John A. Hostetler, and Gertrude E. Huntington. "Fertility Patterns and Trends among the Old Order Amish." *Population Studies* 33 (1979): 255–76.

Esau, Alvin J. *The Courts and the Colonies*. Vancouver: University of British Columbia, 2004.

Evans, Simon M. "Alberta Hutterite Colonies: An Exploration of Past, Present and Future Settlement Patterns." *Communal Societies* 30, no. 2 (2010): 27–64.

———. "Dispersal of Hutterite Colonies." Master's thesis, University of Calgary, 1973.

———. "Hutterite Agriculture in Alberta: The Contribution of an Ethnic Isolate." *Agricultural History* 73, no. 4 (Fall 2019): 656–81.

————. "The Hutterites in Alberta: Past and Present Settlement Patterns." In *Essays on the Historical Geography of the Canadian West*, edited by L. A. Rosenvall and S. M. Evans, 145–71. Calgary: University of Calgary Geography Department, 1985.

————. "Some Developments in the Diffusion Patterns of Hutterite Colonies." *Canadian Geographer* 29, no. 4 (1985): 327–39.

————. "Some Factors Shaping the Expansion of Hutterite Colonies in Alberta since the Repeal of the Communal Property Act in 1973." *Canadian Ethnic Studies* 45, no. 1–2 (2013): 203–36.

————. "Spatial Bias in the Incidence of Nativism: Opposition to Hutterite Expansion in Alberta." *Canadian Ethnic Studies* 6, no. 1–2 (1974): 1–16.

Evans, Simon M., and Peter Peller. "A Brief History of Hutterite Demography." *Great Plains Quarterly* 35, no. 1 (Winter 2015): 79–102.

————. "Hutterite Colonies and the Cultural Landscape: An Inventory of Selected Site Characteristics." *Journal of Amish and Plain Anabaptist Studies* 4, no. 1 (Spring 2016): 15–81.

————. "The Hutterites Come to Alberta." *Alberta History* 63, no. 4 (Autumn 2015): 11–19.

————. "Mapping an Ethnic Isolate: The Diffusion of Hutterite Colonies across the Prairies and the Great Plains." *Great Plains Quarterly* 38, no. 4 (Fall 2018): 357–86.

Flint, David. *The Hutterites: A Study in Prejudice*. Toronto: Oxford University Press, 1975.

Francis, R. Douglas, and Herman Ganzevoort. *The Dirty Thirties in Prairie Canada*. Vancouver: Tantalus, 1973.

Frideres, James S. "The Death of Hutterite Culture." *Phylon* 33, no. 3 (1972): 260–65.

Friedmann, Robert. "A Hutterite Census for 1969: Hutterite Growth in One Century, 1874–1969." *Mennonite Quarterly Review* 44 (January 1970): 100–105.

Friedmann, Robert, John Hofer, Hans Meier and John V. Hinde. "Hutterian Brethren (Hutterische Brüder)." *Global Anabaptist Mennonite Encyclopedia Online*. 1989. https://gameo.org/index.php?title=Hutterian_Brethren_(Hutterische_Br%C3%BCder)&oldid=167706.

Friesen, Gerald. *The Canadian Prairies: A History*. Toronto: University of Toronto Press, 1984.

GAMEO (*Global Anabaptist Mennonite Encyclopedia Online*). Last modified November 25, 2020. https://gameo.org.

Gietz, Ron. "The Potential for Soybeans in Alberta." *Alberta Agriculture and Forestry*, August 2014.

Gillis, Charlie. "A Built-In Advantage." *Maclean's* 123, no. 50 (December 27, 2010): 25.

Gloy, Brent, Michael Boehlje, and David A. Widmar. "The Great Margin Squeeze: Strategies for Managing through the Cycle." Purdue University Center for Commercial Agriculture. January 1, 2015. https://ag.purdue .edu/commercialag/home/resource/2015/01/the-great-margin-squeeze -strategies-for-managing-through-the-cycle/.

Government of Alberta. *Report of the Hutterite Investigation Committee.* Edmonton: Queen's Printer, 1959.

———. Select Committee of the Assembly. *Report on Communal Property, 1972.* Edmonton: Queen's Printer, 1972.

———. Special Advisory Committee on Communal Property and Land Use. *An Interim Report to the Minister of Municipal Affairs, October 1973.* Edmonton: Queen's Printer, 1973.

———. Special Advisory Committee on Communal Property and Land Use. *Report to the Minister, October 1974.* Edmonton: Queen's Printer, 1974.

———. Special Advisory Committee on Communal Property and Land Use. *Report to the Minister, October 1975.* Edmonton: Queen's Printer, 1974.

Graham, Laurie. "Hutterites Elect Unique Body to Run Affairs of Each Colony." *Lethbridge (AB) Herald*, August 26, 1965.

Gross, David, comp. *Schmiedeleut Family Record.* 3rd ed. High Bluff MB: Sommerfeld Printshop, 2003.

Gross, Leonard. *The Golden Years of the Hutterites.* Kitchener: Herald Press, 1980.

Gross, Paul S. *The Hutterite Way.* Saskatoon: Freeman Publishing, 1965.

Guenther, Lisa. "A New Venture." *Country Guide*, April 9, 2015.

Hartse, Caroline. "Social and Religious Change among Contemporary Hutterites." *Folk* 36 (1994): 109–30.

Hauer, Matt, Jack Baker, and Warren Brown. "Indirect Estimates of Total Fertility Rate Using Child/Women Ratio: A Comparison with the Bogue-Palmore Method." *PLOS ONE* 8, no. 6 (June 2013).

Hausmann, Sascha Samuel. "Working at the Hutterites: Motivation in a Communitarian Group." Master's thesis, Freie Universitat Berlin, 2017.

Hiebert, Jerald. "The Story of a Pure Church: A Study of Dariusleut Alberta Hutterites, 1918–2000." Master's thesis, Regent College, 2001.

Hoeppner, Ken. *The Ordinary Genius: A Life of Arnold Platt.* Edmonton: University of Alberta Press, 2007.

Hofer, John. *A History of James Valley Hutterite Colony, 1918–2018.* Elie MB: James Valley Book Center, 2019.

————. *The History of the Hutterites*. Winnipeg: W. K. Printer's Aid, 1982.

————. *Treasures of Time: The Hutterian Brethren of Cartier*. Elie MB: Rural Municipality of Cartier, 1985.

Hofer, Kelly. *Hutterites: The Things I Saw Growing Up as a Hutterite Teen.* San Francisco: Blurb Books Canada, 2016.

Hofer, Samuel. *Born Hutterite*. Saskatoon SK: Hofer Publishing, 1991.

————. *The Hutterites: Lives and Images of a Communal People*. Saskatoon SK: Hofer Publishers, 1998.

Holzach, Michael. *The Forgotten People*. Sioux Falls SD: Ex Machina Publishing, 1993.

Hopkins, J. Castell. *Canadian Annual Review of Public Affairs*. Toronto: Canadian Annual Review, 1918.

Horsch, John. *The Hutterian Brethren, 1528–1931: A Story of Martyrdom and Loyalty*. Goshen IN: Mennonite Historical Society, 1931.

Hoshowsky, Robert. "Alberta-Based Manufacturing Expertise." *Business in Focus*, October 1, 2018.

Hostetler, John A. *Hutterite Society*. Baltimore: Johns Hopkins University Press, 1974.

Hostetler, John A., and Gertrude Enders Huntington. *The Hutterites in North America*. New York: Holt, Rinehart and Winston, 1967.

Howard, Joseph Kinsey. "The Hutterites: Puzzle for Patriots." *Pacific Spectator* 2 (Winter 1948): 30–41.

Huntington, Gertrude E. "Ideology, History, and Agriculture: Examples from Contemporary North America." *Culture and Agriculture* 13, no. 45–46 (1993): 21–25.

————. "Living in the Ark, Four Centuries of Hutterite Faith and Community." In *America's Communal Utopias*, edited by Donald E. Pitzer, 319–51. Chapel Hill: University of North Carolina Press, 1997.

Huntley, Susan. "Discrimination against the Hutterites: The Racialization of a Religious Community in Rural Montana." Master's thesis, University of Montana, 2000. ScholarWorks (5527). https://scholarworks.umt.edu/etd/5527.

Hutterian Brethren. HB *Directory*. http://www.hutterites.org/directory.

Ingoldsby, Bron B. "The Hutterite Family in Transition." *Journal of Comparative Family Studies* 32, no. 3 (2001): 377–92.

Ingoldsby, Bron B., and Suzanne R. Smith. "Public School Teachers Perspectives on the Contemporary Hutterite Family." *Journal of Comparative Family Studies* 36, no. 2 (2005): 249–65.

————. "The Role of Discipline in Hutterite Child Rearing." *Family and Consumer Sciences Research Journal* 37, no. 3 (March 2009): 284–97.

Ingoldsby, Bron B., and Max E. Stanton. "The Hutterites and Fertility Control." *Journal of Comparative Family Studies* 29, no. 1 (Spring 1988): 137–42.

Janzen, Rod. "The Hutterites and the Bruderhof: The Relationship between an Old Order Religious Society and a 20th Century Communal Group." *Mennonite Quarterly Review* 79, no. 4 (October 2005): 505–44.

———. *The Prairie People: Forgotten Anabaptists.* Hanover NH: University Press of New England, 1999.

Janzen, Rod, and Max Stanton. *The Hutterites in North America.* Baltimore: Johns Hopkins University Press, 2010.

Janzen, William. *Limits on Liberty: The Experience of Mennonite, Hutterite, and Doukhobor Communities in Canada.* Toronto: University of Toronto, 1990.

Joern, Antony, and Kathleen H. Keeler, eds. *The Changing Prairie: North American Grasslands.* New York: Oxford University Press, 1995.

Jones, David C. *Empire of Dust: Settling and Abandoning the Prairie Dry Belt.* Edmonton: University of Alberta Press, 1987.

Kant, Joanita. *Gentle People: A Case Study of Rockport Colony Hutterites.* Brookings SD: Prairie View Press, 2011.

———. *Hutterites of South Dakota: The Schmiedeleut.* Coral Springs FL: Lumina Press, 2006.

Katz, Yossi, and John Lehr. *Inside the Ark: The Hutterites in Canada and the United States.* Regina SK: Canadian Plains Research Center Press, 2012.

Kells, Edna. "Hutterite Commune." *Maclean's,* March 15, 1937.

Kephart, William M. *The Encyclopedia of Religion.* Detroit: MacMillan Reference, 2005.

Kirkby, Mary-Ann. *I Am Hutterite.* Prince Albert SK: Polka Dot Press, 2007.

———. "New Bishop for Schmiedeleut 1 Hutterites." Polka Dot Press blog, September 12, 2017. https://www.polkadotpress.ca/single-post/2017/09/12/new-bishop-for-schmiedeleut-1hutterites.

Knight, Demi. "Magrath Area's Rockport Hutterite Colony Still Flipping over Pancakes after 90 Years." *Prairie Post West,* April 13, 2018.

Kobayashi, Audrey. "Multiculturalism: Representing a Canadian Institution." In *Place, Culture and Representation,* edited by James S. Duncan and Ley Duncan, 205–6. Toronto: Routledge, 1983.

Kraybill, Donald B., and Carl Desportes Bowman. *On the Backroad to Heaven: Old Order Hutterites, Mennonites, Amish and Brethren.* Baltimore: Johns Hopkins University Press, 2000.

Kraybill, Donald B., Karen M. Johnson-Weiner, and Steven M. Nolt. *The Amish.* Baltimore: Johns Hopkins University Press, 2013.

Kraybill, P. N. *Mennonite World Handbook*. Lombard IL: Mennonite World Conference, 1978.

Laing, L. M. "Declining Fertility in a Religious Isolate: The Hutterite Population of Alberta, Canada, 1951–1971." *Human Biology* 52, no. 2 (May 1980): 288–310.

Lehr, J., and Y. Katz. "The Hutterites' Dilemma: A Closed Society Confronts Diversity, Multiculturalism and Globalization." In *Understanding Diversity: Canada and India*, edited by Om P. Juneja and Sudhi Rajiv, 25–36. New Delhi: Creative Books, 2010.

Lehr, John, Brian McGregor, and Weldon Hiebert. "Mapping Hutterite Colony Diffusion in North America." *Manitoba History* 53 (October, 2006): 29–31.

Lobb, Harold O., and Neil McK. Agnew. *The Hutterites and Saskatchewan: A Study of Intergroup Relations*. Regina SK: Canadian Mental Health Association, Saskatchewan Division, 1953.

Loeb, Mark, Margaret L. Russell, Lorraine Moss, Kevin Fonseca, Julie Fox, David J. D. Earn, Fred Aoki, et al. "Effects of Influenza Vaccination of Children on Infection Rates in Hutterite Communities: A Randomized Trial." *Journal of American Medical Association* 303, no. 10 (March 2010): 943–50.

MacDonald, Robert J. "Hutterite Education in Alberta: A Test Case in Assimilation, 1920–1970." In *Western Canada: Past and Present*, edited by Anthony W. Rasporich, 291–316. Calgary: McClelland and Stewart West, 1975.

Maendel, Linda. "Who Will Help Recycle This Bag?" *Hutterian Brethren* (blog). May 30, 2012. http://www.hutterites.org/category/news/page/6/.

Magrath and District History Association. *Irrigation Builders*. Magrath AB: Magrath and District History Association, 1974.

Mange, Arthur P. "Growth and Inbreeding of a Human Isolate." *Human Biology* 36 (May 1964): 104–33.

Manning, Richard. *Rewilding the West: Restoration in a Prairie Landscape*. Oakland: University of California Press, 2011.

Marsh, James H. "Alberta's Quiet Revolution: 1973 and the Early Lougheed Years." In Payne, Wetherell, and Cavanaugh, *Alberta Formed*, 643–74.

McCurry, Michael W. "A Study of Recent Hutterite Outmigration in South Dakota." PhD diss., South Dakota State University, 2008.

McGarvey, Dan. "Alberta Village Fights Plan for 'Horrible' Animal Feeding Operation on Nearby Hutterite Colony." CBC News, February 20, 2018. https://www.cbc.ca/news/canada/calgary/animal-farming-carmangaye-1.4540303.

Meinig, Donald W. "Cultural Geography." In *Introductory Geography: Viewpoints and Themes*, 97–104. Commission on College Geography, Publication No. 5. Washington DC: Association of American Geographers, 1967.

Melland, John F. "Change in Hutterite House Types." PhD diss., Louisiana State University, 1985.

Miller, Timothy. *Communes in America, 1975–2000*. Syracuse NY: Syracuse University Press, 2019.

Moore, Sandra. *Southeast Alberta Energy Diversification Report: Our Region, Our Jobs, Our Communities*. Medicine Hat: Economic Development Alliance of Southeast Alberta, 2017. http://www.seedsalberta.ca/uploads/1/0/9/3/109320257/seedsmarch2017report.pdf.

Morgan, Geoff. "The Power of Change." *Alberta Venture*, October 1, 2010.

Morgan, Kenneth. "Mortality Changes in the Hutterite Brethren of Alberta and Saskatchewan, Canada." *Human Biology* 55, no. 1 (February 1983): 89–99.

Morgan, Kenneth, and T. Mary Holmes. "Population Structure of a Religious Isolate: The Dariusleut Hutterites of Alberta." In *Current Developments in Anthropological Genetics*, vol. 2, *Ecology and Population Structure*, edited by Michael. H. Crawford and James. D. Mielke, 429–48. New York: Plenum Press, 1982.

Nikiforuk, Andrew. "Community Life." *Equinox* (May–June 1987): 23–43

The Nine. *Hutterites: Our Story to Freedom*. Kearney NE: Risen Son Publishing, 2013.

Nonaka, K., T. Miura, and K. Peter. "Recent Fertility Decline in Dariusleut Hutterites: An Extension of Eaton and Mayer's Hutterite Fertility Study." *Human Biology* 66, no. 3 (June 1994): 411–20.

Ogilvie, Margaret H. "The Failure of Proportionality Tests to Protect Christian Minorities in Western Democracies: Alberta v Hutterian Brethren of Wilson Colony." *Ecclesiastical Law Review* 12, no. 2 (May 2010): 208–14.

Palmer, Howard. "The Hutterite Land Expansion Controversy in Alberta." *Western Canadian Journal of Anthropology* 2 (July 1971): 30–38.

Payne, Michael, Donald Wetherell, and Catherine Cavenaugh. *Alberta Formed Alberta Transformed*. Vol. 2. Calgary: University of Calgary Press, 2006.

Peter, Karl A. "The Death of Hutterite Culture: A Rejoinder." *Phylon* 40, no. 2 (1979): 189–94.

———. *Dynamics of Hutterite Society: An Analytical Approach*. Edmonton: University of Alberta Press, 1987.

Peter, Karl A., and Ian Whitaker. "The Acquisition of Personal Property among Hutterites and Its Social Dimensions." *Anthropologica* 23 (1981): 145–56.

———. "The Changing Role of Hutterite Women." *Prairie Forum* 7 (1982): 267–78.

Peters, Victor. *All Things Common: The Hutterian Way of Life.* 1965. Reprint; New York: Harper and Row, 1971.

———. "The Process of Colony Division among the Hutterites: A Case Study." *International Review of Modern Sociology* 6, no. 1 (1976): 57–64.

Petersen, Hans J. "Hilldale: A Montana Hutterite Colony in Transition." *Rocky Mountain Social Science Journal* 7 (April 1970): 1–7.

Pluzhnikov, Anna, Daniel K. Nolan, Zhiqiang, Tan, Mary Sara McPeek, and Carole Ober. "Correlation of Intergenerational Family Sizes Suggests a Genetic Component of Reproductive Fitness." *American Journal of Human Genetics* 81, no. 1 (2007): 165–69.

Popper, Frank J., and Deborah E. Popper. "The Great Plains from Dust to Dust." *Planning* 53 (1987): 12–18.

Pratt, William F. "The Anabaptist Explosion." *Natural History* 78 (1969): 9–23.

Preston, Brian. "Jacob's Ladder." *Saturday Night* (April 1992): 30–38, 76–80.

Radtke, Hans D. *The Hutterites in Montana: An Economic Description.* Bozeman: Montana State University Agricultural Experimental Station, 1971.

Rampton, Roberta. "Urban West Growing." *Western Producer*, December 7, 2000.

Redekop, Bill. "Hutterite Colony Carving Out Epoxy Niche." *Winnipeg Free Press*, March 7, 2018.

Rich, Mona. "Hutterite Defectors: A Qualitative Assessment of Ebaugh's Role-Exit Model." Master's thesis, University of Manitoba, 1995.

Rideman, Peter. *Confession of Faith.* London: Hodder and Stoughton, 1950.

Riley, Marvin P. *The Hutterites and Their Agriculture: 100 Years in South Dakota.* Brookings: South Dakota State University, 1979.

Riley, M. P., and D. R. Johnson. *South Dakota's Hutterite Colonies, 1874–1969.* Bulletin 566. Brookings: South Dakota State University, 1970. https://openprairie.sdstate.edu/agexperimentsta_bulletins/566/.

Rockyford and District History Book Society. *Where We Crossed the Creek and Settled: Rockyford.* Rockyford AB: Rockyford and District History Book Society, 1980–84.

Rogers, Everett. *Diffusion of Innovations.* 5th ed. New York: Simon and Schuster, 2003.

Rogers, Rob. "After Centuries of Farming, Hutterite Colony Expands into Building Construction." *Billings Gazette*, October 15, 2017.

Ryan, John. *The Agricultural Economy of Manitoba Hutterite Colonies.* Toronto: McClelland and Stewart, 1977.

———. "Hutterite Settlements in Rural Manitoba." In *The Pressures of Change in Rural Canada*, edited by Michael F. Bunce and Michael J.

Troughton, 92–101. Geographical Monograph No. 14. Downsview ON: York University, 1984.

Sanders, Douglas E. "Communal Property Decision a Month Away." *Edmonton Journal*, October 2, 1965.

———. "The Hutterites: A Case Study in Minority Rights." *Canadian Bar Review*, 42 (1964) 225–42.

Sauchyn, David, and Alwynne B. Beaudoin. "Recent Environmental Change in the Southwestern Canadian Plains." *Canadian Geographer* 42, no. 4 (Winter 1998): 337–53.

Scheer, Herfried. "The Hutterian German Dialect: A Study in Sociolinguistic Assimilation and Differentiation." *Mennonite Quarterly Review* 54 (1980): 229–43.

Schlabach, Theron F. "The Historiography of Mennonites and Amish in America: Reflections on the Past and Future." *Mennonite Quarterly Review* 81, no. 1 (2007): 49–75.

Serl, Vernon. "Final Report on the Saskatchewan Hutterite Program." Unpublished report for the Saskatchewan Government Committee on Minority Groups, Regina SK, 1958.

Sheps, Mindel C. "An Analysis of the Reproductive Patterns in an American Isolate." *Population Studies* 19 (July 1965): 65–80.

Smith, Bryan, dir. *Born Hutterite*. Black Hat Productions, 1996.

Spiteri, Edward, and Hugh Aylmer Dempsey. *Hutterites: The Hutterite Diamond Jubilee*. Calgary: Glenbow-Alberta Institute, 1978

Solbak, Vern. "Renewable Energy Strategies for Communities in Alberta." October 12, 2016. http://www.infrastructure.alberta.ca/Content/doc-Type486/Production/RenEnStratComAB.pdf.

Stabler, Jack C. *The Changing Role of Rural Communities in an Urbanizing World, 1961–1990*. Regina SK: Canadian Plains Research Center, 1992.

Stabler, Jack C., and M. Rose Olfert. "The Economic Structure of Saskatchewan's Communities." In *Encyclopedia of Saskatchewan*. Regina SK: Canadian Plains Research Center, 2005. https://esask.uregina.ca/entry/economic_structure_of_saskatchewan_communities.jsp.

Statistics Canada. CANSIM Table 004-0126: "Socioeconomic Overview of the Farm Population, Population Distribution for Rural and Urban Centres of the Farm and Non-Farm Population." Ottawa ON: Statistics Canada, 2013. http://www5.statcan.gc.ca/cansim/a26? lang=eng&retrLang=eng&id=0040126&&pattern=&stByVal=1&p1=1&p2=50&tabMo de=dataTable&csid=.

———. "Geosuite: 2011 Census." Catalogue No. 92-150-XBB. Ottawa ON: Statistics Canada, 2012. http://www12.statcan.gc.ca/census-recensement/2011/geo/ref/geosuite-eng.cfm.

———. "Selected Collective Dwelling and Population Characteristics (52) and Type of Collective Dwelling (17) for the Population in Collective Dwellings of Canada, Provinces and Territories, 2011 Census (Statistics Canada Catalogue no. 98-313-XCB2011024)." 2011 Census of Population. Ottawa ON: Statistics Canada, 2012. http://www12.statcan.gc.ca/census -recensement/2011/dp-pd/tbt-tt/Index-eng.cfm.

———. Table 17-10-0063-01: "Historical Statistics, Estimated Population and Immigrant Arrivals." https://doi.org/10.25318/1710006301-eng.

———. "2011 Census of Canada Topic-Based Tabulations: Selected Collective Dwellings and Population Characteristics and Type of Collective Dwelling for the Population in Collective Dwellings of Canada, Provinces and Territories." Ottawa ON: Statistics Canada, 2016. http://www12 .statcan.gc.ca/census-recensement/2011/dp-pd/tbt-tt/Rp-eng.cfm ?TABID=2&LANG=E&APATH=3&DETAIL=0&DIM=0&FL=A&FREE=0 & GC=0&GK=0&GRP=1&PID=102239&PRID=0&PTYPE=101955&S=0& SHOWALL =0&SUB=0&Temporal=2011&THEME=91&VID=0&VNA-MEE=&VNAMEF=.

———. "Type of Collective Dwelling (16) and Collective Dwellings Occupied by Usual Residents and Population in Collective Dwellings (2) of Canada, Provinces and Territories, 2016 Census—100% Data (Statistics Canada Catalogue no. 98-400-X2016019)." 2016 Census of Population. Ottawa ON: Statistics Canada, 2017. https://www12.statcan.gc.ca/census -recensement/2016/dp-pd/dt-td/Download.cfm?pid=109538.

Statistics Canada Agriculture Division. "Trends and Highlights of Canadian Agriculture and Its People." Catalogue no. 96-303E. Ottawa ON: Statistics Canada, 1992. http://publications.gc.ca/ collections/collection_2013/ statcan/rh-hc/CS96-303-1992-eng.pdf.

Stevenson, J. C., P. M. Everson, and M. H. Crawford. "Changes in Completed Family Size and Reproductive Span in Anabaptist Populations." *Human Biology* 61 (1989): 99–115.

Stoltzfus, Duane C. S. *Pacifists in Chains: The Persecution of Hutterites during the Great War*. Baltimore: Johns Hopkins University Press, 2013.

Swan, Jon. "The 400-Year-Old Commune." *Atlantic Monthly* 230, no. 5 (November 1972): 90–100.

Taber, Sarah. "America Loves the Idea of Family Farms. That's Unfortunate." *New York*, Intelligencer, June 16, 2019.

Teichroew, Allan. "Military Surveillance of Mennonites in World War I." *Mennonite Quarterly Review* 53 (April 1979): 95–127.

———. "World War I and the Mennonite Migration to Canada to Avoid the Draft." *Mennonite Quarterly Review* 45 (July 1971): 219–49.

Thomas, Kenneth Charles. "A Survey of Hutterite Groups in Montana." Master's thesis, Montana State University, 1949.

Troth, H. W. "Migration of Milltown Colony of the Hutterian Brethren May Mark the Passing of Sect from South Dakota." *Sioux Falls (SD) Daily Argus-Leader*, December 18, 1922.

Unruh, John D. "The Hutterites during World War I." *Mennonite Life* 24 (July 1969): 130–37.

U.S. Census Bureau. "Table P12: Sex by Age." 2010 Census Summary File 1. Washington DC: Bureau of the Census, 2010.

———. "2010 Census Block Boundary Files." August 15, 2013. ftp://ftp2 .census.gov/geo/tiger/TIGER2013/TABBLOCK/.

von Schlachta, Astrid. "Anabaptists and Pietists: Influences, Contacts, and Relations." In *A Companion to German Pietism, 1660–1800*, edited by Douglas H. Shantz, 116–38. Leiden: Brill Publishing, 2015.

———. *Die Hutterer zwischen Tirol und Amerika: Eine Reise durch die Jahrhunderte*. Innsbruck: Universitätsverlag Wagner, 2015. Translated by Werner Packull and Karin Packull as *From the Tyrol to North America: The Hutterite Story through the Centuries* (Kitchener ON: Pandora Press, 2008).

———. *Hutterische Konfession und Tradition (1578–1619): Etabliertes Leben zwischen Ordnung und Ambivalenz*. Mainz: Von Zabern, 2003.

———. *Täufergemeinschaften: Die Hutterer*. Mainz: Institut für Europäische Geschichte, 2011.

Vulcan Chamber of Commerce. "A Brief to Premier Peter Lougheed." February 23, 1973. Calgary AB: University of Calgary Law Library.

White, Katherine J. Curtis. "Declining Fertility among North American Hutterites: The Use of Birth Control within a Dariusleut Colony." *Biodemography and Social Biology* 49, no. 1–2 (2002): 58–73.

"Whiteshell Colony Farms." *Whitemouth River Valley: Visitor and Community Guide, 2017–2019*. http://www.rmwhitemouth.com/Home/DownloadDocument?docId=f0395614-7ce7-4831-876a-cc22a64eecd9.

Willms, A. M. "The Brethren Known as Hutterians." *Canadian Journal of Economics and Political Science* 24 (August 1958): 391–405.

Winkelbauer, Thomas. "Die Vertreibung der Hutterer aus Mähren 1622: Massenexodus oder Abzug der letzten Standhaften?" In *Glaubensflüchtlinge: Ursachen, Formen und Auswirkungen frühneuzeirlicher Konfessionsmigration in Europa*, edited by Joachim Bahlcke, 207–34. Munster: LIT, 2008.

———. *Österreichische Geschichte 1522–1699: Ständefreiheit und Fürstenmacht; Länder und Untertanen des Hauses Habsburg im konfessionellen Zeitalter (Teil 1)*. Wien: Carl Ueberreuter Verlag, 2003.

Young, Gertrude S. "The Mennonites in South Dakota." *South Dakota Historical Collections* 10 (1920): 470–506.

Zieglschmid, A. J. F., ed. *Das Klein-Geschichtsbuch Der Hutterischen Bruder.* Philadelphia: Carl Schurz Memorial Foundation, 1947.

———. "Must the Hutterites Leave Canada?" *Christian Century* 64 (October 1947): 1269–71.

Zwarun, Suzanne. "The Model Citizens Nobody Wants as Neighbours." *Toronto Globe and Mail,* March 7, 1972.

Index

Page numbers in italics indicate figures.

buffalo, 8, 210

buildings, 20–21, 24, 42, 45, 168, 170, 172, 174, 187, 189–90, 193, 217, 238, 240, 243–44; agricultural, 160; bungalows, xxi, 175–76, 186, 189, 191, 194; commercial, 242; common, 173, 177, 181; duplexes, 175–76, *186*, 186–87, 256; smaller, 169, 179

Burleigh, Walter A., 2

Burns, John, 158

Bushrod, Gillian, 155

Butte Colony, *178*, 179

Calder, James, 16, 33, 36, 37, 42

Calgary AB, 31, 33–34, 56, 64–65, 72–73, 135, 137, 142, 144, 198–99

Cameron Farms Colony, 160

Cameron Ranch, 59, 64

Campbell, Douglas, 52

Camrose AB, 56, 95

Canadian Census, 35, 109–10, 113, 169

Canadian Pacific Railway, 24, 45, 143

CanAm Colony, 242

canola, 198, 200, 204, 209, 239–41

Card, Joseph, 46

Carlier, Oneil, 232

carpenters, 12, 20, 179, 205, 207, 219, 226, 228, 240, 241

cattle, 10, 18, 45, 74, 103, 140, 150, 160, 198, 200, 202, 203, 204, 210, 214, 222, 223, 248

Cayley Colony, 94, 247

Cedar Grove Colony, 88

census, 7, 22, 107–10, 120, 121, 196, 198

Census of Canada, 22, 110, 113, 121, 131

Chakravarti, A. K., 44

chickens, 74, 78, 140, 160, 199, 200, 205, 210, 214–15, 217, 239, 241

children, 21, 23, 25, 29–30, 80, 111–13, 115, 118, 120, 125, 127–28,

129, 132, 142, 150–52, 154–56, 163, 208

Choteau MT, 57, 96

churches, xv, xvii, 52, 129, 170, 173, 179, 182, 189, 258

clan groups, xvi–xvii, xx, 70, 72, 74–75, 79, 81, 84–85, 91, 106–7, 120, 139–40, 191–92, 251–52, 257–58

Claresholm AB, 64, 232

Clark, Bertha, 21, 107

Cleardale Colony, 193, 241

Clear Lake Colony, 93, 159–60, 248

Clearview Colony, 137, 211, 245, 275n51

Cloverleaf Colony, 275n51

Cluny AB, 64, 269n8

Codesa Colony, 94

Cold Lake AB, 94

Collins, Jeff, 229

colonies. *See individual colony names*

colony density, 87, 94, 99

colony designs, 170, 176, 185, 189, 192; geometric, 194; innovative, 174, 192; nontraditional, 191; original and radical, 189; radical circular, 192

colony managers. *See* managers

Communal Expansion Bill (1961), 57

communal lifestyle, xv, 1, 217, 224, 227, 254

Communal Property Act (1947), 54–56, 58–60, 62–66, 75–76, 83, 85, 95–96, 99, 130–33, 136–39, 141, 145, 147, 154

Communal Property Control Board, 58–59, 63, 65, 75, 91, 133

Community Welfare Association, 52

companies, Hutterite-owned, 98, 157, 213–14, 230, 240, 242–47, 250; food-processing, 283n33; metal fabrication, 237; mortgage, 46; renewable energy, 230

Dominion City Colony, 8
Donalda Colony, 157
Doukhobors, 35–36, 39, 267n11
Dowling, Robert (minister), 133
driver's licenses, xvii, 139, 141
droughts, 1, 3, 10, 44–45, 143, 217
Drumheller AB, 27, 61, 64–65, 134, 157

Eagle Creek Colony, 273n10
East Cardston AB, 41, 182, 182–83
Eastend Colony, 288n100
Eaton, Joseph, xx, 106–7, 111–23, 116, 219, 253
Eberhard, Arnold, 192, 227
Edmonton AB, 56, 94, 134, 144, 210, 214, 237, 245
Edmunds County, 54
education, xix, xxi, 31, 33–34, 36, 124, 128–29, 132, 142–45, 150–56, 205, 208, 213, 226–27, 259; high school, 153; postsecondary, 153; sex, 152
Edwards, Bob, 33
egg farmers, 203, 231
egg production, 102, 214
eggs, xviii, xxi, 45–46, 153, 196, 199–200, 202–3, 209–10, 214–15, 217, 222
elders, 14, 22, 59, 82, 133, 135, 137–39, 141, 146
electricians, 179, 205, 228, 236
Elie MB, 18, 20, 36, 38
Elmspring Colony. *See* Old Elmspring Colony
Elm Spring Colony AB, 6, 10
Emerson, Lee, 33
"enemy aliens," xviii, 34, 46, 51–54, 56–61, 63–66. *See also* hostility toward Hutterites
Enertech Global Manufacturing, 236
engineers, 233, 236, 245

enterprises, 74, 106, 162, 195, 208, 225, 234, 241–43, 247, 253; agricultural, 126; eclectic, 247; geothermal, 236; industrial, 140, 237, 248; intensive livestock, 205; nonagricultural, 140, 228; nonfarm, 219–20, 225, 235, 251–53, 256
Entrup, Helmut, 137–38
Entz, Johann (minister), 41
Esau, Alvin, 130, 142
Europe, 1, 12–14, 31, 37, 50, 192, 227, 232–33, 286n66
Ewelme Colony, 41, 60, 269n8
excommunication, 227
exemption from military service, 13, 16, 35
exemption from taxes, 141
expansion, xxi, 7–8, 49–52, 57, 58, 65, 70, 75–76, 82–83, 84, 86, 94, 96, 99, 129, 131–32, 135–38, 146–48, 155–60, 215, 216–17, 221, 223, 253, 254, 256; control and limiting of, 161; restricting, 147. *See also* demography

families, 80, 111, 126, 142, 181; size of, 111, 113, 125
Faulkton SD, 243–44
fertility, 1, 18, 113, 115, 117, 122–23, 125, 126, 127, 128
fertilizers, 157, 203, 257
First World War, xxii, 96
flocks, 3, 12, 39–40, 74, 103, 203, 211, 214, 224
flooding, 3, 8, 10, 17–18, 133, 234
Fordham SD, 90, 269n7
Fords Creek Colony, 96, 194
Fort Leavenworth KS, 15
Fort Lewis, 15
Fort Macleod AB, 32–33, 149

Hofer, Joe, 137

Hofer, John, 245, 288n97

Hofer, Joseph, 60, 151

Hofer, Michael, 23–24

Hofer, Samuel, 125, 142, 157, 207

hogs, 140, 144, 158, 160, 200, 202, 204, 207, 209–10, 212, 223–24, 238–39, 241

Holden Colony, 237, 251; manufacturing, 238

Holliday, Alex, xiv

Holmes, Mary, 118

Homestead Act, 2, 262n6

honey, 45–46, 129, 199, 211

Horsch, John, 107

horses, 24, 45, 50, 239

Hostetler, John, xx, 172, 181

hostility toward Hutterites, 14, 31, 33, 34–35, 37, 38, 39, 40, 41, 42–43, 50, 52, 54, 57, 59, 61, 63, 65, 66, 75, 96, 99, 115, 130–33, 135–36, 143, 145, 147, 148, 149, 152, 154–55, 156, 159, 160, 161, 227, 250, 254, 256, 258

host society, xviii–xix, 103, 105, 125, 129, 132, 141–42, 147, 153, 185, 192, 218–19, 255–56

House of Commons, Canadian, 33, 37, 42

houses, xxi, 20, 23, 29, 74–75, 179, 182, 184–87, 191, 193, 237, 243–44, 246, 250, 255; communal buildings, 179; detached, 186; existing, 177; frame multistory, 174; high wood-frame, 256; ice, 12, 211; large, 18, 20; long, 172; modern, 125, 175; motel-style, 193; multifamily, xxi, 177; new, 21, 243; nontraditional, 184, 191–92; overflow, 190; prefabricated, 190; single-family, 191; smaller,

174, 186; stone, 10; two-story wood-frame, 185

Huntington, Gertrude Enders, 192

Huron Colony, 8, 18, 45, 47, 212–13, 280

Hutchinson County, 11

Hutter, Jacob, xvii, 116

Hutterite beliefs, xix–xx, 34, 39, 60, 77, 104–5, 114, 120, 122, 129, 132, 139, 147, 150, 152, 153, 155, 161, 195, 224, 227, 248, 249, 253

Hutterite gender roles, xv, 22, 78, 207, 283n22

Hutterite landholdings, 62, 87, 149, 197

Hutterite land purchases, 58, 65, 134

Hutterite settlement, 18, 54–56, 58, 64, 70–71, 74, 94, 96, 102, 268–69n1; control, 146; dense, 83, 98; patterns, xviii, 54, 73, 88, 139

Hutterite women, 21, 23–24, 25, 29, 32, 113–15, 115, 117, 122–23, 127, 142, 205–7, 206, 216, 239–41, 244, 247, 276n57, 283n22; unmarried, 122, 148; working in teams, 244, 247; young, 103, 112, 123–24, 127, 148, 154, 207, 216

Hutterville Colony, 47, 140, 141, 250

Huxley AB, 56, 98

Hynes Lake Colony, 248

Iberville Colony, 21, 40, 47, 239

imagery, aerial, of Hutterite colonies, 109, 168, 179

income, 46, 102, 223, 230, 234–35, 240–41, 251

industry, 98, 223, 226, 233, 256; building supply, 249; cattle feedlot, 238; hospitality, 240; meatpacking, 213; new light, 257; oil, 132, 238. *See also* manufacturing